THE
DECLINE
OF
CAPITAL

THE
DECLINE
OF
CAPITAL

Arthur Jones

THOMAS Y. CROWELL COMPANY

Established 1834 / New York

The column by Senator Stephen Young, "Straight from Washington," is reprinted with his permission.

Extracts from *The Enterprising Scot,* by W. Turrentine Jackson, are reprinted with permission of the Edinburgh University Press.

Designed by S. S. Drate

Manufactured in the United States of America

Library of Congress Cataloging in Publication Data

Jones, Arthur, 1936–
  The decline of capital.
  Includes index.
  1. Capital—United States. 2. United States—Economic conditions—1961–
I. Title.
HC110.C3J65   332'.041'0973   75-35953
ISBN 0-690-01045-1

10 9 8 7 6 5 4 3 2 1

Foreword

by Paul E. Erdman

"Americans have to be educated to the great American facts of modern life—that this country has peaked as a self-sufficient nation endowed with a potential for constant growth."

These words of Arthur Jones summarize the theme and purpose of this book: growth in America is dead, and the people of this nation must be told the truth and warned about the consequences.

Pessimistic, yes. But those who are expecting yet another spectacular gloom and doom scenario along the lines produced by pseudo-economists of the Harry Browne ilk will be disappointed. First, because Jones is a literate man. But more important, because Jones is not playing to the crowd. His is not a dramatic story of a "Great Crash" to be followed by the "Greatest Depression Ever Told." His basic point is "merely" that the curve of our national economy, which, throughout our history, has allowed for universally rising expectations, is no longer ascending. That the sixties in the United States were the years of the last great boom. The last! That our economic future has already begun—signaled initially by the 1971 devaluation of the dollar, and confirmed by the 1973 oil embargo. It is not a future which will culminate in a catastrophic collapse, but rather something much less exciting, something which will prove to be quite tedious and trying: a future in which, in Jones' words, "recession is permanent"—note recession, not depression—and where inflation is ever-present. Again, not dramatic runaway inflation, but a more boring process of slow but constant erosion of wealth. In my terms, we are therefore not about to be struck by lightning as a nation; we are just going to gradually sink in quicksand.

From the basic proposition—the end of growth—Jones then states the corollary: "where there is no growth, there is no capitalism." In other words, we of this generation are witnessing the beginning of the end of the capitalistic system, that system upon which this nation and its institutions have been built. Again, it will be a nondramatic event. "U.S. capitalism, presently under duress, is increasingly to go the way of capitalism in all Western nations—to become first a minority economic factor, then a mere economic quirk, as the bulk of capitalistic wealth is redistributed and savings eroded."

The corollary of the decline of capital: the demise of the middle class.

Far out? Hardly. In my opinion, all we have to do is look across the Atlantic to Great Britain. There is where the Industrial Revolution which spawned modern capitalism began, and there is where capital is in the most advanced stage of decay. The process can already be traced historically. The loss of the empire following World War II meant the end of Britain's "self-sufficiency" as an economic entity. Her captive natural resource base was gone. This led to a slowdown and ultimate stoppage of economic growth, and to ever-widening balance of payments deficits. This caused the demise of the pound sterling as a world currency, and a loss of faith by investors, both domestic and foreign, in the future profit potential in the United Kingdom. As private investment slowed, the government felt it necessary to fill the gap, both by taking over industry after industry and by inflating the economy to double-digit rates to create at least the illusion of increasing wealth. The masses—read labor unions in the case of the United Kingdom—wanted more than illusions. So the British government had to increasingly tax the rich—read the middle class—to maintain civil order. Net result: stagnation, inflation, and taxation have combined to sound the death knell of capitalism and the middle class in the United Kingdom.

Can that happen in the United States? Arthur Jones says yes, and makes a very convincing argument for the fact that not only can it happen, but that it already is happening.

Why? Because the preconditions for constant growth, that process which allowed the Great American Economic Machine to produce

ever-increasing wealth on a truly vast scale, no longer exist. These
are: cheap energy, cheap raw materials, low rates of inflation, low interest rates, and cheap venture capital.

True? Let's start with energy and raw materials. Jones states,
"American wealth, like Spanish wealth, was just there for the taking.
And Americans took it." Indeed they did. Until it had been so depleted, in so many key sectors, that there was simply not enough left
to support 215 million Americans in the style to which they had become accustomed. The case of oil is so obvious that it hardly needs
amplification. As long as America had an exportable surplus of crude
petroleum, it controlled the world price. Cheap domestic energy meant
cheap production costs for American industry, strong exports, and an
almighty dollar which ruled the world. Ditto for iron ore, so long as
the Mesabi deposits were still there in abundance. Ditto for coking
coal in the East. Ditto for silver, for zinc, for copper, for forest products. American capital did not have to search, or compete internationally, for raw materials. It had surplus supplies of virtually
everything at home, at prices American capital—not world
markets—determined. Discovery and exploitation of these natural
riches created instantaneous wealth. It was the basis for the Standard
Oils, the Anacondas, the U.S. Steels of our nation, and it was these
giant corporations which basically formed the basis of the capitalistic
system which created sufficient wealth to make the American society
the most affluent in the history of our planet.

But, as Jones points out, those days are over. Domestic wealth creation through the constant recurrence of discoveries of valuable deposits of natural resources has peaked. We no longer have surplus
supplies which allow us to control domestic prices. We are at the
mercy of the shahs, princes, and sheiks of the Persian Gulf, and the
dictators in Central Africa for an increasing proportion of those energy and raw material resources which we as a nation need just to
sustain our current standard of living. We have to trade off, through
the international price mechanism, more and more of our domestic
production to just stay even. As time progresses, our situation as a nation is bound to deteriorate further.

What about low interest rates and low rates of inflation? Our entire
system is geared to the maintenance of such conditions. It was assumed that as long as we had a Federal Reserve Board, acting re-

sponsibly in regard to the creation of money supply, these preconditions for continued American economic growth would remain. Wrong again. The U.S. government has lost control of the dollar, and it is highly doubtful whether it will ever regain control in the historical sense. Following World War II it was universally assumed that the total internationalization of commerce and finance was the only sure path to global continuing prosperity. Money had to be allowed to move freely across borders, along with goods and services. Under the aegis of the multinational corporations and banks, money did indeed move internationally: in fact, money has moved completely out of the reach of national control. You would, however, hardly suspect this by reading this country's newspapers. A monthly joke are those articles by American financial journalists dissecting the latest figures on M-1, M-2 through M-7, pronouncing—also on a monthly basis—that the Fed is getting things back under control. Totally ignored is that vast pool of dollars—not included in any of the "M's," yet amounting to at least a quarter of a trillion dollars—Eurodollars which float around the world totally out of the reach and control of the Fed, but still totally accessible to those economic entities which the Fed is supposed to be controlling. So much for the *real* power of our central bank.

And this pool of uncontrolled dollars is being added to at a continuing high rate, year after year. It can be fed by the citizenry, the corporations, but ultimately is fed by the governments of almost any country on earth, through the exchange mechanism. A continuing buildup of such funds is inevitable, because throughout the world deficit spending is regarded as the *only* antidote to recession and unemployment. The result is an uncontrollable process of rapid global money creation, and rapid global money creation must produce high rates of inflation—globally, including, of course, the United States. And high rates of inflation make necessary, ipso facto, high rates of interest. Unless the United States intends to reverse almost every international monetary and trade liberalization program it has sponsored during the past 30 years, this process will continue. So much for those two other key elements necessary for continuing American economic growth—low rates of inflation and low interest rates.

Which leaves us with the future of the price and availability of equity capital—venture capital, that which makes capitalism go round. Is it still available? Ask any corporation, any bank, any entrepreneur which has tried to raise risk capital lately. It is very, very difficult to find, and those who do find it must pay the world for it in terms of dilution. Why? Because Americans have lost faith in Wall Street. They no longer believe that corporations are going to grow and grow, and produce ever-greater income, profits, and dividends. Through some collective reasoning process which, perhaps, only Jung could have explained, millions of American investors sense that the ball game is over; that the preconditions for American growth have been lost. They somehow feel what Jones' book articulates: the age of capital (and thus of capital gains) is over.

If this is true, then a vicious circle has been created: no new equity capital, no future corporate growth; no future corporate growth, no new equity capital. I suspect, unfortunately, that the history of Wall Street during the past few years tells exactly that story.

Add this all up, and what do you get? I hate to give away an ending, but the last paragraphs of this book indicate where the author thinks we are going: "down, down, down." Jones, however, has not just thrown up his hands in dismay. Instead, he has come up with a whole series of suggestions as to how we as a society can be schooled to cope with what is coming, allowing for an orderly retreat from plenty.

The Decline of Capital is obviously not a book that offers much comfort to those of us who feel that something has gone basically wrong with our economic system. It should offer even less comfort to those economists and social "scientists"—including those of the New Left—who, during our generation, have so arrogantly claimed that they have the knowledge to control inflation, deflation, recession, unemployment, and just about every other economic evil that heretofore has plagued society. They do not have such knowledge, and the current state of economic affairs attests to the bankruptcy of their concepts and the national policies to which they have given rise. They still apparently believe that all that is left for our national leaders to do is to merely fine-tune a growth economy that is essentially unchanged from a decade ago. They could not be more wrong. We have passed over a threshold into a new economic situation. The brief age of American affluence is already waning. Our challenge today is to find ways to cope with the disheartening problems of the new era, an era of secular stagflation.

Our nation desperately needs a Great Debate on this subject. I hope that this book spurs such a discussion.

Acknowledgments

Fine words, I wonder where he stole 'em.

Jonathan Swift

The words worth stealing were stolen from a variety of sources. The time—weekends, evenings, holidays, and, finally, a 12-month leave of absence—was stolen mainly from my wife and children. To them this book, along with my thanks—and apologies.

Rodger Beehler, philosophizing somewhere in Canada, gave the earliest boot to my seat of talent with a short but brutal note castigating the introduction and outline some four years ago. He was on target, and I kept his advice masking-taped to the oak paneling behind my typewriter.

J. Carl Cook curled up in an armchair and curled his bottom lip as he read the first draft. His criticisms during the early Henley days wrecked that summer, but improved the manuscript immeasurably.

For four years my friend Dero Saunders cajoled, encouraged, guided, and rebuked me to seeing the manuscript finally completed, and finally published.

Dero, executive editor of *Forbes* magazine, Latin scholar and master of English usage and drollery, copy read all the drafts pencil in hand. He saved me from myself, and saved the book from 40,000 words too many. Any touches of quality hidden among the generality of this work are directly or indirectly attributable to Dero Saunders.

Those who worked their way through various drafts—offering criticism and guidance en route—included Ross Nicholson, Barbara

Wolfson, Joseph Nye, Sr., Joseph Nye, Jr., Annie Dobinsky, and Jim Flanigan. To them my thanks for a thankless task.

Forbes editor Jim Michaels carved his initials into one or two places—and the main trunk of the story benefited from his attention. Geoffrey Bell, economist, journalist, banker, and bon vivant, packed a wealth of guidance and information into a short, sharp review of the second draft. Encouragement and enthusiasm came from various colleagues and cohorts at *Forbes* magazine, with much help from Peggy Everett, and at the *Financial Times* of London. Colin Abson, the *Financial Times* librarian, was unfailingly cheerful when I wanted information and figures—and usually told me where to go. Miss Forrester at the Henley library was very helpful. In England, Janet Smith typed 100,000 words of original draft, and Elaine Popovic labored through the pencil marks and staples of the next one. Jean Blake, my executive secretary in America, tied all the loose ends together and got me to the press on time. Derek Turner of Henley-on-Thames and the British Museum, by his calm, unruffled responses, gave me the confidence to rely on my historical material. Jim Srodes, my Hollywood correspondent, had his particular insights.

My wife, Margie, had the good sense not to read a word of the manuscript until it appeared in book form. My daughter, Christine, caught sight of the manuscript one day and asked: "Do you just copy chunks out of other people's books, Daddy?" Not quite, but Jonathan Swift might have enjoyed the joke.

Michael hung up the Do Not Disturb sign on the study door. Ian took it down each teatime. The banks of the Delaware River at Frenchtown, New Jersey, and of the Thames at Henley, were—in their own separate ways—sources of inspiration, too. The book was completed in the heartland—Kansas.

To them, and to my circle of friends, my Arrogant Sheep, "who view these things with curious eyes, and moralize," my thanks.

A.J.

Frenchtown, New Jersey
Henley-on-Thames, England
Prairie Village, Kansas

1971–1975

Contents

Prologue   1

1 Dependence Day   17

2 How the World Turned—On
   U.S. Capitalism   37

3 It's a Threat! It's a Savior!
   It's Supergovernment!   77

4 The Beleaguered Capitalist   99

5 Goodbye, Middle Classes! Goodbye,
   Capitalism!   138

6 The Decline of Capital   163

7 Austerity   183

   Epilogue   195

   Index   197

Prologue

Joseph S. Nye was 35, and a railroad bond trader with Wall Street's Freeman & Co. But it was the Depression. Railroads were bankrupt. The stock market was practically dead. Many considered capitalism to be in its final state of collapse.

Nye was not listening. He was busy studying the bonds secured by railroad mileage. In the years prior to the massive railroad reorganizations of the 1890s and 1900s, many railroads had taken out mortgage bonds, using the track as security.

When reorganization came, these smaller railroads, with their mortgage bonds, were swept up into the larger systems. The result was that a system like the Chicago and Northwestern Railroad, for example, consisted in part of the former Des Plaines Valley Railroad. And the Des Plaines Valley Railroad had outstanding a first mortgage secured by some of its track.

Straightforward enough. Railroad bonds secured by mileage were depressed, too, just like every other bond and investment. But Nye, instead of fretting, was thumbing through the Copeland Traffic Density Maps. After all, the railroads were still running, and freight, while not as much as previously, was still being carried.

Ten percent of all the U.S. track carried some 50 percent of all the U.S. railroad traffic. Some defaulted bonds were worth more than other defaulted bonds based on the value of the traffic carried on the particular mileage.

Nye was betting that the economy would eventually recover, and was busily working out what all these various depressed bonds were worth. He was establishing value, one bond to the next. His reckoning was accurate enough.

He worked out the "net ton mile per mile of road per dollar of funded debt." In simple terms he could figure if the income from that track was sufficient to cover its mortgage interest—even though the system was in bankruptcy.

In this way, by finding a formula by which to measure the value of the bond, Nye was creating a market in them.

Gradually Nye became recognized as an expert in the field. Other dealers and institutions came to him to make a market, and to tap his knowledge.

Nye—at the depth of the Depression—was trading in the very essence of the value-and-market capitalist system. The monetary value of an item was being established by a generally accepted authority. Those prepared to trade in that item (railroad bonds) were using Nye's general evaluation. But the final price was being determined by supply and demand.

Wall Street was in the doldrums. But, among people prepared to accept the reality of depressed conditions, trade continued. For they accepted the current value of the railroad bonds. They were worth whatever income was being generated by the track across which the railroad freight traffic was carried. As long as the economy was ticking over, at however low a rate, trading continued.

Another young fellow, Robert M. Macrae of Seattle, Washington, dismayed but not defeated by the Depression, was buying railroad bonds through Nye. Finally Macrae came east, to visit the railroad bond expert.

"Do you, by chance, ever buy anything but railroad bonds for yourself?"

Nye looked over this drawling, skinny westerner as they lunched.

"Well, I bought a stock for myself today which you would never buy. American Ice preferred. I paid 22½ for it on the New York Stock Exchange, and it pays no dividend."

Refrigerators were coming in. The iceman did not come around the way he once had.

Macrae laughed, somewhat derisively. "An *ice* company? Now why would you waste your money on that?" he asked.

Nye explained that while the ice company was losing $1 million a year, it was all a book loss. That was the amount of the depreciation account. "They are only using old machinery to compress and freeze water—they really have nothing depreciating. In effect they are putting $9 a share in the bank for the stockholders. I feel this stock will go to $100 a share one day.''

Nye was willing to go over the figures to show him. But no, Macrae did not want that. He preferred to surprise Nye by telling him that he, Macrae, with his clients, represented the biggest single holding of American Ice preferred.

''We think alike, Mr. Nye, we're always buying value.'' (Some time later, to the satisfaction of both, American Ice preferred was bought in at $100 a share.)

On July 12, 1974, Nye finished the front page headlines in the *Wall Street Journal*. He had already read the *New York Times*. Then he had gone through the *Journal* and was back on its front page. He put the newspaper to one side and looked out at the view. Through the huge picture window he could see nearly 40 miles across the rolling dips and hills of prime New Jersey real estate. It was a tranquil scene.

At first glance, Nye looked like a tranquil man. At 71, age was treating him well. He had slowed down a little physically. But his 5 foot 9 was erect when he walked. And there was nearly always a twinkle in his hazel eyes. The years were giving a slight parchmenting effect, the patina of old age, to his facial skin.

When concentrating, Nye screwed his eyes closed (Stanley Laurel, of Laurel and Hardy, did it equally well). He stopped concentrating.

''I'm going, Ellie,'' he said.

He was dressed for the office, in pinstripes and with shoes shined. But Nye had been retired for four years. The office these days was in the garage, or rather, above the garage.

He walked into the kitchen. Smiled at his wife, Ellie. She smiled back: ''Don't forget you've got a lunch today, Joe.''

''I won't.''

But as he left the house and walked along the path toward the garage, he wasn't really thinking about lunch. It was about the headlines. Nye on the inside was nowhere near as tranquil as Nye on the outside.

Self-made and wealthy, Nye was turning 56 years' experience on Wall Street over in his head. Had he seen it all? he asked himself.

Recession was moving toward depression. The inflation rate was desperate. Interest rates were heading for historic highs. The stock market was challenging historic lows.

Nye walked past the swimming pool. He would take a quick swim before dinner as he usually did.

He had seen a lot since starting as a runner with Freeman & Co. on July 1, 1918.

He had educated himself. He learned from the lectures at New York University and the New York Chamber of Commerce. Evening after evening he spent at the New York Public Library's main branch at Fifth Avenue and 42nd Street filling notebooks in longhand. He was committing to memory the writings of the classical economists of the day, Irving Fisher of Yale, Taussig of Harvard.

Nye read widely, debated keenly. He learned from the skilled, intuitive people he had worked with, and from the duds, the failures, and the get-nowheres.

Memories of the panic of 1907 were still fresh on Wall Street when he had started there. He was a young man from New Jersey raised by two aunts after his mother died. They had all gone through the slump of 1914. Then through the post–World War I slump and inflation. The U.S. 1913 dollar lost 52 cents by 1920. That was inflation.

Unemployment rampant in 1974 and getting worse? But that had happened before, too.

Daring times? When the Depression had struck Wall Street, Nye had ordered the stock market ticker and the wire machines removed.

"Don't look at the market. Buy and sell value," he had told his staff.

Buy and sell value. He unlocked the garage doors, a smile bringing out the Stan Laurel in him. Well now, did he believe in his own judgment or didn't he? He had been relying on himself all his life. No point in running scared now.

Across the garage and up the stairs. At the top he unlocked the door which led into his pied-a-terre-cum-office. It was a fine retreat. An apartment, fully equipped, with an office to one side. File rooms, records, memories—and work to do. He quickly settled down and started going through the folders on his desk.

Was it really different this time? The United States always had had plenty of oil. Now the Arabs had it and were holding the country for ransom, more or less. The United States had always had copper and iron ore enough to export, if necessary. But now large quantities of these were being bought outside.

The money once spent in the United States was being spent outside the United States to buy commodities the country once had supplied to itself. That, too, was different, at least on the present scale. And that trend would continue. The nation's appetite was too large. But large appetites had built America. People not settling for what they had, people working for more. The dollar twice had been devalued. Imagine that.

Was the nation living beyond its means? Yes. And that was bad. The banks were out of control—the Bank Holding Company Act had turned them loose. They were overloaned and those loans were undersecured. The banks were a real risk factor.

Was the market still vital? Was this the end? Would the petrodollar drain pull all the money away? Would the tremendous shifts in the world's surpluses plunge the Western capitalist system into a disastrous dive from which it could not recover? Was the United States in that plunge?

Nye looked at one of the folders on his desk: Thiokol.

What had he been doing with Thiokol? On June 11, 1973, he had bought 1,000 shares at between 9⅞ and 10¼. Later that year, as a shareholder, he had called up the company chief executive officer, Robert Davis, and made a date to go to Bristol, Pennsylvania, to look over the company—and Davis.

Musing, Nye reminded himself that in going to see Davis he had acted out a two-line thought he had long accepted. Someone once had said: "A corporation is but the shadow of the man." He, Nye, liked what he saw in Davis, and liked the way the company was being run. But he stopped buying. He was satisfied just to study the interim reports for a while.

Then, early in 1974, ignoring what the newspapers were saying about the economy, Nye added an additional 3,100 shares.

And here it was July. What to do? He dialed a number in Seattle, Washington. Once he had exchanged hellos with a secretary, he was put through to Bob Macrae.

"Bob, good morning."

"Hi, Joe. How are you this morning?"

It was the same Bob Macrae from the railroad bond and American

Ice preferred days. The two men had hit it off, and had been friends, colleagues, and business cohorts ever since. They called one another at least three times a week. Some weeks they called one another each day. Rarely did one make a business decision without bouncing it off the other. Always they were candid—and listened carefully to what the other had to say.

"What do you think of the market, Bob?"

"Trying not to think about it, Joe. Seriously though. There's a lot of bargains."

"Bob, I'm going to go deeper into Thiokol. I'm thinking of buying a few thousand more shares."

"You know that stock, Joe, you *know* if it's any good. I'm just about to do the same with those two I've been following: Foote Minerals and Leslie Salt."

"Thanks, Bob, talk to you later. Bye, love to Jackie."

"So long, Joe. Love to Ellie."

Nye put down the phone, picked it up again, and dialed his stockbroker. He bought another 3,300 shares at between 13 and 14. The price dropped. In November 1974 he took in a further 2,000 at 11½, and in December more at 9½. No matter how bad the headlines, Nye each time made a decision based on the value of the company, what it was capable of earning. The worth of what was behind the paper that was being sold, that was a part of it; the quality of the men running the company, that was the rest of it. One had to assume the economy would eventually bounce back.

Sure the old days were gone. And yet, were they? Robert Macrae had gone back to buying those defaulted senior mortgage railroad bonds. The hopes were that Amtrak and freight carriers would have to get their house in order one day because they, too, used those heavily trafficked tracks. Now, as in the thirties, the interest would have to be paid off; the bonds would have to be liquidated.

Nye and Macrae, capitalists confident in their skills, and in the continuing viability of the capitalist free market system, were following "value." Their judgments were based on the current and future financial worth of the entity they bought. They were prepared to accept their own judgment, and to pit that judgment against the judgment of the marketplace at some time in the future.

They were operating on basic skills, depending on an element of luck, and hoping they were right.

But they were doing all this when the United States was in the most serious economic tailspin since the Depression. They traded as they always had, even though far-reaching fundamental changes were taking place in the U.S. economy, in the value of the U.S. dollar, in the role of government in the private sector, and in the pressures on government to provide an ever-increasing array of social services.

George Kozmetsky turned the key to start up his gray Jaguar. Austin, Texas was experiencing a sudden torrential downpour. The dapper dean of the Graduate School of Business at the University of Texas was soaking wet. But he didn't notice. He was talking business.

Business is much of Kozmetsky's life. The cofounder of Teledyne, an electronics growth stock in the sixties, Kozmetsky sold out most of his interests—$5 million worth—to plunge into business education. At the University of Texas graduate and undergraduate business colleges, he was giving his enthusiasms full throttle.

In the summer of 1974, when the U.S. economy appeared close to its nadir, and the Wall Street future was a matter of open conjecture, what was Kozmetsky telling his business graduates? Had they a future?

Through studies, through inspiration, and through optimism, Kozmetsky was plugging his students into "asset and balance sheet management." It is one more way of looking at the basic financial worth of the entity. Take, for example, a real estate trust. Break it down to its component parts, get rid of the money losers, and do whatever is possible to maximize the moneymakers. Not a complicated formula. But, as a process, asset management demands an unemotional look at the fiscal worth, that is, the current and potential market value of the entity.

Asset management is not unlike what the British call "asset stripping." Buy something as cheaply as possible, strip away what is valueless, and walk away with what is left. The time to buy bargain-priced assets is when the market has become fearful about buying anything.

So it was in 1974 that Kozmetsky was working hand-in-glove with his students—and with a real-life real estate investment trust in which he had a small stake—to give those graduate students experience far removed from the normal classroom and case study routines.

Not just real estate, but finance. Kozmetsky posed to Professor David Huff whether a survey would show if a savings and loan office could thrive in Texas. Huff's group narrowed the search down to two cities. In one of them, Austin, Huff and his student group persuaded a savings and loan institution to open an office. And one of the graduate students moved into the organization as an executive trainee.

In such ways George Kozmetsky was tackling economic hard times. More than that, he was turning out future businessmen at a period when business was in disrepute, the economy in dire straits, profits at a minimum, and confidence in the market system at an all-time low.

Kozmetsky could proceed full steam ahead in spite of the storm.

Earlier in 1974, Dr. Henry Kaufman, a senior partner at Salomon Brothers, a Wall Street securities firm, spoke at a Conference on Wall Street and the Economy. His address to the audience at the New School for Social Research was carried in an edited version the following day on the *New York Times* Op Ed page.

Kaufman was chilling in his observations of the U.S. scene. To many, his cure seemed more severe than the problem. To get out of the inflationary entrapment the United States was experiencing would require, said Kaufman: ". . . a program of national austerity including, among other things, increasing incentives to save, taxing inflationary profits and wages . . . and controlling the total credit creation process."

Improved prices for their market-ready pigs were not enough for the hog farmers of the Missouri Ozarks, 500 miles south of meat-packing Chicago. The farmers wanted to make sure that the housewife bought pork products once they reached the supermarket. In 1975 Ozark hog farmers were trying to bring about an improved image—and cultivate some understanding by the consumer of what it costs the farmer to produce such essentials.

In an attempt to get the message across, Roland (Pig) Paul,

founder of the National Feeder Pig Show, invited 17 consumer activist housewives from the Chicago area, as the show's guests, for an Ozark weekend.

The women, members of Chicago's Citizens Action Program, came with husbands and children and stayed several days with local farmers. The Missouri Ozarks is a beautiful area of rolling, and sometimes rugged, forested hills, and lush farmland.

But when the tourists and fishermen leave at the end of the summer the Ozark economy relies exclusively on farming and allied local industry.

To the consumerists from suburban Chicago, the Ozarks was a different world. Two Americas were coming face to face. The Chicagoans, in their mod gear, with their determined ways and political-action oriented plans, were equally an education for the Ozarks farmers, many of whom were substantial men of agribusiness.

The Chicago Citizens Action Program is no mere loosely knit gathering of local housewives. Born out of the high meat prices of 1973, the CAP has formed into a strong consumer-lobby unit, one that moves into direct action against specific supermarkets and supermarket chains.

What CAP members do is to distribute "pledge" cards among shoppers. Shoppers who sign promise to spend their food dollars only in stores which agree to negotiate with CAP leaders. CAP already has several thousand pledges worth, in the words of Mrs. Jean Schakowsky, CAP leader, "about $1 million or so each week in food buying power."

Food store managers, or supermarket chain executives—in a high-volume, low-margin business—cannot afford to take too many chances when faced with the adamant housewives. So they negotiate with CAP on specific items, explain the shelf prices, and show who gets what profits from where.

Mrs. Schakowsky and the other CAP members are aware enough to realize that the battle cannot be fought only with shopping carts in supermarket aisles. That is why they accepted the farmers' invitation. Mrs. Schakowsky was the featured speaker at a gathering of hog farmers during the Feeder Pig Show.

The politically astute Mrs. Schakowsky had believed the consumers and the farmers could find a common cause, and that it would start both groups on the road toward lower prices for all. The Scha-kowskys, guests of pig raisers Mr. and Mrs. Robert Hinds, enjoyed themselves immensely. But their social activist hopes never took roots in the Ozark soil.

The consumers argued that high prices were due to high farm prices and high corporate profits taken by the packers and the super-markets. The farmers saw the high prices as due to high labor costs on the farms and in the factories.

The gap between consumerist and farmer was wide enough to show just how pluralistic this society still is. The socially pleasant weekend could not bridge the city-dweller versus country-dweller gap.

Rural Americans like the Hindses are examples of the rugged Amer-ican independent, members of ex-Vice President Agnew's "silent ma-jority." They ask no help, and are prepared to be self-sufficient under their own steam, or to fall by the wayside.

Chicago, which has a long heritage of social action involvement, was an urban seedbed of many core-city programs that eventually made an impact on America's "War on Poverty" in the sixties. Life is tough in a different way. U.S. inflation and recession have made deep inroads into middle and lower-middle class metropolitan America.

For 25 years, give or take a recession or two, the U.S. economy has pulled everyone a little closer to affluence. People have experi-enced financial and social "upward mobility." Middle and lower-middle class America—gauged middle class by virtue of having dis-cretionary disposable income for nonessentials—is not accustomed to having to share out some of its gains.

But the United States no longer has the growth that got Americans where they are today. There is an enormous national debate going on as to whether that growth can ever return. All that the Chicago con-sumer-active housewife sees, however, is not national inflation, but bacon at $2 a pound, and a one-pound canned ham at $3.45.

The farming Hindses see only the high price of feed grain and the need for enough profit to keep them in business. They know about the big cities, where garbage collectors make $18,000 a year. The farmers fail to see the logic of the urbanites' complaints.

The Schakowskys and the Hindses both know that life—economic life—in the United States is changing. No American capable of reading a daily newspaper, or watching the television news, or trying to balance a household or business budget can avoid acknowledging that fundamental changes are taking place. But few Americans know how, or why.

Americans have no clear understanding of where much of their wealth came from. They do not know what it means to go from being completely self-sufficient to relying to a major degree on imports. They do not know what has given them their high standard of living. They do not know what is taking it away.

What lies ahead politically is more disagreement, not less, over who is going to foot the bill for higher U.S. prices as U.S. inflation and the U.S. recession continue apace.

Weekends in the Ozarks simply add to the frustrations.

It was a rather "schmaltzy" photograph even by public relations standards. George Weyerhaeuser, president of the Weyerhaeuser Co., agreed to feed the corporate ducks at the corporate pond in front of corporate headquarters. The corporate photographer clicked away, and the corporate annual report for 1973 carried the photograph inside the front cover.

The senior vice-president was at hand with a plastic bag of Wonder bread should the ducks display any interest. They did not—at least not in the photograph.

There was nothing "schmaltzy" about George H. Weyerhaeuser's words alongside the picture:

"There is no doubt that while the free market does provide the greatest good for the greatest number, its workings at times fall most heavily upon the poor, the underqualified, and those who must live on fixed incomes."

Enlightened self-interest comments from the head of a $2.3 billion sales corporation?

"We simply do not have as a nation enough understanding of the complexities of our economy and of its relationships to world economics, for price controls to work."

Weyerhaeuser was concerned because he knew that the price for his company's basic products, wood and paper, would shoot up during 1974 when the annual report came out. Weyerhaeuser was prepared to leave those prices, and the pricing system generally for national and international business, to work themselves out:

"Those complexities are handled automatically and best where the buyer's dollar determines what is needed within the free market mechanism." But he again qualified himself, because of the effect that the free market system would have on "the poor, the underqualified and those who must live on fixed incomes."

The effects of the free market system, "particularly in a time of inflation, are ones which must be recognized, and dealt with. Public policies and funds are needed to deal with them."

In 1972, Gabriel T. Kerekes, an economist at Hoening and Strock, was quoted in *Business Week:*

"Our entire political and social trend is to slow up industrial growth." It was a companion to the rhetorical question Frederick Heldring, then vice-chairman of the Philadelphia First National Bank, had asked in 1971:

"What if the consumer of the future turns out to be less materialistic and, *as a result, demand sags?"*

What is it that we are living through? Why can men like Nye and Macrae and Kozmetsky continue on course, when others like Weyerhaeuser and Kaufman and Kerekes can see fundamental changes in the economy?

The answers are present in the complexity of capitalism itself. But that complexity does not mean that the trends are too confused or confusing to be discussed. Is capital declining? Yes. Is capitalism dead? No.

What is happening is that capital's sphere of operation is contracting.

Imagine Western capitalism as a huge, multi-ringed circus. When railroads are nationalized that removes one of the rings from the circus tent for there no longer is a market in the common stocks of the railroads. Government bonds to finance that nationalized railroad will still be in the tent, in the government ring.

If one of the circus rings is the aerospace industry, picture the industry as a troop of performing horses, each corporation a horse, each horse an investment possibility. Where once there were 20 publicly listed aircraft manufacturers to invest in, now there are perhaps 8. Remove 12 horses from the ring. The show still goes on—but with fewer performers. The horses are joined by a dog act—the airlines themselves. But the airlines are in trouble; start to remove the dogs from the ring, one by one. When the government has to step in and totally subsidize them or jointly own the airline industry, as in Britain and France, remove the diminished dog act from the aerospace-airline circus ring and put the dogs with the others in the government circus ring.

The picture is obvious. The government ring is getting crowded with acts no one else wants, or no one else can afford. Many other rings remain in the same tent, but the number of rings is becoming fewer, and the number of performers in each ring is dwindling.

That is what is happening to capitalism.

What was nominally free enterprise capitalism (in spirit if not always in practice) gave way to mixed economies in the Western nations as the government became more involved. Within those mixed economies there still existed a fairly vibrant free market sector.

Today the freedom of the capitalist corporation in that sector, the corporation in which Nye and Macrae invest, is being curtailed to such an extent that the future behavior, investment patterns, location, quality and profitability of the corporation is determined as much by pressures outside the market as by internal corporate needs to maximize profits.

Yet even as its freedom of operation is curtailed, this heavily regulated, heavily taxed, and closely watched and criticized corporation remains—and is expected to be—the economic dynamo of those Western democracies. Its profits provide taxable incomes, its growth provides jobs, and its potential attracts the investors' money.

For government and private citizen, for democrat or technocrat, for fascist or socialist, the dilemma is real: can any of these traditionally capitalist democracies adjust to being something other than a capitalist democracy without losing the economic vitality—for all its boom-and-bust problems—that capitalism affords? (Sweden, that much-heralded social democratic state, remains almost totally capital-istic—only 5 percent of its industry is government owned or con-trolled. The government is social democrat and pragmatic—it does as little as possible to hinder the export competitiveness of its capitalist corporations.)

The story of the problems facing U.S. capital is a comparatively recent tale. For all intents and purposes, the U.S. economy peaked on December 31, 1965. That was the crest of the Final Boom.

By the mid-sixties, post–World War II U.S. capitalism appeared to be working for the majority, even though the nation was heading into a period of great social turmoil. The turmoil, black-white friction and the riots, were in part a reflection of the extent to which a large mi-nority had been left out of the all-too-obvious prosperity.

And yet, directly and indirectly, all Americans were benefiting from this final festival of affluence. Through corporate profits and ad-vancing share prices investors were reaping benefits. Through rising wages and greater job opportunities the work force was improving an already high, by Western standards, standard of living. Through in-come redistribution, Social Security payment increases, and new so-cial programs the least fortunate in society were experiencing assis-tance after years of neglect.

Energetic capitalists, working unhindered by government in the more-or-less free enterprising marketplaces of the United States, pro-duced that Final Boom of 1964–66.

Capitalist democracies have permitted a man to make a fortune meeting the needs of his fellow men. Capitalism swelled because in-vestors felt that the profits accruing from the investment and efforts that produced fortunes were a right rather than a privilege, and be-cause the society at large did not dispute that right.

But much is changing.

Capitalism is contracting. Return on investment is shrinking be-cause the capitalist corporation no longer has the freedom—or cli-mate of opportunity—to maximize its profits the way it once could.

Corporate capitalism requires constant recharging with capital and reinvested profits to continue its vibrancy and growth. The capitalist mode of production depends on an abundant supply of cheap raw ma-terials, big markets and outlets for manufactured goods, constantly improving technology, an efficient marketing system, consumer confidence, and government support for all but those who abuse the system.

The investment of capital, the promise of a return on capital, is *the* Western system for exploiting new ideas, like the auto and the airplane; for exploiting new-found wealth, like the coal deposit or the oil field; for exploiting natural advantages, like a damp climate for spinning cotton, or a lower wage area for lower production costs.

Capitalism thrives on newly released capital (like savings invested for the first time, or increased disposable income from rising wages). Capitalism is the system in which the wealth is redistributed among those who share in the exploit, and in which the wealth is reemployed to seek, create, or exploit more wealth.

The "capital" of this book is money, wealth, profits or credit available for investment and the creation of more money, wealth, profits or credit.

The "capitalism" of this book is the market system that encourages and enables that capital to be invested profitably at reasonable risk.

The "decline of capital" refers to the continuing diminution—for all the reasons discussed—of money, wealth, profits and credit available for investment; to the diminution of opportunities for corporate and capital growth; to the diminution of return on the capital invested; and to the inability of the market system and the corporate sector to encourage or enable what capital there is to be profitably invested at reasonable risk, or to convince or demonstrate that this market system is indeed an honorable system worthy of widespread public understanding and support.

This capitalist system as described is being seriously questioned even though capitalism is still the dominant force in the society, be it the simple capitalism of the small investor seeking interest on his deposit in the bank, or a return and hoped-for capital gains on a rich portfolio.

Challenged is the all-pervading capitalist ethic of American life: the expectation that a man or woman will be rewarded for individual effort expended in a particular way.

The United States is a Western, industrialized democracy built on and by capitalism, resting on codes, laws, traditions and habits that are a part of a capitalistic way of life. This way of life has produced, promoted, and—until recently—extolled a capitalist ethos that affects both government and individual, that governs personal and public affairs, both national and international.

Given these facts, the most difficult thing for many Westerners, and certainly for most Americans, to accept is that what has happened in the past—economic opportunity for all in a booming economy—can never happen again.

Some sectors of the economy may flower and spurt forth and the Kozmetskys will spot them early; some industries and corporations may flourish and the Nyes and Macraes will invest in them; but the great outpouring of wealth that was the United States for its first two centuries is ended.

There is a new economic reality now.

Why will those good old days not return?

The boom of 1964–1966 will not repeat itself because in those years inflation was only 2 percent per annum. Japan was still a customer, not a competitor. The adverse balance of payments (at $2.6 billion) raised few eyebrows at home or abroad. There was cheap energy, energy galore. There were plenty of raw materials and the prices were right for industrial nations. The dollar was still rock solid. And as for trade, why, in President Kennedy's words in 1963, "60 percent of the goods we import do not compete with the goods we produce."

Every single item on that boom shopping list has taken a marked turn for the worse.

1

Dependence Day

The United States, with the exception of one or two
minor minerals, and rubber and coffee, produces everything necessary for her own consumption and manufacture,
and much to export. Food materials of all kinds she has in
abundance, enough to support a much larger population
than her own . . . *this country could be blockaded for
centuries without fatal suffering.* We produce 60 per cent
of the world's copper, 66 per cent of the world's oil, 75
per cent of the corn, 60 per cent of the cotton, 52 per cent
of the coal, and 40 per cent of the iron and steel; yet we
have only 6 per cent of the world's population and 7 per
cent of the world's land.

Harold Underwood Faulkner
American Economic History
Harper, 1924

Fifty years ago, when Harold Underwood Faulkner wrote, the United
States was a very independent nation indeed. The United States still
has about 6 percent of the world's population and 7 percent of the
land, but it could not be blockaded for long without some suffering.

For nearly two centuries the United States has lived primarily off
the natural raw material wealth it found in nature's bank, plus the
wealth generated by its inventions and technology (a considerable
amount of wealth), the accumulated capital of past industrial boom
periods, and, until recently, a huge income from overseas sales and
investments.

The wealth of North and South America has always been there just for the taking. As Cortes' companion, Bernal Diaz del Castillo, re-marked: "We came to America to serve God, and become rich."

Historian James Douglas put it this way 60 years ago: "In the discovery of the North American continent, and in the exploitation of its resources, private enterprise has generally taken the lead of government initiative."

North America has been to waves of European adventurers, traders, investors, capitalists, and emigrants what Spain was to the Phoenicians, then the Romans, then the Moors: a place to get rich. Many arrived from other motives, too, but they knew in advance about the economic opportunity.

Eighteenth-century England wanted the American colonists to run the country as a giant "extractive industry." Today the industrial nations would prefer the emerging raw-material-supplying nations to remain storehouses of extractable wealth rather than become burgeoning manufacturing states.

British eighteenth-century Prime Minister Walpole made no attempt to enforce the English "extractive industry" preference, and American industrialization grew rapidly. Faulkner attributes George III's attempt to return to the "old commercial policy" (suppressing industry, emphasizing raw materials exports) "as the greatest of all causes of the American Revolution."

Not that a successful revolution made much difference to the source of what became the commonwealth, or the common wealth, of the United States. It still remained primarily extractive, and continued to do so right into this century.

American wealth, like Spanish wealth, was just there for the taking. And Americans took it.

W. Turrentine Jackson, in *The Enterprising Scot,* describes the following event in Nevada at the turn of the century:

James L. Butler and his wife, driving a pack-train through the wasteland, picked up stones to hurl at their recalcitrant burros and recognized the rock as mineralized quartz. On a return trip through the region they gathered some ore samples and turned them over to the district attorney of Nye County, offering him half-interest in the claim for the assay fee. The lawyer, equally impoverished, offered half of his half to an Austin engineer who learned that a ton of the ore would produce 80 dollars in gold and 600 dollars in silver. The partners later returned to the richest outcrop at Mizpah Hill and staked off every foot of ground. They filled two wagons with ore and started back to Austin. The rush to Tonopah was on.

Tonopah's final contribution to American wealth was $125 million worth of precious metal.

Farfetched? John G. McLean, president of Continental Oil, said it again, to *Forbes* magazine, in 1971:

> This is where a natural resource company really makes its money—in the instantaneous creation of wealth, in the appreciation of value that takes place when you put down an exploratory well and discover a big new oil or gas field, or go out with a core drill and stumble onto a new uranium or copper prospect.

The United States has had thousands of Tonopahs, in agriculture, mining, manufacturing, technology, commerce, and cheap labor.

What most affects the U.S. future, however, is that many Tonopahs have been exhausted, and there are few domestic new ones being discovered. Look at the problem as expressed by a report to the U.S. Senate Committee on Finance. Did the researchers who prepared the "Steel Imports" staff study for the Senate Committee on Finance in 1967 realize the significance of what they were presenting?

> The rapid expansion of the U.S. steel industry between 1890 and 1930 was based on the low-cost, high-quality iron ore deposits of the Mesabi, and the world's best coking coal near Pittsburgh . . . [combining] with the waterways of the Great Lakes—an inexpensive means of transportation. These nature-given advantages, when added to the entrepreneurial drive of a people [possessing] the first continent-sized free market, without traditional bonds of social classes [but] with a broadly-based educational system, was bound to outdistance the Old World. These factors helped attract immigrants and build up an industrial economy without peer. Steel was the foundation of this economy and has remained its backbone.

The study laments the "expected early exhaustion of the high-grade direct shipping iron ore of the Mesabi." U.S. steel production, which rose steadily for the first half of this century, declined between 1957 and 1973, and recovered "only during the capital goods boom of 1964–66." The U.S. steel industry's plight and future, as described for the U.S. Senate, can be taken as a very adequate description of U.S. dependence day problems.

> The century-old dominance of the United States and Northern Europe in the world steel economy was based on the industrial revolution of the 19th century, propinquity to iron ore, coking grade coal, and technical ability of their populations.

The world steel industry today is characterized by the emergence of two new giants, the USSR and Japan, and of some 36 new, small steel producing countries. The expected early exhaustion of the high-grade direct-shipping iron ore deposits of the Mesabi sent U.S. geologists all over the world in search of other iron ore deposits. The success of these missions led countries like Canada, Mexico, Venezuela, Brazil and Australia to build up their steel industries using the newly discovered native ores. Furthermore, new low-cost tranportation by boats in the range of 50,000 to 150,000 (nine years later 250,000) tons, combined with lower investment costs for steelmaking facilities [due to] the use of basic oxygen converter process and continuous casting, have given other countries the chance to build up their own steelmaking facilities.

The development of Mesabi low-grade ore into taconite pellets signals the way in which advanced technology can aid a declining raw materials situation. But new ore-refining capability does not eliminate the basic trend, though it does fortunately prolong the rundown period.

Today the U.S. has 28 percent of the world's copper reserves, consumes more than 27 percent of world output, and imports 15 percent of its needs. U.S. oil reserves are 6.8 percent of known world reserves, but the United States is consuming around 30 percent of annual global output. The United States produces 82.5 million tons of iron ore annually (1971), consumes 122 million tons, some 19 percent of world steel production.

Some estimates for the 1980s suggest that the United States will require more than half of all oil going to industrial nations, and almost twice as much as its present consumption.

These figures will remain fairly accurate even though prices, supplies, and alternate sources may marginally affect them. They make the point that the United States has to cope with a totally new concept of economic vitality (for the optimists), or survival (for the pessimists).

Now the country is having to start living off its earnings. The difference is the difference between two billionaires, between H. L. Hunt and D. K. Ludwig. Hunt, the oil billionaire, found his money in the ground, pumped it out, and sold it. Eventually some of the profits were invested outside the natural resource areas, but the bulk of his money came from a consumed-once commodity. Ludwig's money came from trading, a much tougher trick. Fundamentally the font of his wealth was the profits accruing from boats owned, charters won in fierce competition, contracts fulfilled. Obviously, Dan Ludwig eventually invested some of his profits in natural resources, too. But the point is that the United States has been getting the bulk of its money Hunt-style, and now is faced with survival Ludwig-style. Nor is there any choice. As things presently stand the United States must become a manufacturing nation so skilled that it can compete internationally with goods manufactured increasingly from natural resources it has had to buy in the world market—against nations which have never known any other way of life.

If America's resource story can be told in dramatic terms over the discovery and decline in native iron ore, oil must be discussed in strategic terms. Fifty years ago, in a very different demand situation, the United States could boast most of the world's known recoverable oil reserves and almost unlimited quantities of natural gas, of which it now consumes 57 percent of annual global output. Today the United States *can be blockaded* over oil, and could be permanently damaged by prolonged interruption of that same oil flow.

To a lesser extent, that blockade situation exists in dozens of raw material product areas that Americans daily take for granted. For its first 150 years, the United States was a boy with so much candy that no matter how much he ate he always had some to give away. For the next 25 years, he could eat as much as he wanted provided he gave very little away. Today he cannot supply enough to meet his very large, and increasing, appetite, and must, for the first time, go to the world's candy stores and stand in line like everyone else to buy it.

He is still wealthy enough to buy it. The total worth of the United States today equals the total of all the natural resources still remaining; all the resources used and converted into money, credit, and goods; the total savings and investments of all Americans during the past 200 years; the value added to every raw product fashioned and converted by American industry; the fees received from the technology produced; and the profits returned from abroad by the money sunk into other nations. U.S. wealth is all this, minus that which has been consumed, and that which has—through war, neglect, or planned obsolescence—been wasted.

Raw material wealth once spent with abandon must be preserved.

Americans should understand that domestic raw materials have two measures of value: they are at hand as captive supplies, and U.S. capital does not have to leave the country to buy them.

When Americans were buying from each other their natural resources, their petroleum and copper, their iron ore and their lead, the money stayed home, in the United States, and was part of the vast infrastructure of domestic wealth which, through its multiplier effect and taxes, contributed to economic stability up and down the economic ladder. They sold products to each other very cheaply. That money is being spent, and increasingly will be spent, outside the nation, but far more of it is needed to buy the same quantity as before.

The United States is self-sufficient in coal and corn. The National Coal Association puts present U.S. coal reserves as sufficient to last between 400 and 2,000 years at current consumption levels. The Department of Agriculture reports that Americans consume about 500 million bushels of wheat annually, and in really good harvest years the United States produces four times that amount.

The United States has, of course, much more than coal and corn. There are vast acreages of other food resources of a staggering variety. Cattle and sheep ranges, hog farms and chicken farms, all capable of converting the grasslands and produce into protein, make most Americans the best-fed people in the world. The United States has much land, much timber, and large—if not self-sufficient—quantities of many minerals, though barely adequate fresh water resources.

The resources alone, however, are not enough to maintain a standard of living anywhere close to that enjoyed by the majority of Americans today, and to have to rely on them alone would mean a major reallocation of how the United States consumes its resources, who may use them, and for what purposes. Yet Americans must gear themselves for a reallocation of resources. Modern energy and modern materials, consumed without thinking, are the modern appurtenances which allow social commentators to talk about people having increased leisure time. (Leisure time is not merely the hours spent away from the office or job; it is primarily the lack of essential duties to perform during those hours away from work.)

There are two ways of looking at the U.S. raw material dependency problem. The first is by looking at a commodity, oil, which the United States must get from a variety of nations. The next way is to look at a single nation, in this case, Canada, on which the United States is dependent for a variety of resources. In neither case is the situation particularly reassuring

Using these two examples, oil and Canada, it is possible to understand what dependency actually means in political and economic terms. These two can represent all the natural resources the United States imports, and all the nations on which the United States depends.

Americans need to understand how deeply they are now engaged in that tricky arena of international resource politics, that so many nations—mindful of their need to have government acting within the boundaries imposed by foreign economic policy—have been practicing for decades, or in some cases centuries. *Resource dependency makes domestic economic policy just that much more difficult, domestic politics just that much more awkward, international diplomacy essential—and suspicion inevitable.*

Domestic oil shortages mean, for example, that economic decisions must be subjected to the scrutiny of national political and security needs. Diplomacy becomes much more than the mere exchanging of notes in areas of mutual concern.

Actual dealings are complicated by the "suspicion factor." Many Europeans, most particularly British Conservatives, are continually suspicious of the Soviet Union and Soviet military maneuvering to discomfort and reduce the Western nations. One British cabinet member provided an example of the "suspicion" view of "resource politics" when he said: "Russia, quite simply, is encircling Europe's oil supply. It can choke off the supply if we are not careful. But if the Soviet Union is encircling our supplies, it is encircling U.S. supplies, too."

A British missile deployment expert, summing up the delicate nuclear stalemate in missile-counting at around the same time, provided another example of the suspicion factor when he said: "There was nothing in the Nixon-Moscow round to prevent the Soviet Union from building up a massive lead over the U.S. purely by replacing existing missiles with ones having independently targeted multiple warheads. The count would remain the same, but the U.S. is outgunned. What is there then to stop the Soviets from establishing a Middle East quarantine area through which all tankers must pass?"

Amid this political doomsaying (of a degree which makes ecological doomsaying appear lighthearted), what boded significant was not the missile-man's outgunning concern, but his huge leap forward to the conclusion that with such strength the Russians would act against oil supplies. Overreactions or not, these nuances, of the type with which resource-short European nations have been playing for decades, are increasingly being taken into consideration by the United States also, in those areas where its economic interests are likely to be pressured.

The following is taken from a 1974 bulletin written by Ross Nicholson, an institutional investment advisor. It is light years removed from Wall Street-oriented investment bulletins of only 12 months earlier:

> In ten years, the Soviet navy has expanded its fleet of submarines enormously so that it can be used in blockading operations in the Atlantic and Pacific, it has broken the virtual American naval monopoly in the Mediterranean, and it has replaced Britain as the most powerful navy in the Indian Ocean. With the right mixture of ships, submarines, weapons, and location, the Soviet navy appears to be able to provide a variety of responses in a naval confrontation and this factor suggests that the Soviet navy will be as effective a political tool as the British navy was in the 18th and 19th Centuries.
>
> The Soviet navy realises it has attained a tremendous bargaining position, and it is doubtful if the radical Arabian boycotters would have been able to induce the conservative Saudi Arabians and other Gulf states to join the boycott without its presence.

Those who are aware that the British government owns 49 percent of British Petroleum (BP), because it wanted to ensure oil supplies for the Royal Navy, may not know that the longest standing oil reserves in Alaska, dating back half a century themselves, are U.S. Navy oil reserves.

Because the British, and the other European governments, have lived with these shortages of vital resources, they regard American profligacy with its own oil as a dual dread: first, it means the United States has joined that group of Middle Eastern oil users subjected to political and economic pressures because they have no alternative sources for extra supplies; and second, it means the United States can no longer be the crude oil supplier of last resort for troubled Europeans, as it was during Suez and the 1967 Arab-Israeli Six Day War, when European supply lines were cut.

The United States still has some room to move. But not much.

What makes the Middle East doubly expensive is that in addition to the dollar cost there is a political price to pay. Compromise is not an economic or political card the United States has often had to play.

The Middle East is a more volatile area even than it appears—and there has been nothing to suggest tranquility. The Arab-Israeli situation is recent by comparison. There is, first and foremost, a deep and lingering resentment that festered for a century under the swaggering dominion of European nations and for half a century under the oil men.

Bitter memories, such as those held by educated Iranians, of the freedom with which the Russians and the British divided up the country into spheres of influence, are wounds that take a long time to heal, and then still leave a scar.

Past colonial subservience, the Westerners usually regarding the domestic populations as inferior beings, is more than sufficient to account for retaliation. But the complexities do not end there, any more than they would with an end to the Arab-Israeli dispute.

There are cultural and national disputes, boundary and legal disputes, on top of deep-seated anticolonial passions. Acted out within this framework of hostility and hate are the disputes and disagreements and war-talk between the Middle Eastern nations themselves. Look at just three nations.

Iran is a Muslim nation, but the people are Aryans. Its western neighbors, Iraq and Saudi Arabia across the Persian Gulf, are Muslims too, but Arabs. Iran is a constitutional monarchy with the fastest growing economy in the area, civil, almost friendly, toward the West. Iraq is a nationalization-prone socialist state with a slowly rising standard of living, a sad contrast to Iran to the eyes of the impartial observer. Saudi Arabia is a monarchy.

There is a measure of civility currently between Saudi Arabia and Iran, but Iraq and Iran are constantly in a state of war preparedness, and both maintain troops and emplacements along their mutual border.

How these Middle Eastern nations see themselves may eventually be more important to freely flowing oil than how they appear to outside investors and oil-dependent nations.

Libya, under Colonel Qaddafi, had been gradually squeezing the foreign oil companies to see how much pain they could take. Qaddafi expropriated the British Petroleum holdings and reserves in Libya "simply to punish the British government," which had not prevented the Shah of Iran from claiming possession of some islands at the mouth of the Persian Gulf over which the British government had had some mandate before removing itself from east of Suez.

Algeria, which has only 8 billion barrels of crude oil reserves but trillions of cubic feet of available natural gas, provided little compensation to the French when it took over the French oil and gas interests. The resultant trauma on French industry has had the French scurrying around ever since for new and more reliable sources. International economic relations between France and the United States, never particularly happy since De Gaulle's day (it was Pompidou who announced the dollar was to be devalued at the Azores meeting in 1971), were not enhanced by the ease with which America's El Paso Natural Gas was able to get tentative U.S. government approval to import Algerian natural gas out of fields not too much earlier nationalized from under the French owners.

That the French went ahead alone with an oil-for-arms deal with Saudi Arabia, at a period when the United States was calling for a united front by oil consumers against the producers, was scarcely surprising. This type of relatively petty international contentiousness is not something the United States has had to lower itself to deal with in the past. But this is the nature of "resource diplomacy" and "resource politics."

There is another, deeper, meaning to the rapid coming together of the Arab oil producers to form an apparent united front. The nations all are Muslim, the "holy war" is not just between Muslim and Jew in the Arab-Israeli war. To a limited extent, one is witnessing a revival of Islam, a revival that many Muslims regard as necessary, just as many Christians are looking to Christianity to reclaim a role as a vigorous social apostolate. In neither case is the reality yet approaching the hopes.

Pakistan, Turkey, Indonesia, and Albania all have majority Muslim populations. There are "three great minorities," in China, the USSR, and black Africa.

The Muslim nations of the Middle East therefore see themselves as part of a major world group with its own sense of history.

W. Cantwell Smith, in *Islam in Modern History,* reminds Westerners that roughly since the Second World War, every major Muslim community has been in charge of its own affairs—as effectively as is feasible in the kind of world in which we live.

As any Islamic state "is not a form of state so much as a form of Islam," the Westerner must look on individual Muslim nations as states to be distinguished

not so much from other kinds of state—liberal, democratic, fascist or whatever—as from other expressions of Islam as a religion. . . . Muslims are unlikely to become Western liberals or Western humanists, or even secular liberal humanists in the specifically Western fashion.

Cantwell Smith reserves a special brand of scorn for those Western political leaders who, in dealing with the Muslim nations, "have apparently adopted in practice the absurd as well as offensive doctrine that man lives by bread alone."

Given these feelings, aggravated by the treatment Middle Eastern nations have received from Western governments and Western oil men, possibly the Muslim populations have a few grudges to work off, a sense of history to fulfill, a mission for social justice, and certainly an economic platform from which to address the world.

Just as Vietnam brought about a taste of the inflation that hastened U.S. dollar troubles, so the Middle East war brought about the energy crisis through the Arab use of oil as a political weapon. But the rapid rise in price of crude oil, the sophisticated awareness of the producers that they need no longer be dictated to, and now, their interest in slowing down the rate of production to preserve their reserves, were all in the cards.

Like the decline of the United States' economy, the emergence of the Arab oil powers as global powers who had to be listened to happened in a relatively short time. The impact of both has been impressive, almost awesome.

Oil producing countries, be they Muslim or not, are not entirely free agents over oil.

Only with continued revenues can they buy the prosperity that will enable them to hold on to domestic power. To risk economic downturn is to risk a coup. The shahs, sheiks, emirs, presidents, and prime ministers cannot afford a major global recession, either.

Oil producers need the income to fight their wars, or keep their peace, depending on their preferences. They need that income to make their voices heard in the world bargaining and conference centers. And they need it for all their specifically nationalistic, domestic, and politico-religious reasons.

As long as the producers can control the prices, they control their revenues. The oil-exporting nations have rapidly developed an international view of resource bargaining, capitalistic profit-taking, global monetary affairs and their own strength that is highly sophisticated and growing more so. They also are aware of the costs borne by the industrial nations of the West and by Japan, and are not hesitant about dictating terms.

These terms involve strategic and national political and economic considerations. It is not an area where governments can permit capitalist interests, profit, return on equity to balance the scales. Nor will it do so—except where domestic governments of oil import-dependent nations are able to perform a fine balancing act between national interests and corporate interests.

In the politics of global raw materials bargaining, for political it now is, the needs of the corporation come a poor third, well behind the national-interest demands of the seller, and the national-interest requirements of the buyer.

Diminishing domestic oil supplies merely serve as one example of how discontent grows when expectations are dashed. Consumers fall back to saying "why doesn't someone do something about it," and because the government is the only "someone" the public believes can do something, the government's hand in the national economy is strengthened, and its arm lengthened.

Vox populi is a snarl when adults accustomed to easy mobility are unable to get gasoline for their family car; when they feel guilty about not turning the heat down to 65 degrees; when some segments of the financial world can produce healthy, or even record, profits at a time when the householder cannot even maintain the value of the dollar in his pocket.

For oil there are non-Muslim sources, non-OPEC (Organization of Petroleum Exporting Countries) sources, but not in locations or quantities that make any immediate difference to America's dependence on Middle Eastern suppliers. The Soviet Union sells some of its crude oil in Europe. China potentially can use crude as payment for international purchases.

North Sea oil, expensive to find and bring ashore, may do wonders for beleaguered Britain's borrowing power in the world money markets, but in spite of U.S. corporations' being involved in much of the exploration and production, North Sea oil is unlikely to go to the United States. Total known North Sea reserves would last the United States only a few years. Yet the North Sea's development for oil and gas is an indication of how one small import-dependent trading nation was sufficiently preoccupied with supplies to get the oil found and delivered. Britain's economic needs, its balance of payments problems, and most of all its suspicions concerning the Soviet Union's oil-blockading potential, has lent urgency to the British quest for its own oil reserves.

Urgency, but not panic, is what the United States has to bring to a review, then a policy, then a program, then action, to cope with the shortages in energy and raw materials that will bedevil its future and are bedeviling its present.

As the search for more oil and energy alternatives expands, with even more government intervention and support, one can note in passing that in 1968 the Office of Coal Production in the United States gave a $10 million contract to Consolidation Coal and Continental Oil to bring a pilot plant on stream that would produce "competitively priced high-octane gasoline for around 10 cents to 13 cents a gallon out of coal."

That miracle is not yet upon a waiting world, and by 1974 the U.S. National Coal Association was calling for a $2 billion a year, internationally financed research program capable of obtaining from coal the versatility currently gained from crude petroleum through the range of its products. If nothing else, the jump from a $10 million one-shot experiment to a call for $2 billion annually shows in which direction Western nations are turning—toward government for intervention.

Coal research and development spending for fiscal 1975 in the United States has already shot up to $414.5 million. It was only $85 million in fiscal year 1973.

Present demands for natural gas are producing expensive programs such as the one to ship liquefied natural gas from Algeria to the United States, and the once much-discussed—but now unlikely—possibility of a joint U.S.-Japanese venture tapping vast natural gas reserves in the Soviet Union. Any nation with abundant supplies of natural gas will be keen to sell to the United States, but gas is one more dependency issue.

There are hopes that U.S. oil and gas reserves can be increased. Alaska is one such hope: there are offshore possibilities; there is much speculation about the oil and gas potential of the Florida Gulf Coast. There are hopes for the alternative energy sources. Hopes and drives for new ways of doing things are much of the spark in U.S. industrial life, and a challenge for its scientists and engineers. Whether the private sector can afford, or indeed will attempt, always to fund the research and development that could unlock these alternatives, again points to the U.S. domestic tendency toward greater reliance and interplay between private and public sectors.

The Western world has been critically short of strategic materials previously, and nations other than Middle Eastern nations have exploited their natural advantage. What will the Middle Eastern nations do with their money? Arm. And industrialize. But nations with a sense of history, and the Arab nations have that sense, must feel they can make their voices heard and their weight felt in world affairs.

Three centuries ago tar was as important to the maritime aims of England, the Netherlands, and France as oil is to the industrial aims of the West today.

Sweden was the great monopolist. Swedish historian Kurt Samuelsson set the scene in *From Great Power to Welfare State:*

> As woodlands had been depleted all over Europe, Sweden and Finland possessed virtually the only remaining forest reserves. This favored position was ruthlessly exploited (by Sweden) to create high prices.

Samuelsson explained that Sweden, in addition to a monopoly of copper and a near-monopoly of iron exports, held

> the monopoly of tar products [that] constituted [for Sweden] a commercial supremacy without which politico-military expansion would have been unattainable.

No wonder the French, the Dutch, and the English were so attracted to those North American forests. (And the interested reader might look closer at what happened to Sweden after the monopoly was broken. At this juncture, however, one is not suggesting that the OPEC oil cartel could be broken.)

So much for the scarcity of a single commodity. The pitfalls of dependency on a single nation, while different, are equally serious, and in similar need of understanding.

U.S. investments in Canada in 1969 exceeded $35 billion, and represented nearly half the book value of *all* U.S. global investment. In no nation does the "host" nation's political-nationalist feeling make more sense than in Canada.

There is almost more U.S. investment in Canada than there is Canadian investment. Canada gains much from U.S. money being placed in its lands, industry, and commerce, but in terms of national spirit, that is, the need for a feeling of independence, Canada feels constricted.

A government-created entity like the Canadian Development Corporation, which is there to buy into those major outside corporations that dominate segments of Canadian industry, is a peaceable reaction to that domination. Canada's bid for Texas Gulf Industries, which gets most of its profits from Canada, is a classic alternative to the more familiar expropriation and nationalization of less moderate nations.

Americans to the south of the 3,000-mile U.S.-Canadian border scarcely know of their dependency on Canada let alone possess a feel for Canadian attitudes toward it.

Canada supplies 66 percent of U.S. newsprint, 84 percent of its asbestos, vast quantities of minerals and forest products, plus $2 billion annually in dividends, profits, and payments repatriated south. U.S. interests control 97 percent of the Canadian auto industry, 97 percent of the Canadian rubber industry, a total 46 percent of Canadian manufacturing, and in the six years up to 1969 merged or took over 600 Canadian corporations as part of U.S. global expansion. A firm grip on Canadian manufacturing means a ready market for U.S. component products within that manufacturing, which is a guaranteed export outlet for U.S. goods, coupled with a guaranteed supply of completed products from a subsidiary capable of pouring wares back across the border for sale in the United States.

The Canadians know they are in a difficult situation. They have to sell energy to the United States, yet they do not want any more U.S. investment than they already have. This frustration is repeated, and will continue to be repeated, in all those nations that smart under a sense of being dominated by outside interests. Oil and gas from the

Canadian Arctic may help strengthen Canada's hand slightly, but Canada has one resource in greater quantity than any other nation in the world, and one vitally important to the United States in the future: fresh water. One-sixth of the world's fresh water is in Canada, and U.S. consumption is straining its own national supplies to the limit.

As it does with practically every other resource, the United States consumes more water per capita than any other nation in the world. In the absence of nuclear desalinization projects, or a rapid cleanup of the ruined bodies of its own water and rivers, the United States must once more turn its attention to Canada. But this time the United States will have to adopt something more cap-in-hand than its previous investment programs north of the border: that is because water is Canada's last nation-to-nation bargaining tool with the United States. And the price will come very high.

The United States decline into import-dependency for raw materials and energy needs is usually fashioned—by Canadians and others—into a single line of attack: that if the United States had better allocated its resources, curbed its population rise and the existing population's appetite, the overall easing of pressure on world raw material supplies would be noticeable, and the effects admirable.

But curbing populations and appetites to levels that match resources is easier said than done. By historical cycle, or social circumstances, rather than by any U.S. governmental design, the population's rate of growth of the United States has been declining. But that does not mean the phenomenon will continue. The enormous appetite remains.

There are two other areas, virtually untapped, from which the United States can draw raw materials. Neither of them will provide cheap resources, but both will be U.S. national territory: Alaska, and the offshore continental United States.

As the North Slope oil has shown, the environmental, political, and economic costs and consequences of taking anything out of Alaska can run very high indeed. But the pressure for reliable oil supplies means the pipeline becomes a reality, and rather expensive U.S. crude oil from the Alaskan North Slope, next door to those long-held U.S. naval oil reserves, will flow south to the "lower 48."

Alaska, which is one-fifth the size of the continental United States, and has two-thirds of the entire U.S. coastline, is a treasure house of minerals. U.S. interests raped Alaskan river beds for copper long before Charlie Chaplin's gold rush.

In that vast wilderness bordering the Canadian Yukon and Northwest territories, and close to British Columbia (where so much resource extraction, indeed plunder, has already occurred) is a U.S. state with coal and copper, cobalt and chromite, asbestos and sulphur, gold and pumice, graphite and platinum, gypsum and phosphate, iron and nickel, limestone, marble, marl, and mercury.

The U.S. Geological Survey has adequately indicated general source deposits, though the actual amounts and the unknown economic costs of extraction add a further question mark to this last magnificent land, which lies uneasy on a bed of wealth of the type and scope which peopled the United States, and created its standard of living.

Those who have fought, and lost, the battle of the Alaskan pipeline, scarcely have begun to grapple with what next happens to Alaska. The $100 million S.S. *Manhattan* tanker project, which bore Esso's flag to the Northwest passage, it was hoped would provide an oil transportation system instead of, or in addition to, a pipeline. Arctic winters and the shifting polar ice cap do not allow year-round navigation, even with a fleet of icebreakers.

But solid minerals and ores, copper, iron, nickel, and gypsum, do not require year-round transportation. They can be stockpiled, and collected in the short open season.

Offshore territory, sovereign land on the continental shelf, is another equally difficult but nationally owned storehouse for the near future.

The politics of seabeds beyond the 12-mile limit, or the eventual prevailing limit, will be anything but internal. The mad scramble for seabed wealth will result in the spoils going to the strong, not to the weak; to the industrial nations, not to the agricultural nations; to the currently wealthy, not to the currently poor.

As the largest single user of global resources, the United States, too, looks at the world seabed; and as the home base of the majority of the world's largest mineral and resource extractive corporations, U.S. industry, commerce, and finance similarly ponder the wealth under the sea.

Casual exploiters are already scooping up pyrolusite nodules from the Atlantic deep-seabed, not an easy harvest, but a profitable one once the technique has been mastered. But these casual excavators are operating in a limbo of "who owns what" and "who has jurisdiction over what." The world's nations have not yet even agreed on a phrase to describe these areas of "seabed beyond the limits of national jurisdiction." And while commentators might point to the already accomplished division of the North Sea undersea area, which permitted the nations bordering that sea to divide up and apportion the seabed, the problems of undersea jurisdiction have scarcely begun.

In a world where national governments are less known now for generosity of spirit, or for seeking to further the aims of the least well-advanced nations, the length of debate to resolve globally a proposal such as this can be imagined only with difficulty. Within the United States there is deep disagreement as to how far out from the shoreline the national offshore jurisdiction should stretch.

While most countries now claim sovereignty only 3 or 12 miles from their coasts, Peru has claimed 200 miles, and Iceland is unilaterally doing the same. The Norwegian government is committed to extending its fishing rights to 50 miles offshore.

But nations that claim sea rights claim rights to the seabed underneath. As long as 12 miles was the limit, the U.S. Navy (and other navies) could move freely throughout the world. An extension of legal offshore jurisdiction is not merely an economic problem.

There may be sufficient resources under the sea to meet the needs of the world's most prodigious user, the United States. The political and economic *costs* are still unknown.

What does become apparent is that the research, exploration, and development costs of bringing new areas of exploitation, like Alaska or the ocean bed, into production are fast exceeding the point at which they can be met by money from the private sector and the corporations involved. Just as the Boeing 747 may prove to be the last civil airliner to be developed almost exclusively by private money, and without governmental loans, so the Alaska pipeline may prove to be the final major energy undertaking not calling on government participation, government loans, or government profit guarantees.

The effect on capitalism of major multinational and major domestic corporations undertaking staggeringly expensive projects in joint ventures with government, or by themselves, if the government guarantees a definite return, will change the nature of capitalist enterprise.

It is sufficient at this point to restate that the absence of an abundant supply of cheap resources for the mighty production sector of the United States means a lowering of the U.S. standard of living. The scarcity of sources of "new wealth," cheap new wealth like Tonopah or the East Texas oil fields, will increase the cost of living on an ever-rising curve. The substitution of expensive-to-buy, expensive-to-find, expensive-to-extract raw materials for what previously came easily and cheaply will further increase those production and living costs by an order of magnitude. An increasing reliance on government to hold down prices, to fund or participate in the costs of new capital-heavy essential projects, and the advent of the corporations trading their expertise and participation in the projects for a governmentally guaranteed return, will alter completely the nature of the U.S. economy, as it is altering the nature of all Western economies.

When the economic fabric of these Western industrialized democracies changes, the political and social fabric changes, too. But these points must wait for further discussion.

As this discussion reaches the juncture at which the United States needs to spend globally money it once kept at home, to find money other than in its domestic raw material treasure trove, the narrative must look at the immediate alternatives, alternatives long profitably explored by Western capitalism: world trade and worldwide investment.

Domestic wealth creation in the United States through the discoveries of valuable deposits of mineral resources has peaked; the technological wealth created by inventions and systems easily marketed and profitably exported has slowed; the profit margins of the mighty industries increasingly reflect higher costs, the rising cost of replacing existing plant, and the justified demands from workers seeking pay claims to stay abreast of inflation; future expansion plans are crimped by expensive money at the bank and the lack of interest shown by the investing public in new stock market offerings. From the investing point of view, the return on investment is unsatisfactory.

Valuable profits from exports, and dividends, interest, and royalties from overseas investment, have long been a salutary factor in the income column. But globally, too, the ease with which the United States sold its products, invested its money in the growth sectors of other nations, and enjoyed majority stakes—even total ownership—of new ventures in other nations is a fading memory.

Indeed, though overseas investment had been a source of delight and high profits, with European nations facing higher inflation rates than the United States, many U.S. multinational corporations will not be quite so gleeful about their expansionist habits of the late 1950s and early 1960s.

The international marketplace is now a bazaar crowded with haggling hawkers. Nations are jealously protecting their growth sectors, and governments are demanding a major stake when foreign corporations come calling with development plans.

2

How the World Turned —
On U.S. Capitalism

International business is a real law of the jungle. We watch
what they do. The more sophisticated we become, the
more we realize in how many areas they can take money
out of our pockets. They have their tricks, so we have to
have our tricks.

Abol Gessam M. Kheradjou
Iran Industrial and Mining
Development Bank

Between 1950 and 1970 exports from the United States rose from $10
billion to $43 billion. Over the same 20-year period the book value of
U.S. corporate multinational expansion went from $12 billion to $80
billion, with the actual value today something more than $200 bil-
lion.

What those figures tell is this. Rapidly increasing U.S. exports
were a great contributor to the American income and the American
standard of living. These ever-increasing exports were new wealth,
just as the raw material discoveries had been.

Exports were followed as a natural progression by U.S. investment
overseas, usually manufacturing investment, using highly valued
(Charles de Gaulle believed them to be overvalued) U.S. dollars.
There was new wealth here, too, buying up the manufacturing capacity in other lands, primarily European lands, or building up new facilities there.

U.S. corporate policy was to stick close to the growth sectors of global industry. Returns from this new investment were high: at least 12 to 20 percent on average has been suggested, to compare with 10 to 12 percent in the United States. Much of the extra profit margin being squeezed out of Europe in the early years included the natural profits possible with sophisticated management techniques, being early in growth areas (computers, electronics, pharmaceuticals), or starting up new factories and marketing networks before the domestic competition presented a serious challenge.

This surge of U.S. corporate multinational expansion meant that, beyond just adding dividends from abroad to the income of the United States, U.S. corporations were establishing, taking over, or expanding foreign industrial manufacturing capacity that, in many situations, could compete directly with U.S. manufactured goods. U.S.-owned corporations account for almost 25 percent of Britain's exports, and that figure is still rising. Major blue chips listed on the New York Stock Exchange were tying their profits to overseas earnings dependent on economies other than that of the United States. Some 40 percent of the largest U.S. corporations by 1974 were receiving better than 25 percent of their total profit from their multinational subsidiaries; and for companies like IBM that figure was nearer 50 percent. Much of this overseas expansion was done with a highly valued dollar that in fact was cashing in at bargain prices.

Today the export growth curve from the United States has slowed markedly. The ability to earn quick new wealth from global multinational expansion similarly has slowed. National interests of foreign nations at a time of uncertainty and austerity press just as heavily, perhaps more heavily, on the U.S. subsidiary as they do on domestic corporations. European inflation rates, generally higher than those in the United States, mean production there is not necessarily more profitable now than U.S.-based production—and the margins squeezed out of newly acquired markets and manufacturing capacity, the advantages of superior management techniques and advanced technology have been eroded. There is competition as never before, and the dollar no longer has the buying power that makes snapping up foreign corporations such a bargain.

There has been a second wave of U.S. multinational corporate expansion: banking and financial services. These too have contributed to U.S. income as profits were made by expanding trade, and by squeezing profits out of doing old business in new ways.

But first, U.S. exports.

About a century ago, when the first supplies of cheap meat from the American West landed on the docks at Liverpool and Dublin, there were near-riots as people fought to buy it. Low-priced beef from the American ranges was raising the nutritional standards of Europe. (Even today, those gauging the development of a developing nation run their finger down the "per capita meat consumption" column to see how it has increased as that nation's economy has expanded.)

The United States was not concerning itself with the European diet, however; it was bringing on one more new product to be bought up in the world marketplace. The reason U.S. beef was popular was because it was cheap.

Grain from the U.S. plains long brought cheap bread; U.S. products, from clocks to broadcloth, were selling around the world because they were high in quality and low in price. They were high in quality because the United States had produced generations of tinkerers and inventors, technologists and scientists, who came up with new ways of making new and better products. They were cheap because the same technology found new ways of making them more cheaply, and because the resources to make them—labor plus minerals plus power—were cheap when totaled up against the manufacturing costs in other countries.

Labor was cheap because the continued waves of emigrants from Europe kept wages down; minerals and power were cheap because they were produced domestically from relatively low cost sources. Production costs also were cheap because intense competition kept prices down and margins narrow, at least in those industries not dominated by monopolies, trusts, or cartels. (Free enterprise was so successful in keeping profits down that by the end of the nineteenth century not one of the 40 major sugar corporations in the United States was making a profit, Faulkner writes.)

As any modern housewife can verify, beef—even U.S. beef—is no longer cheap. It is not landing on the docks of Liverpool and Dublin, though beef from Dublin has been known to land on the docks in New York. U.S. grain, caught up in international commodity speculation, government-to-government trading, and increasing demand, is not providing the world with cheap bread.

Clocks made in America generally stay in America: they cannot compete in price, though they might in quality, with clocks made in Japan. The European Economic Community is a trading bloc, a customs union, that makes the American clock more expensive in Britain or Germany than a French clock that cost the same to make.

American cloth—but not U.S. blue jeans—bowed out of world markets under the pressure of Taiwanese or Hong Kong textiles. U.S. technology, still supreme in computers and a few other key products, now has many rivals abreast of it in aerospace, electronics, consumer goods—areas where U.S. technology long brought premium prices in the world marketplace.

Puerto Ricans settling on the mainland, Mexicans coming up from the South, were recent influxes of cheap labor. Illegal aliens from Central and South America are the latest. American corporations today set up manufacturing facilities in low-labor-cost areas outside the United States. The corporations may be saving on production costs, but not necessarily to the benefit of the U.S. consumer, or the U.S. economy, or U.S. exports and balance-of-trade. But they do make a profit.

Domestic mineral supplies and cheap power are no longer providing the price advantage to U.S. exports, but dollar devaluations and a lower rate of inflation in the United States—in relation to the other major exporting and trading nations—have maintained the marketability of many U.S.-manufactured exports. Devaluing the dollar, lowering prices through lowering the value of the currency, does something to restore the selling advantage, but that is offset when increased amounts of the currency have to be used to buy the same amounts of raw materials.

During the 1964–66 boom aerospace was a prestigious, profitable, expanding industry with a high export component. U.S. aircraft dominated the civil air routes. U.S. manufactured goods dominated most markets in the fifties and early sixties, because the United States' manufacturing capacity, industrial inventiveness, and capital availability had come out of World War II virtually unscathed. The United States, as conventional economic history tells, did fill the needs of a war-torn world short in capital and consumer goods.

During the boom years, U.S. aerospace sales, commercial and military, were sometimes little more than extra production runs on aircraft already bought in huge numbers by U.S. airlines and the U.S. military. With the United States as the world's single largest aircraft market, any aerospace manufacturer needed a strong sales success there to carry production and development costs; after that the profits started to mount rapidly.

Free world air forces patrolled the skies and fought their post–World War II skirmishes and "police actions" in large numbers of U.S. made aircraft. From SAS (which has bought at least one of every new aircraft the McDonnell-Douglas Corporation has built) to Britain's BOAC (which, despite its own British-built VC10s, bought a large Boeing 707 fleet), all European airlines were ready customers for the high-quality, low-cost airliners. Low cost? In purchase price and in passenger-mile revenues, U.S.-designed and -built aircraft experienced little competition.

The jumbo jets naturally followed the pattern of previous sales: plenty for the U.S. domestic airlines, followed by massive sales to the rest of the world. Not only did Boeing's 747 entry coincide with a downturn in the world economy, meaning fewer passengers, and a probable permanent near-leveling of the new-business curve, but its cost and capacity threw airline economics into a spin.

The dynamic aerospace market in civil airliners has flown into rough weather, and turned more into a saturated replacement market than an outlet for an ever-expanding industry. And this was before rapidly rising oil costs added to airline operators' woes.

The world's airlines already had just about enough capacity to see them through the decade. Many of them, still saddled with their pre-jumbo jets, turned back their 747s, delayed deliveries, or were stuck with excess capacity on the tarmac and in the hangars. There was even talk of 1,000-seater aircraft, but not much talk of who would finance them or who would be able to purchase them.

Europe has long been the United States' biggest customer for exports, including military aircraft. In Europe, the French, British, German, Swedish and Italian aerospace interests, in little combines or in big consortia, would like to fill the needs of their own market. European governments would like them to, too. But price and quality still matter, and the United States apparently has them. In what was

termed "the sale of the century," General Dynamics Corporation
sold $2 billion worth of aircraft to the Netherlands, Norway and Den-
mark, outselling not only the European products, but also those of
Lockheed, Boeing, LTV Aerospace and Northrop.

European air forces can take their pick of the British-built Jaguar
or Harrier aircraft, the Dassault product range, the Saab range, or the
MRCA (multi-role-combat-aircraft), a joint product of most major
European aircraft manufacturers. In this protected market, which
once welcomed Vought's aircraft-carrier-based fighters, the F-111,
the Sabers, and the rest, the U.S. sales teams try to maintain a
toehold. The competition is government-funded, government-sup-
ported and government-will-buy domestic interests.

The Belgian national airline Sabena bought 10 Hercules aircraft on
the understanding they would be assembled in Belgium. This is yet
another way in which the U.S. hand is being weakened. Aircraft and
engines, civil and military avionics and weaponry are all losing their
previous advantages. So, in Europe, the single most important market
for U.S. civil and military aircraft since the end of World War II, the
increasing tendency toward European-wide mergers in the industry,
the local buying preferences of national governments anxious to keep
their aircraft industries functioning and their high technology teams
together, and an already-underway series of joint military and civil
aircraft ventures mean far tougher sales for U.S. aerospace export.

Iran, Japan and a half-dozen other potential customers come to
mind. But the bloom is off the aerospace export-sales rose, and one
more boom-time money spinner has lost much of its luster.

Aerospace was just one export industry in which the United States
had a head start over the competition in the fifties and sixties. In
aerospace, and in many other profitable lines from air conditioners to
electric toasters, the United States has lost that head start.

Much of the money that fueled the U.S. economy in the fifties and
sixties was from this new wealth in trade and overseas investment.
Look at the staggering proportions it reached.

Touch down as a tourist or business executive in Brussels, the new
capital of the new Europe in your European-owned U.S.-built Boeing
747. After arrival take a taxi, a German Ford (U.S. owned), along
the highways to the Rue de la Loi and the Brussels Hilton.

As the taxi makes its energy crisis 80 km.p.h. (50 m.p.h.) journey

along the highways, running on gasoline supplied by U.S. oil mul-
tinationals, the neon signs along the highway provide, for the visiting
American, nice touches of home: Exxon, Culligan, Holiday Inn,
IBM, and RCA are just a few.

What is behind the signs? A gigantic U.S. corporate presence in
Belgium. Total foreign investment in Belgium between 1959 and
1969 was nearly $2 billion; 55 percent of that was U.S. investment.
The pace has slackened since.

In the seventies RCA opened its new semiconductor plant at Liege,
leaving its research and development facilities back in Somerville,
New Jersey; Mead Corporation opened a new paper factory near
Brussels with a daily capacity of 180 tons; its joint builders were
Coppee Rust, a joint venture owned by Evence Coppee et Cie. of
Brussels, and Rust Engineering, which had Litton connections.

(Not all those European or Belgian acquisitions were bargains.
Westinghouse, late into Europe, ended up by buying Belgian electrical goods manufacturer ACEC. By 1975 Westinghouse was seeking ways to significantly reduce its European connection.)

In fact, it matters little that a visitor from North America has
landed in Brussels. Had his Air France 747 touched down at Paris
Orly, and had he been driven to the Paris Hilton in a French-built
Simca (owned by the U.S. firm Chrysler), he would see many of the
same corporate signs along the highway, and be reassured that
beyond the highway are the homes of the ordinary French businessmen, built by Levitt.

Geneva, Dusseldorf, London, it hardly matters where, because the
scene is the same. Though with less impact, Tehran, Rio de Janeiro,
Hong Kong, and Sydney carry versions of the same flashing signs
that signal the U.S. corporate presence.

Belgium and France are two European nations that between them
represent a fair cross-section of conditions and attitudes within the
Common Market. The multinationals, in the days when they were
just the foreign subsidiaries of U.S. corporations, were welcomed for
the investment they represented, the jobs and industrial stability they
created—though when they went after key or prestigious industries
(the British Rootes automobile group, or France's Jeaumont-
Schneider electrical group) there were national outcries.

Often, during the fifties and sixties, when U.S. interests moved with a vengeance into Europe, everyone was pleased. Stockholders in U.S. corporations were happy because U.S. companies could make more on their investments. When, in the middle and late sixties, the last of the major U.S. manufacturers not already established in Europe moved in—Chrysler into Germany, for example, or Deere into France—it was an acceptable use of the manufacturing, capital-raising, managerial, and marketing abilities that U.S. corporations possessed.

There were other factors at work. *Fortune* magazine commented on them in July 1972:

as a new product becomes established in the domestic market, it is increasingly exported, particularly to other high-income, high-wage countries. When those foreign markets reach some critical size, however, it becomes worthwhile to manufacture the product there.

How much of the overseas expansion has been at the expense of the United States' ability to manufacture at home, and to export from home, there is no adequate way of finding out. By no means all of the $80 billion spent in overseas expansion would have been invested instead in the United States, lowering production costs, improving technology, developing export-oriented products, but that does not mean none of it would have.

Even assuming the repatriated profits and dividends from overseas investment equal the amount of money the United States could have gained from domestically manufactured exports, there is still another factor. That $80 billion has had a multiplier effect, through jobs, service industries, tax-supported facilities for nations other than the United States.

The United States has not exported all its export industry, but it has exported much manufacturing, much investment, that is a loss to the domestic economic infrastructure of the nation. For as long as a new plant overseas promotes exports from the domestic U.S. factory, multinational corporate expansion is aiding the U.S. economy. Where the foreign-based factory takes on new markets, ships low-cost parts back to the United States to make U.S.-produced goods more competitive, who can complain? But where that new factory replaces the U.S. factory, by taking away its potential new investment, its potential new markets, its existing exports, its existing jobs, the United States suffers a net loss.

If nothing else, the foreign-produced goods of U.S. corporations could be competing with the U.S.-produced goods of the same corporation, or goods that might have been produced in the United States had investment been made there instead. Black & Decker was selling drills made in Maryland directly to the Japanese, which means that Black & Decker is a highly competitive manufacturer. But Black & Decker in Maryland is not manufacturing the bulk of those highly competitive drills: the Black & Decker factories around the world do that. Black & Decker is probably doing the right thing, from the point of view of corporate strategy, corporate profitability, and historical development. Its factories in Europe mean its goods are inside the EEC tariff walls; Black & Decker is making its entry into the Eastern European market from Europe, which it possibly could not do from the United States.

Yet it is difficult to believe that a Black & Decker capable of selling U.S.-made products in Japan could not similarly have produced the sophistication, in manufacturing and sales, to sell U.S.-made products competitively almost anywhere in the world.

Even if royalties and dividends from overseas investment equal the amount exports would have brought, repatriated profits are not as good as "visible" exports.

To speculate that perhaps $40 billion of the $80 billion spent on U.S. investment overseas could rather have been invested in the United States is to say very little. Perhaps there was no economically feasible way in which U.S.-owned manufacturing facilities opened up in Mexico—providing jobs for Mexicans, and a multiplier effect to the Mexican economy—could instead have been opened up in Newark, New Jersey, providing jobs for Americans and a bolstering to the infrastructure of the U.S. economy.

Look at it this way. Remember that in 1965, when President Johnson asked U.S. corporations to improve their individual balance of payments, International Harvester replied that for every dollar it exported it "brought back $4.67." But when International Harvester can advertise, in the European edition of *Time:*

From the European Common Market—two new International tractors—92 HP and 110 HP it means, if nothing else, that U.S. export potential in International Harvester tractors from U.S. manufacturing plants has one more competitor. Dollars from dividends are good dollars, and for the average corporation they are as good as dollars from exports. But for a national economy, which gains the multiplier effects of the export industry's profitability, export dollars are much the better value.

Global competition against U.S.-made exports is intense, and national pressures against U.S. multinational corporate expansion and financial investment have curbed the freedom of operation that multinationals enjoyed a decade ago.

The types of pressures being applied against the U.S. multinationals and U.S. (and other foreign) investment are many. There is pressure on IBM in Europe to become a separate corporation so that European interests can have a stake in its European profitability and what actually has developed is a series of European corporations controlled and owned by U.S.-based interests. Involved in the IBM instance are emotions ranging from nationalism to dislike, motives ranging from greed to fear.

General Motors was long under pressure in Australia to provide equity participation for Australians in GM's Australian holdings. GM's unwillingness to do so caused Australia to open wide the doors of competition—by inviting in the Japanese auto manufacturers.

The GM corporation serves as an example of the mixed fortunes and unpredictable future of the U.S. multinational as global exporter and global investor. General Motors purchased its presence in Europe by buying Opel in Germany, Rootes Group in Britain. It was the heyday of the auto as rapidly rising European living standards opened up a huge domestic European car market.

But GM went into Iran in 1971 on Iran's terms (GM as a minority stockholder in its own factory), not on GM's terms. That is how much the world has turned. Corporations seeking investment in developing nations, where a period of rapid growth promises to unleash new domestic markets, suddenly find themselves up against governments as sophisticated and demanding as themselves. The odds have been evened up.

Americans surveying their own world trade future should not forget that Europeans and the Japanese have been much hungrier about succeeding in it than Americans. They had to be. The total European Economic Community gross national product is $625 billion, but most EEC income comes from the EEC's 40 percent stake in world trade. Exports are, for the United States, a $55 billion affair at the bottom end of a $1,000 billion-plus economy.

Neither socialists nor capitalists worry much about ideological maxims in international trade. World trade, like domestic politics, is the art of the possible.

To assume that the Soviet Union primarily engages in international trade as a huge loss leader for international political gain is inaccurate. To assume the United States has always kept as separate as "church and state" its foreign political policy and the overseas investment policy of privately held U.S. capital is equally inaccurate.

Samuel Pisar, in *Coexistence and Commerce,* rightly insists that "undeterred by Marxist dogma that 'business is theft,' the Russians and their imitators have found it expedient to adopt, wholesale, many traditional institutions, laws, and practices conceived and perfected by private merchants over the centuries." Pisar reveals the sophistication of Soviet wit in these matters, when he recounts an incident from the early sixties:

I was startled to hear a Soviet Deputy Minister say, "Your Attorney General Robert Kennedy should give me a medal for the way I compete with the major international oil trusts." Considering the aggressive Soviet forays into the world aluminum, tin and oil markets during the late Fifties, the remark was not entirely in jest.

How much benefit accrues to the United States from Soviet trade depends on what form the trade takes.

Parsons and Whittemore is one U.S. corporation that has sought Soviet business. But a $150 million pulp plant built by a U.S. corporation in the Soviet Union does not necessarily mean $150 million in sales to the U.S. economy. If the pulp machinery is built in the United States that is one thing, but if built by a U.S. subsidiary in Europe, quite another.

By 1975 the U.S.-Soviet trade entente had cooled because the U.S. Congress was tying Soviet Jews' emigration to the trade bill. Vladimir Alkhimov, Soviet Deputy Minister of Trade, told U.S. officials that the Soviets in 1975 diverted trade worth $1 billion away from the United States toward Europe. According to the *Financial Times,* Harold Scott, president of the U.S.-U.S.S.R. Trade and Economic Council, said Alkhimov explained Soviet action as direct retaliation for the congressional decision (the Jackson amendment) linking Soviet Jewish emigration to the most favored nation trade status Russia was seeking.

U.S. exports to the Soviet Union had already dropped from $1.4 billion in 1973 to $961 million in 1974.

(Not only the United States is finding trade with the Soviets an on-again-off-again affair. The Japanese have withdrawn from a much heralded deal to develop Siberian oil and gas.)

The reality, however, *Financial Times* writer Peter Zentner suggests, is that each $100 million in credit advanced by the United States to the Soviet Union for trade purposes is worth about 60,000 U.S. jobs.

It was suggested in the previous chapter that "resource dependency makes domestic economic policy just that much more difficult, domestic politics just that much more awkward, international diplomacy essential—and suspicion inevitable." The same holds true for trade dependency also. And these basic facts about the complex nature of international raw materials acquisition, and international trade, have to be included as part of the basic American education— for the people and for the politicians.

The whole nature of trade is changing. The emphasis is on self-supporting deals. The Parsons and Whittemore pulp plant is an example. Parsons and Whittemore France would buy cellulose from the Soviet Union plant Parsons and Whittemore constructs. Technological development is paid for with the goods extracted by that development. The idea is not new, but the extent to which that "self-supporting" mechanism is built into international investment and trade is new.

Trade of this nature is more barter than cash purchasing or selling.

More countries are participating in world trade, some of them making inroads into traditional U.S. exports, others not.

Brazilian furniture? With an abundance of high-quality woods from an abundance of forests, the Brazilians are now in the world furniture export business—to the tune of millions of dollars annually, with the natural advantages of cheap resources and cheap labor.

The United States is the world's tobacco exporter, and Japan was its third largest customer in 1966. Now Japan is growing tobacco in South Korea and India.

Brazil is selling its iron ore to Eastern Europe in exchange for Czechoslovakian machinery; the Austrians are building trucks for Greece. The Danes—who manufacture advanced machinery, foundry equipment, electronics goods—have steadily been increasing their sales to China; organized their own 1972 Peking trade fair, and joined the Swedes among the Scandinavian countries seeking to have an early stake in China's new trade rapprochement with the West.

There are many areas of technology where the Europeans and Japanese do not lag behind the United States.

In aerospace, missiles, and weaponry, U.S. experts concede that Europeans are "up alongside us in the state of the art." Though the computer makers of Europe cannot match IBM's range of products— nor touch its 62 percent of the market—they can compete in concert. European computer corporations will yet emerge as much larger factors than they are today, if only from some EEC desire to stop IBM from dominating the European market.

Many nations have good technology to challenge the United States. Until recently, Britain's Rolls Royce powered 50 percent of the free world's commercial airliners and a significant percentage of its military craft.

The Japanese have been a special case where world trade is concerned, especially in vying for sales in the U.S. marketplace. By the middle of the seventies it is a chastened Japan that realizes the nature of trading dependency; that sees it moved too fast; that understands—after Indonesian students burned Japanese cars, and many Asian countries point to "the Ugly Japanese"—the tough side of economic imperialism.

Japan in the middle seventies is scared about its economic future, especially its supply of oil. And only a few years earlier could the Japanese launch a VLCC tanker, with a brochure carrying the words of Mrs. W. Tajitsu as she launched T.T. *World Mitsubishi:*

Oil
You come deep from the bowels of time.
You are rich and powerful,
and you can shape the future of man.
The World Mitsubishi will carry you, oil, over the
rolling oceans, with birds and the wind as escort.
The sun follows us,
but we will race that golden ball
with stars for new found friends.
Night lends
a phosphorus carpet beneath our feet,
Then a welcome world will greet us,
and you, oil, will live again.

Domestically, the Japanese became competitive by developing skilled labor—almost as skilled in as many fields as American labor—at about one-third the cost of U.S. labor. Not just in price, but in quality also, the Japanese made themselves competitive.

Japan's rise to world trading dominance in certain products indicates how serious the competition is. Japan's trading strength comes as much from the interlocking nature of business and government as it does from aggressive marketing.

Not until 1966 did the United States find that no matter which industrial pie it dipped into, it came up with Japan's thumb on its plum.

Steel: Japan had nudged West Germany out of third place behind the U.S.S.R. and the United States. Japan had gone from $3 million sales in electronic data processing equipment early in 1963 to $70 million by late 1974. A humble item such as ceramic tiles: U.S. tilemakers reported that sales were increasing by 12 percent annually, and Japan was getting 60 percent of the increase.

Japanese inroads into transistor radios, motorcycles, cameras, baseball gloves, sewing machines and optical goods are part of the U.S. economic folklore, and scarcely need repeating.

Nor could the Japanese feel badly about their ever-bigger bites of the U.S. market: they had watched U.S. corporations such as National Cash Register ringing up giant strides in Japan ever since 1947. There were the minor slights, too, apart from the "all look alike" attitudes and the "transistor salesman" descriptions.

When a Japanese team visited Washington to see if it could participate in the $10 billion planned expenditure on U.S. mass transit, the team was told that the Mass Transit Act of 1964 specifically forbade foreign equipment. The Japanese would instead make their presence felt in other ways: Sony Corporation's sales quadrupled in the four years to 1965, and increased a further 30 percent in 1966; Panasonic, the largest seller of portable tape recorders in the U.S. by 1966, had entered the country only in 1961; Mitsui, the giant Japanese trading company, was by 1966 doing nearly 25 percent of its business in the United States.

It would finally be the United States, laden with resources and technology, which would "holler 'Uncle' " to a nation which to survive had to import every ounce of ore, every lump of coal, to produce the metal for the tops of Tokyo-bottled Coca Cola.

In the sixties the U.S. was just beginning to look at Japan for what it was, an increasingly aggressive industrial nation, not just a country of people copying the world's products (the Japanese were now sending teams worldwide to ensure that Japanese designs and trade names were not being copied in "textiles, chinaware, costume accessories and consumer electronic products").

Seemingly from nowhere this nation of 100 million people, with a GNP of $114 billion, where men retire from government at 50 and go into industry, was producing goods for the world: Piedmont airlines had just bought 10 Japanese-built YS 11 turboprops, the world's tanker owners wanted Japanese-built tankers, and the Japanese themselves in 1967 nudged the United States out of fourth place in deadweight tanker tonnage, after Liberia, Norway and Britain. The Japanese had firm contracts with the iron-ore- and coal-producing nations of the world. From Mount Goldsworthy, Australia, and from the Hammersley Investments, Australia—where Kaiser Steel had spent $22 million to sell iron ore to the Japanese—the raw materials were flowing to Japan with a vengeance.

Fighting back with quotas, and pressing for more access to Japanese markets, the U.S. government began intervening on behalf of U.S. export industry. It was the U.S. government that moved to make trade with Japan more favorable to the United States.

That was the situation when the oil crisis struck, with U.S. industry again strengthening the U.S. government's hand as intercessor on its behalf—because that intercession also is in the national interest.

Mitsubishi Bank in 1975 forecast a year of zero growth for Japan. That was how seriously depressed world trade became in the middle seventies. But once Japan bounces back, as indeed it must, the lessons of the last 10 years show U.S. traders how vigorous they must be in the world marketplace.

The best market for U.S. exports has always been with the European countries that make up the EEC in its enlarged form, and with the nations of the European Free Trade Area which brings in the Scandinavian countries. But those countries, where so many U.S. multinational corporations have bases, and with which so much U.S. export trade was done, have severe economic problems. In order to contain domestic inflation, to maintain a balance of payments at all in the face of the huge oil price increases, European nations (and Japan) want to sell without buying. All their balance of trade surplus, if any, is rapidly gobbled up paying for oil.

Where these Europeans once had money to buy from the United States, they now must borrow to be able to afford to buy oil they cannot do without.

Mergers and trade within and between the European nations—plus Japanese trade in Europe over and around tariffs—make it increasingly difficult for the United States to noticeably enlarge its trade with the EEC.

U.S. subsidiaries in Europe will be participating in European trade, but the split personality of the U.S. multinational corporation, headquartered in the United States but exporting throughout Europe from its European subsidiaries, will come home to haunt both in non-U.S. and U.S. domestic politics.

When the U.S. Commerce Department can boast in its "Did You Know" advertisements that "3 out of every 10 U.S. exporting firms have less than 100 employees," that may be little cause for rejoicing. The bigger firms have already established their factories abroad.

A trader is, by nature, a risk-taker. He will buy before he sells. He is not a commission man. A trading nation similarly is a risk-taker. It will produce before it has sold, though it will have made attempts to gauge demand.

Interference with free trade is a great finger-pointing exercise. It is always the other fellow. Before the creation of the European Economic Community (primarily a customs union seeking economic and political uniformity and, perhaps, eventual unity), and Britain's entry into it, writes John Cockroft in *Why England Sleeps,*

for years (and certainly since Imperial Preference was introduced nearly three decades ago) Britain [had] a relatively heavily protected economy.

But who throws the first stone? Anthony Thomas, writing in *The Times* of London, comments,

The fact of course is that most countries with mixed economies subsidize exports indirectly, through tax, credit or other policies, and the United States is, in anything other than the most literal sense, more guilty than most in financing defence research with commercial spill-over potential in its high technology industries.

When the United States, which had dominated the global aerospace market since the end of World War II, points to suggest that the EEC's Common Agricultural Policy—a tariff wall U.S. agricultural products must scale—needs changing, Europeans with long memories and struggling aerospace industries point a finger back again.

CAP, implemented by the EEC in 1966, establishes variable levies against agricultural imports. This has markedly affected U.S. agricultural exports because European farmers, protected by high tariffs, became self-sufficient, and exporters themselves.

When Britain, a major importer of U.S. foodstuffs, entered the Common Market, U.S. agricultural exports were further tariff-handicapped. The U.S. farmer, subsidized in the past by an average of $55,000 a year as the government attempted to limit production, is indicative of America's trade and resource dilemma.

U.S. agriculture's bounty supports the thesis that U.S. wealth in the past has come primarily from an abundance of cheap resources, and secondarily from industry, innovation, and technology (high technology will never be a substitute for cheap raw materials). The U.S. farmer can make the point that if the rest of U.S. industry were as capital intensive as the grain farm, U.S. exports would be globally competitive without relying on changes in the dollar's value.

A stark admission of the value of these cheap U.S. raw materials was revealed indirectly by Americans meeting with Europeans in March 1972 in Versailles. The President's Commission on International Trade and Investment Policy (known as the Williams Commission after its chairman, Albert Williams, head of IBM's finance committee), had a roster of U.S. finance, industry, and labor ranging from I. W. Abel, president of the United Steelworkers of America, to Williams himself.

What was its major concern? Not aerospace, electronics, computers, or further capital investment, but the need for a "major relaxation of your [EEC's] very high protectionism against imports of our agricultural products."

In the arena of international trade the action never stops. But what does it all mean? To the United States, the single Western nation not previously primarily dependent for income from it, it means that this is the arena in which Americans must sharpen their skills, must bring their myriad unexported goods to market, and the arena they must rely on for an increasing percentage of their future income. To the rest of the export-or-die industrial nations, it means the growing presence of an economic giant.

To the United States it means also a continued agonizing over whether it should be exporting goods instead of exporting money. Those 3,600 U.S. corporations that have at least one factory outside the United States may well have been acting in the best interests of their stockholders—and in the medium- to long-term, of the nation. Some corporations can legitimately argue that "we've increased our foreign jobs by 12,000 and our domestic jobs by 21,000." But few corporations could deny that at least some of the capital investment gone abroad could have improved productivity at home, aided domestic exports, brought in export profits. In truth, the vast outflow of capital from the United States in the sixties was a heady mixture of the "flight of capital," a burgeoning of internationalism in the breast of U.S. industry, and the attraction of greater profits elsewhere.

To repeat: not just for the workers, but for the nation, too, a new factory in Mexico, Iran, or Spain may well be one less for Newark, East St. Louis, or the more promising domestic growth areas: the Southwest, the Southeast, and the West.

The argument for overseas industrial investment (to produce goods within markets that otherwise would price U.S.-made goods out with tariff walls, or markets that would otherwise fall to other exporters and manufacturers) is a legitimate one. But that still begs the question of exporting products, money, and jobs.

One could not reasonably expect all the money that has gone into overseas expansion to have remained in the United States creating domestic jobs. There has not been that much room for enlightened discussion and maneuver toward evaluating, in economic terms, the best interests of the U.S. economy and the U.S. people. The labor unions are as shortsighted and self-interested as the corporate manager and stockholder. If $40 billion had stayed home, would the unions have seen that in terms of U.S. competitiveness, increased automation and new techniques would have meant less employment in specific industries, but probably more employment at large as the multiplier came into effect?

Where is the "think tank," supported and given credibility free of political gamesmanship, that brings together government, industry, and labor to provide reasonable outlines as to what the next five or ten years could or should look like? Who else but a combination of congressional, corporate, and labor leaders, perhaps joined by academics, could reasonably be expected to sell a national survival plan to the country at large?

As long as the major structures of U.S. socioeconomic life (government, industry, labor and education) act as if "business as usual" is possible, so, for that length of time, will Americans generally believe that economic life can return to normal after the recession-inflation-unemployment trauma of the mid-decade.

If U.S. corporations domestically based, and U.S. trade unions directly involved, do not come up with workable programs in the light of the changing nature of the U.S. economy, then the U.S. government will have to do so. And the U.S. government may do it badly, or do it wrong. What is demanded is a degree of "statemanship" from management, labor, and government, which none has shown much sign of. U.S. corporations now see world markets "that once were easy outlets for surplus output, . . . being taken over by the Japanese, the Dutch, the Danes, the British and the Germans, with their high technology, and their very strong international marketing," as one U.S. commercial attaché summarized it to this writer.

The best selling aid any U.S. product has ever had was the Made in U.S.A. stamped on the bottom, which meant that the quality could not be excelled by any other nation. "The Germans started outselling the Americans in Iran, when the Americans started reducing their quality," explained a Tehran trader discussing this topic with this writer. A cheapening of goods, part and parcel of the planned obsolescence of the late fifties and early sixties, also dates back to earlier periods of inflation and wage and price controls.

There was that other unique U.S. habit, only now being cured, of the U.S. automakers allowing foreign competition in because they would not keep U.S. products in the low-priced field.

Many American products have never entered the world trade fracas. One U.S. trader explains the problem: the profits from filling a few global orders, as the result of overseas inquiries, may not be worth the trouble involved. Customs forms, currency changes, different languages, have served to keep many small and medium U.S. manufacturers out of the export business. Credit problems, governmental regulations, adapting U.S. products slightly to make them more attractive to non-U.S. users, the problems of finding reliable representatives in the country one would export to, have conspired to allow U.S. manufacturers to trade mainly in their own huge, homogeneous market.

. . . you get out into the U.S. hinterland, and try selling the small manufacturer and his bankers on the idea of export possibilities and you have your work cut out. . . .

What Europe-based U.S. trader Joel Taylor said above refers primarily to trade between developed nations. U.S. exporters run into entirely different problems with developing nations.

World trade is a $300 billion marketplace that is the last bastion of both capitalism and free enterprise, that is, governmental and multinational capitalism and large-unit (national or corporate) free enterprise. One significant new aspect of that world trade is the global "industrial developer" selling short- and medium-term technological and managerial technique and advantage to those in a position to buy it.

Turkey plans an aircraft industry, Iran manufactures automobiles, Spain boosts steel capacity. Zaire's president Joseph D. Mobutu keeps a copy of Jean-Jacques Servan-Schreiber's *The American Challenge* on his desk, and an eye on his copper revenues, with a view to increasing domestic industrialization.

Economic nationalism, a yearning for some degree of self-sufficiency, plus the ambition to industrialize and provide one's own prestigious or strategic goods, has created this new type of trade within world trade. Developing nations anxious to build automobiles, like Iran, can find willing minority stake partners, like General Motors. Turkey's aerospace industry will be built up in conjunction with either U.S. or U.K. aerospace industries, or both. But Turkey will have the majority stake and the final say. That much has definitely changed. What else changes is that these countries then cease to be customers for purchases of these products elsewhere.

Government-to-government negotiations—and international aerospace expansion could involve strategic decisions—are just one part of the major new pattern of world trade development. Wheat for cash, industrialization for oil, gas development in return for gas (packages so huge that governments cannot stand by uninvolved even if the deals are privately consummated) have brought all governments positively and permanently into the world trade arena.

Nor does the government come to the world bargaining tables solely as negotiator. Government is present today in its huge role of state-as-trader.

Explains Pisar, in *Coexistence and Commerce,*

Few realize that the Federal Government of the United States, with its substantial dealings in military hardware, foreign aid and surplus agricultural commodities, ranks only [second to] the Soviet Union as [the] world's largest international trader. . . .

The Commodity Credit Corporation alone, a government enterprise which buys surplus American farm products and arranges for its disposal at home or abroad, has had annual turnovers of as much as $2.5 billion.

The increasing presence of states-as-traders, further reducing certain types of international corporations to a secondary role, not only moves world trade out of private corporations, it further brings it within the scope of political and strategic decision-makers.

The Soviet Union, preeminent in people's minds as the state trader, is not merely a raw-materials producer providing "20–25% of all platinum, 70–75% of all palladium, and 60–70% of all rhodium moving in world trade," Pisar writes. It is the political controller of a vast industrial empire beyond its own national borders. He says,

Comecon countries account for some 30% of the world's industrial output and 20% of its agricultural production, while contributing only 11% to the global volume of international commerce.

Moscow either makes, or rules on, any important industrial, trade, or investment decision made in Comecon countries, just as the central authorities within the Soviet Union make the final decisions about national expansion (into oil tankers), contraction (out of car hire), and incentives (cash prizes for efficient industries, diplomas for efficient workers).

Peter Reddaway of the London School of Economics, in a 1965 *Survey* article on "The Fall of Khrushchev," delineates the extreme choices open to the Soviet Union. Those choices are slightly different from the ones all countries have to make, though the general solution is an attempt to try some of each simultaneously:

> In 1962 two mutually exclusive sets of tactics were being urged on Khrushchev by different pressure groups. One was based on the primacy of economics over politics, and favored decentralisation, economic incentives, and a greater role for the state vis-a-vis the Party hierarchy. The other favoured increased political and economic discipline, to be achieved largely through a traditional type of central direction.

Obviously the Western democracies are not having to choose between state and party, but between state capitalism and private capitalism in many sectors.

Reddaway believes Khrushchev made the wrong choice—for that *particular* point in time:

> . . . it now seems clear that Khrushchev's fairly logical intentions, given his basic philosophy and the political circumstances, of deliberately courting a break with China by drawing nearer to the West (for the sake particularly of economic cooperation), were too radical for most of his colleagues.

Today Khrushchev's economic policies have prevailed, and the break with China is nearly complete. Industrial management in the Soviet Union is becoming increasingly decentralized; there are economic incentives. Perhaps not even Mr. Khrushchev envisioned Aeroflot, the Soviet national airline, advertising on British commercial television. The Moscow Narodny Bank, which has operated in the City of London since 1919, now has better than $1 billion assets and, legend has it, it was a Narodny banker who created the Eurodollar market.

If the Soviet Union is the noncapitalist state-as-trader, Japan must be the preeminent capitalist state-as-trader, in terms of the degree government control affects internal and external commitments. In Japan, such governmental presence is unexceptional; it is the norm. Governmental paternalism toward industry is an extension of the corporate paternalism toward the employee.

State-as-trader international commerce does mean that businessmen are likely to advise on government decisions. In the West, as well as in the Soviet Union, China, and Japan, there is a small corps of people as at home in finance-commerce and industry-commerce as they are in government-commerce. These are truly the technocrats of neocapitalism, men whose role and power the democracy has yet to take into account.

The "dollar diplomats" or "capitalist equerries" are sophisticated animals. To be at once nestled in the financially rewarding arms of private industry, while participating at the highest levels of government decision-making, is having the best of both worlds for men of ambition.

In no sphere is the emergence of the economic diplomat more pronounced than in international banking. The economic diplomat may be arranging international bond issues for major corporations, or medium-sized nations, operating at a diplomatic altitude only ambassadors usually reach. They are variations on the role that started the banking Rothschilds on the route to banking eminence, but assessing the financial credibility of nations instead of rulers.

The diplomats of international capitalism have grown in importance with the advent of multinational banking, especially U.S. multinational banking.

Only two or three U.S. banks opened in London during the nineteenth century, and even into the 1950s U.S. banks found little reason to establish their separate global networks. They were not necessary. New York City was an international finance center.

New York's decline, and London's rise to international eminence during the last decade or so, was due to U.S. imposition of capital controls that "drove most international financing out of the United States."

London offered "a favorable regulatory atmosphere," and the banking business boomed there. In 1969, however, the U.S. Federal Reserve Board agreed to permit U.S. banks to establish "shell" banks in tax havens like Nassau and the Cayman Islands. The idea was that capital controls were preventing smaller U.S. banks from engaging in the international financial market, and the "shells" would enable them to do so competitively.

In international banking, the profits are taxed wherever the deal is recorded. As Ellmore C. Patterson, chairman of Morgan Guaranty, told a London audience in 1972 at Claridges,

> Our London office recently managed a substantial loan to an African country. The business originated in our New York office. The members of the lending syndicate were a group of American, Japanese and Canadian banks. This was not British business in the usual sense. Nevertheless, because this was the most favorable place to do it, the business was booked by our London office, the loan was funded here, and the profits will be taxed here.

Were the deal booked to the Nassau or Cayman Island "shell," however, there would be no taxes to pay on the profits at all, as long as the profits remained outside the United States. "Offshore" banking is a regulatory headache for the home nations of all international banks, much the way international investment funds have been a headache for all regulatory agencies in countries where they were sold.

U.S. banking has changed considerably since the Bank Holding Company Act amendments of 1970. These amendments freed U.S. banks to think in terms of a broad range of financial services that, coupled to the growing tendency of corporations to raise more money at the banks and less in the marketplace, greatly emboldens the future role of banks and banking in the national economy.

Morton Mintz and Jerry S. Cohen, in *America, Inc.,* state:

> Now, because of the insidious one-bank holding device, they [the banks] have moved far from their proper role into other numerous areas of the economy. There has been no more alarming example of creeping (or is it sprinting?) private socialism. If anything, an economy controlled by the sources of money can be more hostile to an enduring free society than an economy controlled by the owners of the means of production.

While Mintz and Cohen concern themselves with the interlocking hold of U.S. banks on the nation's top 200 corporations, many of those same banks have equally powerful linkups worldwide (consortium banking, as it is known, is the creation of banking units jointly owned by major national banks of the leading industrial nations).

Domestic banking patterns are repeated, naturally, in other industrial nations. Look at Sweden before the death of the scion of the Wallenberg family. This was before Enskilda Bank, the Wallenberg bank, merged. The new corporate-banking hegemony is even greater; as Kurt Samuelsson explains:

. . . chief executive Marcus Wallenberg was the man who held the 60 directorates. Ragner Aoderberg, a close relative of the Wallenbergs, held 39, Jacob Wallenberg held 23, and Marc Wallenberg, 22 directorates.

The corporations involved were Sweden's largest and most prestigious. Global names, many of them: Atlas Copco, Alfa Laval, L. M. Ericsson, Saab, and more.

Looking at just one consortium arrangement, the network Mintz and Cohen pointed to can be seen in its full global flowering: Société Financière Européenne, in which BankAmerica Corp. has a 14.3% stake, is (1971) a joint effort with Britain's Barclays Bank (14.3%), Banca Nazionale del Lavoro of Italy (14.3%), Banque Nationale de Paris (14.3%), Dresdner Bank of Germany (14.3%), Algemene Bank Nederland (14.3%), Banque de Bruxelles (14.3%).

BankAmerica Corp. had multinational banking links in Banco Real do Canada, São Paulo (50%), and similar entities based in or covering Geneva, Nassau, Australia, and the Pacific basin.

Six of the world's top 10 international banks are U.S. banks, all have significant tieups with other major banking groups, and those major banking groups in turn have significant representation within their own national corporate structures.

Looking at the City of London (the "City" is London's financial district), where since 1971 U.S. banks have been permitted to compete against British banks for sterling business, it is obvious that serious competition still remains in world banking. As *Fortune* magazine summarized in 1971,

. . . Sophisticated techniques of credit evaluation, computerized financial planning services, faster decision-making than local competitors, plus vast international resources give Americans a distinct edge on British commercial banks as both vie for domestic U.K. business.

The wave of U.S. banking activity in London took three distinct stages. The first was the establishment of branches to benefit from the Eurodollar activity following the U.S. government's prohibition of U.S. domestic borrowing for U.S. corporate overseas expansion in the mid-sixties. In 1965, for example, American Cyanamid floated a $20 million Eurobond, and during that year alone companies such as Monsanto, duPont, Gulf, and Mobil raised $70 million in European bond issues.

In 1968, when the U.S. administration clamped down on direct investment overseas, forcing more and more U.S. subsidiaries overseas to finance their activities in European capital markets, the result was staggering. In May 1968 U.S. corporations raised $1.1 billion in Europe, compared with a total $1.8 billion throughout the whole of 1967. U.S. banks wanted to be part of this money-raising, for these U.S. corporations were their prime customers back in the United States.

Short-term loan activity led to longer-term interests and the development by the late sixties of the multinational lineups as banks of many nations pooled their interests into the global consortia.

A range of specialist banking activities has U.S. banks overseas behaving much like British merchant banks, seeking business from fees as well as from the spread between rates for borrowing and lending. As Ian Morrison in *The Times* wrote, in 1971,

Five years ago it was fashionable for American banks to establish branches in London. Three years ago it was fashionable for them to join forces with other banks in setting up multinational banking consortia. Today it appears to be fashionable for them to form subsidiaries of their own to which the title of "international merchant bank" can be applied.

Financial services and banking also appear to be a major thrust for the dozens of U.S. stockbrokerage firms with branches in Europe. U.S. financial interests—from reinsurance to mortgage banking—continue to increase their grip on European and other financial centers.

There will be concentrated efforts by many governments in this decade to restrict banking multinationalism.

Andrew Brimmer, when governor of the Federal Reserve Board, advocated stronger controls for economic rather than for political reasons. U.S. banks were too easily able to avoid domestic U.S. government curbs—resulting in tight money—by going overseas for Eurodollars.

Discontent over corporate multinationalism is only partly a xenophobic revolt against size and outside dominion. More than that it is a distinct distrust of power not easily subjected to local controls, of outside power not easily identifiable or understood.

U.S. global investment meant that the huge pool of dollars outside the United States provided speculators, including U.S. speculators, a golden opportunity to participate in a handout from a "billion dollar killing," during two dollar devaluations.

The financial multinationals, more than corporate manufacturing multinationals, can create severe problems for their own and other governments by their ability to shift wealth more rapidly than governments can anticipate the shifts, or enforce regulation. Discussing the period immediately before the second dollar devaluation, Federal Reserve Board Governor Brimmer showed that U.S. commercial banks had experienced

a net outflow of $1.3 billion in the few weeks before the dollar was devalued. Another $1.2 billion outflow occurred in the following month. Thus, a net balance of some $2.5 billion of bank funds moved abroad during the period of exchange rate speculation.

Brimmer states that as far as the U.S. commercial banks were concerned, they may not have been speculating against the dollar:

the modest build-up in their balances with foreign institutions may not have reflected foreign exchange activity—since the increases were primarily in dollars. Nevertheless, because of the complexity of the overall situation, such a possibility cannot be ruled out.

Multinational corporations and multinational banks are deeply involved in the vast waves that build up to smash currencies, sometimes out of sheer self-protection, sometimes for speculative reasons, as Brimmer shows,

It has been estimated that speculative movements of capital by international companies into Germany in 1969 accounted for one half of the total capital inflow that year.

The profits can be huge. A banker in Switzerland told this writer,

It's not just restricted to American corporations. I remember talking to a fellow a number of years ago about the 1967 sterling devaluation. He was advising one of the largest Swedish corporate complexes. They played their foreign exchange right, and in a year when they would essentially have had no profits, they ended up with one of their most profitable years in a decade.

That same banker believed that had the United States imposed foreign exchange controls in 1969, at which time the alert participant in world money markets could see what was coming, the dollar devaluations—certainly the second one—could have been avoided.

Banker-economist Geoffrey Bell, commenting in the *Times* on "the vast battery of exchange controls which have been erected in Western Europe and Japan aimed against currency inflows," sees Western controls producing two results: the Eurocurrency business moving from Western Europe, perhaps to Singapore and Hong Kong, and, equally significant, the need for European banks to find more capital "and/or form closer links with other financial institutions."

Closer international banking links, resulting in fewer and fewer, but larger and larger fish in the global pool, have agencies that once concerned themselves with national banking monopolies now looking at the international consequences.

One multinational agency, the European Economic Community, intends to limit the freedom of multinational banking consortia. It will apply the test of whether the banks "prevent, distort or restrict" competition.

Floating exchange rates, fixed parities, and preventing nations from exporting inflation by unloading their currencies constitute the top layer of international financial problems. Rapid currency movements by multinational banks and corporations, and a continuation of the trend toward ever-closer banking linkups, are the bottom layer. The filling in this monetary cake is the currencies themselves. Currencies remain only as sweet as the prevailing national economic conditions behind them allow.

To recapitulate briefly, the U.S. multinational corporation is being watched closely by its own government. The potential victim of eventual investment regulation from Congress, it stands accused by U.S. trade unions of exporting jobs. Multinationals are under attack from "the traditional enemies of business: aggressive trade unions, dissatisfied youngsters, anti-business intellectuals, demanding consumerists, and left-wing influences in the mass media, all of which might coalesce under ambitious politicians." Multinationals are resented by economic nationalists in the countries in which they locate, and are having to reconcile themselves to growing hostility from the trade unions in host countries too.

Look at Britain, a nation which has welcomed, and still does welcome, U.S. multinational investment.

The following is taken from a book review in *The Economist:*

The most serious aspect of the American industrial invasion lies in the fact that these newcomers have acquired control of almost every new industry created during the past 15 years. The place is stated and the date indicated, as the passage continues: "What are the chief new features in London life? They are, I take it, the telephone, the portable camera, the phonograph, the electric street car, the automobile, the typewriter, passenger lifts in houses, and the multiplication of machine tools. . . ." In other words, the place is London and the year 1901, with the writer [Fred A. McKenzie] concluding: "In every one of these, save the petroleum automobile, the American maker is supreme; in several he is the monopolist."

J. H. Dunning, writing for the British Government and Business Economic Advisory Group, brings the same *cri de coeur* up-to-date.

The $6 billion U.S. direct investment in Britain, says Dunning, is concentrated "in the technologically advanced industries, in motor vehicles and in oil refining and distribution." Dunning estimates that "within 10 years between 20 and 25% of U.K. manufacturing output, and more than one third of exports, will be supplied by foreign-owned corporations." As 70 percent of all foreign investment in Britain is U.S. investment, the magnitude of the U.S. stake in the island's economy is both substantial and easily identifiable.

Dunning points to the dichotomy of aims between the final criterion of the foreign subsidiary and that of the British economy: "Whereas, in the final analysis, the foreign firm will judge the success of its subsidiary in terms of the return on the capital invested, the U.K. economy is best served when the local value added by the subsidiary is maximised.''

Britain's Department of Trade and Industry in 1973 followed up Dunning's studies with a look at the "impact of foreign direct investment on the United Kingdom.'' The study narrowed the furor over multinationalism down to "three concerns":

> That multinational companies may be eroding the power of the nation state, that source countries for direct investment capital may impinge on host countries, and the economic consequences for capital receiving countries.

This British study concerned itself primarily with the third attitude, the British government having always given foreign investment a "qualified welcome.'' Of the other two, multinationals eroding state power, or outside capital impinging on host countries, the study merely says that responses to them are "more dependent on subjective political preferences.''

In periods of national economic stress, in the country where the foreign subsidiary is located, the anti-foreigner attitude emerges, rather naturally, from "subjective political preference" and from all corners of the society. In Canada, where the U.S. presence is so dominant, Canadians worry about the prevalence of U.S. professors at Canadian universities, U.S. programs on Canadian prime-time television, U.S. magazines on Canadian newsstands.

Justified or not, once bitterness or hostility does gain hold, it is difficult to discourage, but not so difficult to detect. An article in the *Sunday Times* of London states:

> Factories of foreign firms are among the first to close if there is a recession here or in the firm's own country. The American engineers Sutter Holly shut their Sunderland plant because of the U.S. recession and 150 people lost their jobs.

British firms dependent on the U.S. for export markets are equally likely to feel early the crunch of a U.S. recession, but U.S. firms directed to a European market with a high-technology product— computers, for example—would be among the last to feel it. But the point is a simpler xenophobic one.

If the British government's attitude toward foreign investment and the U.S. multinationals has been "relatively free and easy"—

especially in contrast with the economic chauvinism of France, for example—that is not to suggest it will always remain so. The Trades Union Congress, which is the biggest single factor within the British Labor Party and the source of the bulk of its funds, made its view of the multinational corporation a focal point of its 1972 economic review.

The review called for stricter rules of trade for international firms that direct investment to the sources of cheapest labor; for new regulations by GATT (General Agreement on Tariffs and Trade); for compulsory observance of International Labor Office standards; and for trade union standards so that developing countries do not secure an undue advantage from low labor costs. Given that low labor costs are often one of the few advantages a developing country can offer a foreign investor, it is unlikely that the developing nation will agree to such strictures, whatever agreements the trade unions of the industrialized nations are able to extract from the national and multinational corporations based in developed industrial countries.

The review called for stricter rules of trade for international corporations that direct investment to the sources of cheapest labor.

Not just national labor unions, but the nations themselves, are paying much more attention to what foreign investment may and may not do when it comes in.

The Canadians, for instance, have limited the foreign stake in any Canadian financial institution to 10 percent. The Australians, following in the shadow of the Canadian Dilemma, will be forced to develop their own "buy back Australia" programs.

Australia is a nation of sparsely populated land but healthy agriculture and mineral resource prospects. Land means agricultural production, and according to the *Financial Times,* "two thirds of the rich northern territory, where rainfall is predictable, is already owned or leased by foreign investors. Most are American, with the British second." In Western Australia, where mineral production rose from $43 million in 1963 to $600 million in 1970, in a state producing 76 percent of Australia's iron ore and dozens of other minerals, the controlling names are Amax Sumitomo (American Metal Climax of the U.S. with Japan's Sumitomo), Aluminum Werke of West Germany, and Holland Aluminium—but no Australians. Australia is wine country, and Heinz bought up the Stanleywine Vineyard, while Philip

Morris paid $17.5 million for Lindemans Vineyards. Chase Manhattan Bank has a major stake in developing 1.4 million acres of the Esperance Plains.

There are uranium reserves, and Westinghouse is in there competing against British, German, and Canadian interests; in portfolio investments, the U.S. is gaining on Britain's first place in Australian investments. Between them, the U.S., Canada, and Britain account for 80 percent of all Australian foreign investment. Natural gas interests and the Australian chemical industry have a strong U.S. representation. U.S. oil corporations have either withdrawn from Australian exploration or reduced their interests, because of oil fields drying up and small finds; but the interest in natural gas has never been higher, with a South Australian monopoly on natural gas being held jointly by Broken Hill Proprietary and Exxon, which have $400 million investment in oil and gas exploration and development.

All of these are indications in degree of the continuing U.S. expansion worldwide, either from U.S. corporate bases in the United States or U.S. subsidiary bases in Europe or elsewhere. All add to the growing mantle of U.S. corporate involvement on a world basis, and all point to the fragile structures which make it possible. Economic imperialism? Since 1954, when American Express opened the first U.S. representative office in Australia, seven other U.S. banks have followed, from Bank of America to Wells Fargo. At least five other U.S. banks have stakes in Australian banks.

Canada has been at the forefront of developing a logical approach to coping, preventing, or undoing—depending on its attitude toward a particular corporation or industry—foreign investment.

Australians make no secret of the fact they hope to copy the ever tougher measures Canadians are adopting. When economic and political circumstances permit, Third World and developing countries will want to model their attitude toward foreign investment on Spain or Iran.

Canada's Gray Report, which saw public light of day at the end of 1971 when the *Canadian Forum* leaked it to Canadians, had recommended that government should have "the power to block [foreign] investment . . . that does not accord with the objectives of the Government."

The *Canadian Forum,* an arts and opinion journal, broadened that recommendation by suggesting that a comprehensive program for the control of foreign investment cannot be effectively implemented without a larger program for the economy as a whole . . .

while readers applauded and wrote to the *Forum* that "perhaps the [Canadian] government can be convinced that we are willing to take a backward step, economically, in order to maintain some kind of control over our destiny."

The Canadians are finding marketplace answers to marketplace problems. The governmentally sponsored Canadian Development Corporation, a holding company designed to take equity stakes in foreign corporations, is already moving: its takeover of Texasgulf, Inc., fairly indicates that.

Coping with U.S. domination of the oil and energy sources, the Canadians will need a mix of political and marketplace reasoning, but all countries are capable of constructing politico-economic vehicles to carry out their intentions. Even the managerial supremacy myths of the multinational are being discredited: John Pearson, writing in *Business Week,* suggests

the dispassionate observer would be forced to conclude only that leading multinational companies are in growth industries—both at home and overseas.

Developing nations can develop particular weapons—if they are attractive enough investment opportunities to outsiders.

Spain realized that for the developing nation, the predictable 10-to-15-year period of "accelerated growth" (a phenomenon now identifiable as a catchup phase evident in economies ready to take off, given the capital investment and political encouragement) is a one-time benefit. Like Arab oil, once it is gone, it is gone.

With half its take-off period still ahead of it, Spain developed programs to ensure that the price outsiders paid to join in this accelerated growth, and its concomitant, accelerated profits, was suitably high.

The Spanish state holding company, Instituto Nacional de Industria (INI), took majority stakes in new Spanish enterprises. Future U.S. investment, to add to the $600 million American corporations have already invested, will be much more stringently controlled by the Spanish. These developing countries have realized that during their period of most rapid growth their vibrant economy is their greatest attraction to foreign capital, so they are learning to protect that asset as best they can. U.S. Steel has a large minority stake in a new quarter-billion-dollar steel complex at Sagunto, but the Spanish state has the major share. The Spanish are not allowing foreigners to profit from Spanish moves into uranium refining, and INI took a 60 percent stake in a recent oil refinery complex being established at Tarragona. Where U.S. investment does take place, it is in a joint venture, with the U.S. subsidiary and the local governmental or private investors linking up.

National sensibilities are spared, U.S. technology, management, and investment can still be utilized and encouraged, and the government remains more in control of its economic destiny than even a more advanced nation such as Canada.

The story is repeated in Iran, which has billions of dollars in petroleum revenues to underwrite the cost of its industrial expansion, and where Iranian interests must have 51 percent of every new venture. In the largest ventures, such as the $300-million investment in Iranian copper, the outside presence is limited to Anaconda selling its professional services as a management, exploitation, and development company, on contract, working for the Iranian government—a remarkable change in status for the former owner of vast Chilean copper deposits less than a decade earlier.

If the Canadians are fighting back by buying into multinational corporations; if the Australians hit out at U.S. multinational automobile manufacturers (who refuse to float off equity in their Australian enterprises to Australian investors) by inviting in Japanese manufacturers; if Spain insists on outside investors taking the state as partner; and if Iran insists on outsiders obtaining only a minority stake; then Iranian banker Kheradjou summed up at the beginning of this chapter what has happened:

> International business is a real jungle. We finally realized that these investors had more than one way of taking the profits out of our pockets. And now we know what to do about it.

These are the sentiments, of course, of those nations that can *afford,* or are able politically, to do something about it. Not all developing nations, and few Third World countries, have that sort of power. Before looking at them, however, one must also be aware of the major moves against the multinationals on their home territories. As Pearson states:

> After all, U.S. companies alone now have more than $90 billion invested abroad, and their overseas production is probably approaching $200-billion annually. So even the giant U.S. economy is now significantly affected by the way in which multinational managers allocate production, market their goods, finance their investments, and manage their liquid funds.

As a U.S. Senate Finance Committee report discovered, multinational corporations (the bulk of them American) control about $700 billion in short-term liquid assets, far more than the central governments have to support their currencies. But apart from the multinational ability to frustrate, as Brimmer says, "a country's monetary policy by sending billions of dollars from one country to another on rumors of a currency devaluation," the host country response still is mainly domestic, not international: jobs, domestic investment, and commitment to the home base.

To the host country, these questions loom just as severe: the foreign subsidiary's ability to run down its investment once it has paid off, or if opportunities are more real elsewhere. These worries may be scoffed at by multinational executives coping with long-term investment, but host governments and unions are inclined to see the darker side of the picture.

Controlling the multinationals is a serious debate. Domestic governments can do it—as the Burke-Hartke bill would have done to U.S. multinationals—by altering tax advantages, insisting on profit repatriation, and making other changes. The European Economic Community is beginning to involve itself in the same discussion. And at the United Nations, the biggest question of all finally is being asked: Are multinationals functioning outside the control of *any* and every government in practice, though component parts of the multinational may be subject to local restraints?

Is there, in fact, an offshore capitalism that touches everywhere, like the rotor arm in an automobile distributor, sending sparks through a variety of outlets?

The answer: yes. A multinational corporation cannot have a home, only a headquarters. All investment decisions, including those affecting its country of origin, must be made according to a fixed principle: the maximization of profit. To think otherwise is to allow oneself to fall into the error of assuming there is something other than the spirit of capitalism motivating capitalists.

No single corporation can, or will, do other than follow the needs of its individual corporate entity. The best interests of the United States, or some other economy, are not a primary consideration. This does not mean that national governments cannot sometimes rely on, or use, the tendencies of multinational corporations, or multinational finance, to their own purposes.

For example, it has become a truism that where the U.S. government can negotiate a peace, U.S. investment can follow.

There is no hard and fast historical certainty that nations pushed into peace will necessarily lapse immediately into civil war, anarchy, or ineptitude. There is equally the chance that such nations will be motivated by the need for progress, will industriously seek outlets for their released-from-combat energies, and will prove to be remarkably sound areas for investment.

The U.S. government hoped this would be the case in Southeast Asia. A Marshall-type plan would flood the area with financial and material support, and both North and South Vietnam could find peaceful coexistence rebuilding shattered economies, and reaching new heights of modern economic existence.

A. W. Clausen, president of the Bank of America, expressed these hopes and intentions when he spoke of the "unfulfilled potential" of Southeast Asia's "wealth of natural resources."

That Southeast Asian boomtime has not occurred.

Similar hopes are pinned by some on the Middle East. There are those bankers who regard the West Bank of the Jordan as a potential Taiwan of the Middle East. But these developments take more than a declaration of peace. They take guarantees of peace.

That governments can use the natural appetites of multinationalism and global investment, with a little dig in the ribs to prod investment in the right—meaning politically desirable—direction, does not mean the final coming together of government and business.

Why do developing nations—new ones or old ones—put up with foreign investment coming in if they are so quick to resent it once it is there? Harry J. Robinson in *Prospectus Preparation for International Private Investment,* writes,

> The national and per capita incomes in industrially developing countries throughout the world are generally so low that the funds available for capital formation are inadequate to accelerate industrial growth.

Etienne-Sadi Kirschen wrote:

> We must be careful not to overdramatise the general situation; a growth rate of 2.4% per annum in the standard of living entails doubling every thirty years and would have been thought very satisfactory in Europe, as well as the United States or Japan, throughout the 19th century and the first half of the 20th.

As an aside, many industrial nations adjusting their sights in line with oil prices and the energy shortage may again be well satisfied with 2.4 percent.

How do rich nations help poor nations?

In the quarter century following the end of World War II, the U.S. gave in grants or loans more than $140 billion, and a sizeable portion of that was in loans tied to "Buy American." But the Argentinian economist Arturo O'Connell argues that U.S. "tied" loans to Latin America resulted in additional costs to the Latin American buyer of about 24 percent, the direct result of captive buying.

With a negative balance of trade between Latin American and the U.S. of some $3 billion during the sixties, Latin America, too, is pushing for closer links with the EEC. Hugh O'Shaughnessy in the *Financial Times* said:

> The U.S., though still the largest recipient of Latin American exports, is a stagnant market which compares unfavourably with the fast growth of Western Europe as a market for Latin America. At the same time Latin America is obliged to buy a large quantity of its imports from the U.S. as a result of tied sales between U.S. companies and their subsidiaries in Latin America. These are often unjustifiably expensive as a result of the fast rise in U.S. export prices and of overpricing of goods sent from parents to affiliates. Investigations of these sales in the case of one country in Latin America have shown degrees of overpricing ranging from 25 to 165%.

Looking at Latin America through European eyes, the Europeans are well aware that many currently U.S.-dominated markets on that continent were once European markets, lost during the two world wars.

Britain's Princess Anne and her husband Captain Mark Philips were as much on a trade mission as on a honeymoon when the royal yacht paid Latin American courtesy calls late in 1973. It was a replay 40 years later of the Prince of Wales making similar calls during the Depression.

All developing and Third World nations need investment, but the industrialized nations need only some of the Third World nations. The issues are becoming clear-cut. From the developing world side, Jamaican Minister of Trade and Industry, Robert Lightbourne, told the Jamaican-American Chamber of Commerce in New York in 1970:

Those who drove hard bargains in the early developing stages of young nations and who still believe they can pursue their advantage regardless of which way the winds of change blow, invite extremism to take charge.

From the investors' side, the following was written about the Bahamas in 1970; it could have been written about many developing nations, in any year over the last decade: This comes from the *Darraugh Letter* of June 1970:

. . . How far will the government's "Bahamianization" efforts go? As far as out-right expropriation of property owned by foreigners? This, many investors fear, is the next step on the path the country has been following the past three years.
. . . In its desperate search for new sources of revenue, will the Bahamas government (despite past protestations to the contrary) impose a progressive income tax which will hit foreigners hardest? What *are* the long-range tax plans?

Those Americans who can find little sympathy with Canadians, Australians, Spaniards, Iranians, Jamaicans, or Bahamians seeking control of their own destiny and lands are referred to the Alien Land Act in the United States of less than a century ago. It was all part of a concerted "America for the Americans" campaign, and it was a plank in both party platforms. Turrentine Jackson explains:

The Democratic Handbook [for the Presidential election of 1884] contained a list of foreign holdings to bolster the party's demand for restriction. James G. Blaine, the

Republican candidate, with his slogan of "America for Americans," was more feared (in this case, by Scottish foreign investors) than Grover Cleveland.

Smaller nations realize that alone they cannot adequately defend or promote their interests under the weight of investment onslaughts from industrial nations, Eastern or Western, capitalist or communist.

Algerian Foreign Minister Adbelaziz Bouteflika, speaking to a unique gathering of nonaligned nations in Algiers in 1973, urged the underdeveloped nations to end "domination and exploitation" by outside investment. He also argued that the Third World must develop its own voice, to be heard otherwise:

> The benefits which can result from the peaceful co-existence now underway between the superpowers, and from the trend in Europe toward detente and security, eliminating the danger of a general conflagration, will not extend to our countries and to the whole international community unless we take an active part in the establishment—so far undertaken without us—of an international society based on balance of interests rather than balance of power.

The smaller nations must also come around to the realization that a global economy with some growth for all is possible only when world trade and international investment are expanding. That is not to say global growth must be disproportionate or favor one party over another, simply that without such growth there is nothing to share in.

The Western investor has already changed his attitude toward joint ventures with developing nations to joining with host governments in development, and even to taking a minority stake in those developments.

Wolfgang Friedmann and Jean-Pierre Beguin, discussing *Joint International Business Ventures in Developing Countries,* suggest that

> A generation, perhaps even a decade ago, few American or European enterprises would have accepted such solutions. That they do so now is due to the increasing determination of the developing country to reduce, or eliminate, foreign economic control, at least in vital sectors of the economy, and a growing weight which they exercise in the United Nations, in OPEC, and in other international organizations.
> . . . this [they say] corresponds, on the part of the developed countries, to the growing recognition of limitations of physical and economic power. Big-power diplomacy or military pressures may still be used by the superpowers in countries considered to be in the immediate sphere of influence and security—as the actions of the

USSR in East Germany, Hungary or Czechoslovakia, and the interventions of the USA in Guatemala, the Dominican Republic and the Cuban missile crisis have shown. . . .

But the U.S. government did not dispatch gunboats when Peru claimed a 200-mile sea limit, and started arresting American fishing boats inside the area. The U.S has been reluctant "to use economic sanctions" against countries where U.S. corporations have had properties expropriated.

Aid and development of the "unattractive"—to capitalists—poor nations must be seen as an ethical question.

Most trade in sophisticated industrial products is between sophisticated industrial nations. The United States can offer its agricultural bounties, but it must make money from its industrial goods, too; the corporations must make their profits from industrial goods; the investor must make his gains from them; and the average American needs to be employed somewhere in the industrial or service infrastructure that such manufacturing promotes and sustains.

It is no longer sufficient to have good products, capital-intensive production, strong research and development programs, and highly competitive marketing ability in order to attract capital and sales. The private-sector owned and run, privately funded, capitalist corporations are subjected to new strains; inflation, pressure for price controls, environmental considerations, consumer demands, and reluctant investors. These come on top of increased competitive pressures in the marketplace of the world, and increased difficulties in promoting future growth, expansion, and extracting profits from global capital investment.

It's a Threat! It's a Savior!
It's Supergovernment!

Most U.S. businessmen don't realize that if they give up
some of their troubles to government, they have to give up
some of their privileges, too.

James W. Michaels
Editor, *Forbes* magazine,
in a personal memorandum

The business of America is no longer business, it is government. The
business of government increasingly means the state taking responsibility for national survival: economic, political, and, of course, strategic.

In spite of this, the relationship between government and capitalism, that is, between government and corporate big business, is
arbitrary and ill-defined, and devoid of defensible goals set in the national interest. In other words, the relationship reflects public ignorance of the U.S. economic condition and an abysmal failure by
elected government to attempt to square political and economic realities in the best interests of the country at large.

A massive overview is the government's responsibility.

But the United States still is a victim of shortsighted attitudes
toward long-term economic planning. Congresspersons who plan a
decade in advance for their children's college education, and a generation in advance for their own retirement, fail to promote the same

farsightedness in government on behalf of the national interest. Perhaps they even fail to see the need for it, a worse indictment.

Until big government knows what it needs, intends, or hopes for the national future, it cannot know what it needs, intends, or hopes for or from its capitalist dynamo.

What this means for big business is that it will continue to be "darling'd" and "damned" depending on some interest prompted by the political or economic pressures of the moment. Congress will continue the self-contradicting sorties that are hindering or helping the nation's largest corporations.

The vacillation in the government's attitudes toward big business can only make bad matters worse for the capitalist enterprise.

Government does not know what it wants, or what to expect for the nation's future. Government cannot offer the public options regarding its future because the government does not know what those options are.

The U.S. government continues with a "can do" spirit in "can't do" situations. And what the United States can't do most is continue to approach the future of the nation as if the problems were solvable by daily cabinet meetings, weekend work sessions, or confrontations with crises as they occur.

The nation was caught with its pants down over the second dollar devaluation, and its shirt tails were showing again over oil. The electorate is led to believe that if a situation gets bad enough the government will make it a priority and solve the problem. One suspects in nightmarish moments that most of the politicians and bureaucrats believe it, too.

Because the American public does not know what it wants, does not know what it should want, and does not know what its choices are, the American government never gets down to the basic issues of the society. "The common wealth," the "national interest" are what the nation—people and government—is all about. The question every American isn't asking himself or herself is "What are we doing all this for?"

It goes without saying that we Americans have the government we deserve, and a pretty shoddy government it is.

This state of affairs makes the United States look ludicrous in the eyes of other nations, and reveals the continuing ineptness of political leadership to domestic eyes. What the nation needs is not annual "state of the union" messages, but "future of the union" and "hopes for the union" messages.

Up to now, however, the nation that has produced the most sophisticated management techniques in the world does not even apply the rudimentary skills of a mom-and-pop grocery store to gauging its future.

Where capitalism is concerned, it boils down to the fact that if the government-big business relation is arbitrary, it is because in most matters other than defense the United States is run practically on an ad hoc basis.

If the electorate does not know what it should expect from government—because it does not know what options it has—there is no reason for the electorate to know what it should expect from business—because it does not know the options there, either.

Out of an admixture of ill-conceived economic notions and political half-truths the public is left with the most dangerous of all impressions, that somehow they can eat their cake and have it. Nothing has yet been done to explain to the public that it is either womb-to-tomb security or brief spurts of affluence; that it is either government intervention in the economy with full responsibility for long-term economic planning or a continuation of pants-down-on-stage exposures as crises present themselves unannounced even though they were anticipatable.

It may well be that the United States cannot afford the capitalism it has in the form it has it. But the debate over what U.S. neocapitalism could become, might become, should become, if discussed at all, comes out only in snatches of conversations at economic mad-hatters' tea parties. Instead of taking a serious look at what was, what is, and what might be, the United States is acting as if the final quarter of the twentieth century can be managed with slight variations of "business as usual" and "government as usual."

Instead of concerted efforts, the nation is treated to the ignominious spectacle of partisan sniping and case-by-case industry and corporate inquisition. While it may be politically palatable to attack big business, and big business' conduct in many areas warrants attack, each thrust-and-parry case is an end in itself. Government versus big oil, government versus big IBM, government versus the utilities are the modern version of the gladiatorial spectaculars, everyone sitting around waiting for the kill. It isn't a particularly edifying sight, and certainly is not constructive. What it reveals is how little Congress, in this case, knows about the viability of the corporations that dominate the U.S. economy and what role those corporations do play and *ought* to play in that economy and in the national interest.

The growing antibusiness attitudes within the United States have all the earmarks of a grass roots revolt. Fine, as long as those at the grass roots have constructive alternatives and viable variations on capitalism's main theme. They do not. Even that is not reason enough for letting the corporations have things their own way. The corporations will continue to act out of self-interest, they can do no more.

But the role of government is to channel all the energies and output of the nation into promoting the best good, the common good. After two centuries it still has no way of going about it, and has ended up with a system of political jobbery as an alternative to statesmanship.

Capitalists turning their problems over to modern American government is like the myopic handing their glasses to the blind: once they've done it neither of them can see where they are going.

Businessmen fail to see the direction in which their own action in turning to government is actually taking the entire system.

The capitalist who turns his problems over to government expects the government to resolve those problems in his favor. Businessmen prepared to let government take over their ailing railroads or unprofitable utilities or ocean liners expect (a) to be compensated for the privilege of having a declining asset taken off their hands, (b) to be absolved of any further responsibility for that former asset in the future.

Once upon a time every major Western industrial democracy boasted its elegant queens of the seas. The *United States,* the *Queen Elizabeth,* the *France* symbolized a way of life, they were marks of national prestige and were also transportation across the North Atlantic.

As the jet aircraft gave increased competition to the liners, national governments eventually had to start providing subsidies, in one form or another, to underwrite the continuation of what was turning into an expensive, noncompetitive mode of transportation. So far, all very familiar. The cycle of change in transportation is well known: barges give way to railroads give way to roads and so on. But now take the story beyond the ocean liner-aircraft duel.

Eventually even governments could no longer justify the expense of keeping these floating palaces on the high seas. First the *United States* went into mothballs, then the *Queen Elizabeth* went to the Orient—and to the bottom of Hong Kong harbor—and finally the prestige-conscious French had to withdraw the *France*.

That left the airlines. But if it doesn't make sense to maintain noneconomic transatlantic service ocean liners how can it make sense to maintain competing airlines if competition means uneconomic operations? It doesn't, of course, so—in this case on a different route—the government permits, even encourages, a well-regulated "cartel."

A capacity agreement between TWA, United, and American Airlines enabled them to reduce duplication of "four key coast-to-coast runs." Like two different railroads running on parallel tracks with neither making any profit, the airlines, too, had to rethink their economics, and their capitalism.

And a further step yet. Government has to think in terms of essential services. If competition means an unnecessary excess of energy consumption, whether in aviation fuel or low-sulphur coal, how can government permit that "waste" if it is invited in by big business to "help out" over specific problems? And it is on the specific problems that business wants government help. Business would rarely ask government to take over all the corporations in a particular industry—like railroads—to "rationalize" the entire industry by streamlining it. Business wants only that government take over the unprofitable corporations, or the money-losing segments of those corporations.

But the arguments that made sense as ocean liners gave way to airliners, and make sense as railroad duplication perhaps gives way to a single unified national railroad network, have to make sense for airlines and airline competition, too. There are other factors pressing on the circumstances that would cause the airlines to follow the railroads: low profitability and excess capacity is a competitive problem, but unnecessary consumption of scarce fuel in an excess capacity situation is a national one.

Were government to exercise even the basic rudiments of modern management technique—imagining government as a huge holding company—it would reduce duplication, and pump money into some operations at the expense of others. The U.S. government is not at that stage yet, but the speed with which it gets to that stage depends less on domestic political preferences and more on domestic and global economic circumstances.

Inflation adds one other element to the corporate bidding for the consumer's dollar. When people are squeezed for money, the airlines are not just competing against each other, they are competing also against everything the consumer feels he *has* to have, as opposed to those things he would like to have.

With limited resources, but hopes for a vacation, the consumer may forsake the airlines for the bus lines in order to have a vacation at all. So the airlines compete with the bus lines. But long-distance bus travel is not to everyone's taste, and the potential vacationer may decide instead to drive. And that might mean the airlines competing against the car rental industry, or against Detroit if the consumer decides to add vacation travel money to a new car purchase. The prospect of driving for days over distances an air passenger can cover in hours may discourage the potential vacationer from going any-where at all. He stays at home and buys a pool.

He doesn't have to have a pool. And if his discretionary income has disappeared completely, he will give up a vacation in order to heat his house, drive his car, and perhaps put his children through school. That is what the airlines, and all other industries, are compet-ing against during a period of inflation.

The ordinary citizen believes—though he would not phrase it this way—that "to govern" is not just "the exercise of authority," but the exercise also of "judgment and knowledge," and that these exer-cises are undertaken in the citizen's best interests.

As the role of government in modern life continues to gather mo-mentum, the citizen somehow assumes that the government knows what it is doing, and that the "right" decisions will be made, mean-ing that deteriorating situations will be improved, not worsened.

These are mighty assumptions.

Citizens who expect the government to damp down inflation, solve the energy crisis, ensure full employment and decent living stan-dards, and provide ever more social services are expecting no less than the capitalist did. Neither capitalist nor citizen in these examples expects the government to demand something in return. Both the capitalist and the citizen, despite cynical jokes to the contrary, seriously believe that government can at worst bail them out, at best "improve things."

Western economies are today marked by determined government intervention and control because the electorate wants certain standards to be established and maintained. Government intervention is there by invitation. Jack N. Behrman, in *U.S. International Business and Governments,* states

> Both business and labor in most of the advanced capitalistic countries have encouraged governments to assume more positive roles and greater responsibility for the maintenance of high growth rates and stability.

The United States was the last Western nation that was capitalistic above all else. It no longer is capitalistic above all else, but has a badly managed economy bearing marks and methods of the capitalist tradition.

That is what is meant by *neocapitalism.*

Government intervention in the private sector has passed the point of no return in all Western economies. The only difference, one nation to the next, is in degree. One example could be that in the United States the federal, state, and local governments handle, spend, and pay out 25 percent of the gross national product; in Britain that figure is nearer 50 percent.

But government is not present just to collect and redistribute income. Since the Depression, aided by Keynesian economics and New Deal practical experience, government has been responsible for economic engineering: sufficient engineering to prevent severe recessions or depressions, while exercising enough caution that the golden egg-laying capitalist goose is not killed off.

Robert L. Heilbroner describes the phenomenon in historic terms, in *Between Capitalism and Socialism,*

> the swing toward the state in the twentieth century should be seen, at least in part, as the expression of a new directive force within history—a force comparable to the impact of trade in the Middle Ages or to the development of a market framework and a laissez-faire legal system in the 18th century.

At home, a closeup of this scenario shows that the U.S. government has taken responsibility for engineering the economy through the maintenance of the dollar's value and the adjustment of foreign trade to bring the balance of trade into equilibrium. The U.S. government has taken steps, and will take more, to ensure the viability of certain domestic industries (like shipbuilding and textiles) unable to withstand the pressure of world competition. The central government in the United States will have to take on responsibility for long-term planning in energy, raw materials acquisition and trade needs.

All this is done in the face of the fact that the American people have continued to believe in the free enterprising market system, in capitalism, and believe they still have such a system even though that is no longer the case.

Until recently most Western governments found it "ideologically expedient" to maintain the free enterprise myth. Since World War II most Western governments have been committed to a policy of "full employment" and minimum standards of health, education and social security for all their citizens. Government does all these things aided and abetted by profitable segments of domestic industry, finance, and commerce. Unprofitable domestic segments are supported or permitted to decline by government almost solely on grounds of national security, or regional solvency, or the volume of political clamor.

Ideology is playing less and less a part in this form of economic management by government. When the *Wall Street Journal* in 1972 carried the headline: "Buddying Up. The Role of Government in Business Might Vault if Nixon Is Re-elected," it did not really matter which candidate for president or which political party gained power. The role of government in business vaulted anyway, and will continue to so vault. There are no apparent alternatives.

There are limitations on government. Businessman and citizen assume the government to have a greater range of options than it actually possesses. The demands of a modern society, aggravated by inflation, exacerbated by the expectations of the electorate, are dropped like an abandoned child on the governmental doorstep.

The bundle turns out to be Oliver asking for "more." This Oliver votes political parties in and out of office, which means the government has to heed it as best it can. Heeding the majority in turn means that the interests of big business take second place to the interests of big politics or third place behind outbursts of interest in big economics: national survival.

Business, then, appears before government, justifying a profit, but the "profit" is going to be negotiated. As the tart said to the concubine, "What you're doing makes sense, but it ain't free enterprise." Or, as James Michaels wrote, in a private memo,

> It is fashionable now for businessmen to argue that they should be permitted to make profits because of the benefits these profits will confer on society in the form of reinvestment and more production. Imagine pleading for laws and government help to "permit" them to make a profit! Under those circumstances they don't "earn" the profit, it is "granted" to them.

When government exercises price controls, corporations or entire industries (steel and oil could be two examples) have to go before the bar of public opinion in requesting high enough prices to produce profits. The public could argue that if profits are a "tax" on the public for expansion and modernization, then don't the fruits and the disposal of that tax "belong" to the public rather than to the capitalist?

In a situation where the corporations cannot make enough money—because of a recession, or inflation, or the scale of competition, or declining share of the market, or rapidly rising costs, or whatever reasons—to expand and attract capital, the government is brought in and capitalism shrinks. Said Michaels,

> The businessman pleads for the right to make more profits and accepts in return more social control.

Inflation and rising costs hit the government quite as hard as they hit the businessman and the voter. Once upon a time the voter had something called disposable income to be spent on desires rather than needs; but now he is spending some or all of his desire-money on needs. His disposable income has shrunk or disappeared.

The same can happen to government in like degree. As the narrative looks quickly at the last couple of years to see how government is increasingly brought to the fore of national survival, the possibility of a less affluent government also should be kept in mind. Inflation is not something that governments necessarily can control.

Despite 1974's appearances, with full capacity, high employment and enthusiastic capital spending, the year was really only a continuation of the downturn that followed the Final Boom of 1964–66. There had been a strong "uptick" in 1972–73; there had to be, so much fat had been rendered out of the corporate and economic system. There was the second dollar devaluation, the return to a trade balance, the energy crisis, Watergate, a stock market rally of sorts, and two-digit inflation. By 1975 unemployment remained even though the stock market climbed for a while.

That trade balance was in part the result of the new selling power of U.S. products. They cost less to buy in world markets after two devaluations, and U.S. inflation was generally less than that of the other industrialized nations competing in those markets, further adding to the export advantage of U.S. goods. (Those dollar devaluations also mean that the United States has to pay out more money for global raw materials even if prices remain the same, which they don't.)

The energy crisis was an inevitability, just one that presented itself sooner rather than later. Watergate has not helped domestic confidence—but it is not part of this book. The brief stock market rally was likely because the shakeout had depressed market values below book values and because of a return to profitability by some corporations after the late 1972/early 1973 economic pickup. The 1975 Wall Street rally came because share prices simply had sunk below the value of the corporations they represented.

But there still is inflation.

I believe that there have been two forms of inflation orbiting around each industrial nation, two forms that interacted, sometimes with one in the ascendancy, sometimes the other. There was global inflation tied to rising world prices and domestic inflation tied to deficit spending. The domestic inflation is aggravated by the work force trying to force up wages to stay abreast, or ahead, of the combined inflation resulting from global and domestic causes.

Global inflation, the rapid rise in raw material costs, most probably is "catch-up" inflation. Post–World War II raw materials were probably underpriced in terms of their real consumed-once value, the price they should have brought. The United States and the West, after

World War II, embarked on a spending binge based on the United States' ability to draw the cash straight out of nature's bank of raw materials.

The reason raw materials prices stayed relatively so low is two-fold. First, the United States, the world's largest user of raw materials, had been in the habit of buying raw materials from itself at extremely low prices for more than a century. There may have been government depreciation allowances on some things, but the actual cost of using up these raw materials was never passed on to the domestic U.S. user, and therefore was never reflected in U.S. costs to the industry or the end consumer.

In other words, the Americans sold their own natural resources to themselves too cheaply. In doing so they similarly depressed world prices, because the price of most commodities was to some degree dependent on the cost of U.S.-extracted oil and minerals going to U.S. users and for export.

The second depressant upon raw materials prices was the strong grip buyers had on the marketplace. No wonder all those years of 2 percent inflation were possible, despite incredible new consumption demands being made by nations old and new. Raw materials did not bring the prices they deserved, or were worth.

Western industrial nations *were* prospering at the expense of those supplying basic raw materials, the oil, the ore, the copper, the coffee, and all the other things so readily consumed by the Oliver nations.

Prices started to climb when raw material production began to lag behind demand. Japan supplied the rapid growth in the demand for raw materials.

Simple arithmetic shows what happened. Japan started using ever-increasing amounts of raw materials. Add to those amounts the United States seeking increased supplies from world sources to replace depleted U.S. stocks, and add in an increasing U.S. appetite. Previous rapid growth of U.S. consumption had always been met, *at least in part,* first by increasing domestic extraction or production.

Add to the Japanese and American appetites the tremendous demand surge of the old European manufacturing nations as they geared up their industries in the fifties and sixties. Then add the appetites of the fledglings like Italy (with its astonishing growth to the mid-sixties) and Spain (joining the manufacturing nations) plus all the little demand chirps from places like South Korea, Taiwan, Portugal, and even some African and Latin American nations.

What all these nations wanted most of all, and wanted more of, most of all, was energy: oil. That is, in part, why the problem showed up there first, and why the price escalation has been so marked there, because the producers could not help but notice how the market was slipping from a buyers' to a sellers' situation.

There are other manufacturing needs besides raw materials. These, too, show their global increases: world labor costs have soared; world interest rates are higher. True enough, inflation is eating into them both, but that is at a point further along the inflation cycle.

Suffice it to say that in oil, if in nothing else, catch-up price increases have caught up, and possibly overtaken their own shortfall. They will ease somewhat, for a time. But then the old seesaw effect will start to give the world another bumpy ride. Industrial nations first price their goods in such a way as to "outvalue" raw materials; then raw materials producers price their goods to "outvalue" industrial products.

The cyle of questions posed by the new price of oil—oil which has not quite priced itself out of the market (for there are few if any immediate alternatives)—goes like this:

Can the industrial nations cut back on consumption?
Yes, at the expense of economic slowdown.
Can those nations cut back on the rate of increase of consumption?
Marginally, perhaps. They could do more.
Can those nations come up with alternative energy sources in the near future?
No.
Have the energy consumers the money to pay for the vast quantities of oil at its new
     sky-high price?
No.
Can they borrow to meet these new costs?
Some of them, for a while.
Will the lenders go on advancing money to the oil consumers?
Not unless those consumers can show an ability to meet their obligations.
Will a drop in the price of oil solve the problem?
No, because prices will not drop that far, unless there is a depression.
So what do the consuming nations have to do?
Shake the money out of their economies by streamlining them, eliminating nonessen-

tial spending and directing investment toward those things that either improve the nation's income, or lessen its future reliance on imports, or both.

But doesn't that increase the risk of a deeper world recession, or even a dreaded depression?

Yes, but that's the risk the West has to face.

The 1974–75 recession temporarily (and marginally) cut into the rate of increase of oil consumption in the United States. But it has not altered the ever-increasing dependency of the United States on OPEC-nation oil sources.

Inflation has not gone away. The U.S. economy may be improving, and that improvement will trigger some improvement in Europe. But the United States has done nothing since the Final Boom years to alter the domestic causes of its own inflation: increased reliance on imported materials, increased government spending, increased deficit financing of the national economy.

There are those who argue that deficit financing is not all bad. When the dollar was strong, and when the U.S. economy was not suspect, they were correct. However, the international value of the dollar is not fixed by those who favor deficit financing. It is fixed by economic forecasts, by bankers, and by foreign exchange futures buyers, based on the present and future health of the economy.

Those who would trade in the dollar, or accept it in payment (as do the OPEC nations), will not accept a dollar devalued in advance by government deficit financing. They know that the buying power of that dollar is depreciating because there are more and more dollars representing only the same amount of assets.

The point has already been made: it takes more and more dollars to buy the same amount of oil. That is not merely a reflection of the higher price of oil, it is a reflection, too, of the declining buying power of the dollar itself.

So much for the pattern of global inflation based on rising prices. Now build into the picture domestic inflation from a constantly increasing money supply pouring off the government printing presses. Deficit spending eats into the collected capital wealth of the country; it is a claim against the future. It mortgages the future much the way the profligate use of domestic wealth in raw materials has mortgaged the future.

Inflation fighting shows quickly how few choices are open to a democratic government. Capitalism itself cannot "control" inflation. In inflationary situations in the past (from the early nineteenth century up to the time of John Maynard Keynes' rising influence), inflation was damped down because the governments and the employers had freedom of action.

The major makeweight in the balance was labor. When it was needed it was hired, when it was not it was discarded. Governments with "full employment" commitments cannot easily go the unemployment route in attempting to combat inflation. It would be heinous in a modern society for government to regard labor as the primary means of keeping the national economy in balance, just as it is heinous if organized labor exerts such pressures—as it has in the United Kingdom several times in this decade—that it risks knocking the national economy out of balance.

Some rise in unemployment is inevitable when governments attempt to fight inflation. The continuing debate is over what constitutes a reasonable amount of unemployment. Parenthetically, "reasonable unemployment" is that which affects someone else's job, not one's own. Ervin Miller, an associate professor of finance at the Wharton School of Finance and Commerce, writing in *Lloyd's Bank Review,* said:

> From a moral point of view, one must severely condemn the use of what can be called "administered" unemployment. The authorities are customarily immune to it, and one wonders whether they would use this prescription if they were subject to its impact. At the minimum, those who administer it should lead the way by giving up their own salaries, perhaps by placing them in a trust fund for the unemployed. If one adds to other costs of unemployment psychological costs and possible damage to the skills of those involved, one probably should conclude that the entire costs of administered unemployment should be borne by those who remain employed, or have adequate incomes, with no monetary cost to those involuntarily unemployed.

For all the "right" reasons, Western industrial democracies cannot return to fighting inflation solely with the massive industrial and service industry layoffs of the type that show up so starkly in the newsfilm of the twenties and thirties.

Nor can governments end free bargaining. Many trade union movements in the West are now so powerful that they have established a monopoly position. They *can* dictate terms. They also can add considerable weight to voting governments in and out of office. Governments of the West cannot direct labor as might be done in a totalitarian state.

Wage and price controls are not compatible with the more open ideals of democracy, either. Besides, controls do not work. They did not work for Emperor Diocletian in the third century, and they have not worked since—except as wartime restrictions. The best any nation can get out of wage and price controls, or wage or price controls, is perhaps a short space when controls are first applied, a brief span in which to attempt some other anti-inflationary measures.

Deflation creates a different problem. Governments that promote deflation, cutting down without explanation on the standard of living for the masses, have a habit of being voted out of office. Electorates will take a little medicine for a while, but only until they begin to feel they should be feeling better.

What government does is to keep hopping around from one anti-inflation device to another. Appeals to national need, and private jaw-boning urging labor leaders to moderate wage claims, replaces wage controls. And in the United States, where the trade unions appear to have allowed a reduction in their real standard of living in recent years, that has helped. But for how long will labor absorb that blow?

What governments are hoping for during their hopping is that the momentum of inflation will lose its force. As inflation slows, because of falling raw material prices or modest wage increases or moderate price increases, government might just be riding out a secular sweep over which it had no control at all. Government faced with global inflation may only be able to hold on and hope for the best.

Real options are few in a democracy. Government can look busy while waiting for inflation forces to spend their fury, hoping that the fury does not merely continue to gather force, thus bringing the world to its knees. Real controls: direction of labor, price controls and profit taxes, allocation of resources, simply cannot be applied as anti-inflation weapons except in the extreme. Governments of the West apply instead little bits and pieces of these controls where they can, as opportunity allows, as part of a general scheme of keeping the economy and its imports and exports roughly in balance.

Tight money is just one more short-term attempt to do something.

Government is left trying to make sure that its own spending is kept down. This hits hardest at the public sector, and the public employees. In Western countries with large nationalized industries this shows up very quickly: Britain's railroad employees, miners, postal workers, and the like soon begin to fall behind in wages as the nationalized industries are used to combat inflation. In the United States the same thing shows up in the public and quasi-public areas: teaching, the civil service, nursing, and the other "public" services as government attempts to hold down expenditure.

No European country has succeeded in vanquishing inflation. Germany had the strongest European economy, a veritable economic muscle that still flexes and expands like no other in Europe. Germany's productive capability had Germans believing they could keep their inflation rate lower than other nations. But Germany is export-dependent, too.

Some German industrialists would like their future expansion to take place in the United States rather than Germany. Why? Because in the United States a corporation can still lay off workers when it has no work for them. In Germany, there are no layoffs, no redundancies, without government approval.

German industrialists, knowing the higher cost of U.S. labor, at the same time see the long-term advantages of manufacturing in the United States. Those advantages will remain only as long as U.S. labor allows layoffs as a means of taking up the slack in a slowed economy. Such a situation could change very rapidly, and indeed will one day.

Germans also are showing what neocapitalism looks like. Dr. Ernest Mommsen, chairman of Friedrich Krupp, the big German steel combine, was quoted in the *Financial Times*. He

suggested that private enterprise and the State should join forces in forming committees to negotiate for supplies of vital raw materials with countries or groups of countries which possessed them.

France, with the next largest GNP ($240 billion) after Germany's $340 billion, sees a strong future for itself despite a hesitant present. But whatever the future economic picture looks like—and what may determine France's future is that the political scene has remained too one-sided to endure much longer—France is currently producing no new ways of dealing with its inflation.

Britain, next on the European GNP ladder ($146 billion), is almost too often discussed as a "sick man" to make it worth using in further discussion. Britain has long cushioned itself against many problems, inflation included, at the expense of its vast army of public employees and at the expense of profitability, and efficiency, and capital investment in the nationalized industries.

As Derek Ezra, chairman of Britain's National Coal Board, stated: "Economic obligations to trade viably could be in conflict with social pressures (meaning government pressures) to hold prices." Because the British government prevents nationalized industry price increases (in amounts that could be justified were they to trade viably), an inflation multiplier is temporarily deferred from the British economy, an economy in which the government handles 50 percent of the GNP purse.

In 1972, for example, the British government wrote off $2.5 billion in coal, steel, and post office losses, to say nothing of holding back on needed huge amounts of capital investment to make some economic sense out of them, to say nothing of interim "loans" to keep these—and other industries like the railroads—operating. The problems facing Britain's nationalized industries revolve more around trying to keep down losses than hoping to maximize profits.

Poor Italy looked like one of Britain's nationalized industries. Even its national borrowing power was called into question. For historical and economic reasons, Italy has the greatest penetration by government in what was once the private sector of any European country. Those who would study neocapitalism, the bureaucratization of democracy, and the problems of state capitalism in the future could find no more fertile field of study than Italy.

Here, then, are Western governments, the United States among them, all attempting to fight inflation, all attempting to please the electorate, all attempting to defend democracy. The voters all want their personal interests safeguarded with a minimum of discomfort to themselves, and they generally believe that "government" is capable of doing it.

Governments have not always provided glowing evidence that they have a particular talent for short- or long-term planning in the best interests of the nation. The U.S. government has permitted the nation to sink into dependency on Middle Eastern oil states, depleting its domestic reserves. Successive U.S. administrations have allowed the national fabric to decay and appear devoid of social, moral, or ethical direction. Successive U.S. leaders have done little leading and have provided no standards by which a nation could measure itself.

That Western governments are in fact notoriously poor at economic planning, have few successes at prediction, little sense of imagination, and practically no capacity for daring to do what is fine and admirable for the future rather than what is immediate and expedient does not mean they should not be required to undertake planning and do it well.

Look at two shams and shambles: shipbuilding in Britain and antitrust in the United States.

For all of Britain's shipbuilding heritage, for all the huge quantities of oil Britain has been importing by tanker for generations, for all that Britain's largest corporation is an oil company (British Petroleum, with the British government holding an almost 49 percent equity stake), and in spite of British government support through loans or takeover of Britain's long-ailing shipbuilding industry, succeeding British governments never put two and two together.

The British never gave evidence of their need to join early in the tanker-building boom of the fifties and sixties, and never saw the advent of supertankers for which their outdated and almost idle shipyards could have been quickly prepared had government identified and accepted the opportunity. As it was, British yards were slow to catch on, slow to upgrade, and have managed to miss the boom. With government-inspired hesitancy over capital investment programs, British yards remain, on average, the least cost-efficient in the world. Britannia may have ruled the waves in the nineteenth century, but she was unable to cash in on them in the twentieth century.

Of U.S. antitrust, Anthony Thomas wrote in the *Times,*

> The Justice Department continues to enforce antitrust laws (albeit with such scandalous exceptions as the International Telephone and Telegraph affair) on the assumption that social Darwinism is the norm.

Antitrust is an area of only semiserious U.S. government intervention in the private sector. It always has attracted as much criticism as correction. One side of the antitrust missions appears to be to help the stock market fluctuate—fluctuate, that is, in such a manner that money can be made—by not allowing conditions whereby corporate growth and earnings are absolutely limited, absolutely predictable, or absolutely at the mercy of a monopoly. Wrote Alexander Kendrick, in *Prime Time, the Life of Edward R. Murrow,*

> The new president [William Taft] like the old [Theodore Roosevelt] would soon distinguish between "good" and "bad" trusts. His Supreme Court would order not only the Standard Oil Company to be "dissolved," but also the Tobacco Trust, which from the ducal seat of James Buchanan Duke in Durham, controlled three-quarters of the entire American tobacco industry.
>
> Guilford County, which lay in the fertile Piedmont country between the two great tobacco towns of Winston-Salem and Durham, knew the decision would change nothing. Nobody was indicted, fined or sent to jail for violating anti-trust laws. Roosevelt and Taft were not opposed to the political and economic system. They were merely trying to save it from itself.

A major problem with U.S. antitrust measures is that they are abominably organized, possibly deliberately, to represent legal and corporate confusion at its worst, government inconsistency and lack of direction at its best, and national economic dogma at its most woolly-minded. American antitrust is in need of total overhaul and codification. Gerd Tacke, head of Seimens, the German electrical goods firm, told this writer,

> I tell Americans that their best tariff barriers are their antitrust laws. Antitrust laws in Germany are in many respects much stricter, but they are clearer. In Germany we know what is allowed and what is forbidden. I don't need to say that in Washington, within government, one person has one opinion, the next person has another— perhaps an opposite one.

When James T. Halverson, then head of the antitrust division of the U.S. Federal Trade Commission, decided that the antitrust implication of the multinational corporation "has not received as much attention as it should," he indicated that such a grievous oversight would soon be remedied. His instincts may well be correct, but any antitrust chief is placed in the position of a missionary who hasn't been told about the dogma: the U.S. antitrust credo has not been thought out.

If a public scrivener were told to go into a closet and produce a late-twentieth-century antitrust credo, and if that credo were adopted, it would be the economic manifesto for neocapitalism. It would have to be.

Antitrust has to include government's "buddying-up" to corporations; government's takeover of industries; capacity agreements and well-regulated cartels; the government's responsibility for assisting in vital supplies for industry (which could mean resource allocation or "pooling"); government economic and monetary measures affecting or promoting takeovers, mergers, "rationalization" (streamlining) in the national interest (like export competitiveness); regional cartelization or other measures to cope with regional unemployment; multinational combinations (as with the financial and banking consortia) as "new" (but very old, too) ways of seeking increased market shares; government-business combinations against other trading blocs (for assaults on the EEC, perhaps); manufacturing sales and exporting cooperatives to take U.S. small manufacturers into the global marketplace; plus the effects on business of short-term deflationary economic management.

Antitrust should worry about the stake by the major financial institutions in U.S. business, meaning the consequences of the largest banks influencing and funding the largest corporations. There are antitrust implications of major financial institutions and institutional investors using bloc trading in like corporations within an industry; and the list can be continued.

Simply, the point is this: should anyone produce an economic scenario for U.S. antitrust (assuming one is produced and assuming the scenario to be workable and capable of providing codification for practically all future developments) he will have decided U.S. economic programs and priorities for at least the next quarter-century.

The government as manager is not a welcome thought. Few examples of nationalized industry within the West can be held up to suggest that the work force is more contented, or that labor relations are any better, or that the profit picture is satisfactory. The U.S. Postal Service is just one laughable example. The one fearsome example that the United States is burdened with, its own unique version of the "state as manager," is the military-industrial complex. While volumes of studies and criticism continue to probe this single but huge example of state capitalism in our midst, it can be said to point us in an unfortunate direction. The military-industrial complex is not what a democracy demands it be: observable. The whole thing hides in the government's skirts.

Growing state intervention in the private sector is likely to mean less openness, not more. What may be a democracy's economic net gain could, unless accounted for in advance, be society's and democracy's net loss.

The following paragraph concerns itself solely with the military-industrial complex. Just allow a few phrases to be altered and it could well be describing government intervention in the private sector on behalf of stimulating U.S. export efforts. Key export industries needing government involvement, like defense involvement, could be "justified" on grounds of national interest. Seymour Melman, in *The War Economy of the United States,* writes

> The Government-based management provided capital not only by making available land, building or machinery but also by the Department of Defense guaranteeing loans obtained from private sources. The extension of the scope and intensity of the state management's control proceeded in every sort of decision making. How to produce on quantity price and shipment. The net effect was to establish the state management as the holder of the final decision power, and also to limit the scope of decision left to the managements of the defense contractors, the sub-divisions of the state management.

The "secrecy" involved in the military-industrial complex has already spread to exports, where government helps exporters through export credits and guarantees. But, as Frank Vogl in *The Times* suggested,

> Company executives claim that secrecy is vital because of business competition. Nevertheless, there are certainly some transactions, particularly where Government subsidies are involved, about which the public has a right to be informed.

Anywhere the government and business intermingle there is room for misunderstanding, confusion and mayhem. (The Senate subcommittee on international finance, during a 1974 look at the Export-Import Bank—a classic neocapitalistic state of affairs—was surprised at the size of the sums involved—sums of taxpayers' money spent in supporting the ambitions and profits of corporations like Occidental Petroleum in its phosphate dealings with the U.S.S.R.)

Government is involved in any number of hard-to-justify, difficult-to-do-without expediencies.

Paradoxes such as supporting and subsidizing the U.S. Merchant Marine while permitting U.S. tanker fleets to fly under flags of convenience (known by their U.S. users as "Flags of Necessity," and, as a means of staying competitive, an accurate description it is) shows how easily the U.S. government can reconcile "ideological" preferences with the need for export and overseas competitiveness.

These are the avenues to society along which government travels as it changes character into supergovernment. Fighting inflation, defending the national currency, trading as an entity in its own right, ensuring supplies of vital raw materials, keeping the economy in balance, in all these areas government is expected to wrap its cloak around the national interests tugging at its legs. The protective wrap of government is expected to shield the special interests from the follies of their own actions, from the difficulties of changing circumstances, from a world in which the nation no longer packs a clout labeled "self-sufficiency."

The electorate keeps getting under the government's feet. As the public gets used to the idea of womb-to-tomb security being neither abnormal nor a communistic attitude in a Western democracy, it, too, wants to share the warmth of the government cloak.

Everybody is snuggling in seeking "luxe, calme et ordre," each person, each social group, each lobby interpreting "light, calm, and order" in its own way.

Supergovernment becomes super because everyone expects it to be savior of last resort. There is not one mad rush to governmental protection. Gradually people and special interests go marching in, taking refuge under its skirt like the children under the dame's skirt in *The Nutcracker Suite* ballet.

And if the one or two try to peak out to look at the crowds waiting to come in, what can they say? It's warm and cozy inside. But supergovernment, the omnipotent dame, has not yet started to order everyone around.

The Beleaguered Capitalist

I once went to Manchester with a bourgeois, and I spoke
to him of the bad, unwholesome method of building, the
frightful condition of the working-people's quarters, and
asserted that I had never seen so ill-built a city. The man
listened quietly to the end, and said at the corner where we
parted: "And yet there is a great deal of money made here;
good morning, sir."

Friederich Engels

If the Engels episode above seems dated, try a modern version substi-
tuting Frankfurt for Manchester. Germany's Young Socialists (Jusos)
have been engaged in street battles with police in the heart of Frankfurt's financial district.

The Jusos occupied empty houses rather than allow them to be torn
down to make room for more office towers. A writer for *Portfolio*
magazine reported that on the door of the Association of German Investment Companies there is a notice which reads: "Dear burglar, we
are not a bank. There is no money to steal here. Your valuable time
would be better spent elsewhere."

One investment company official told *Portfolio:*

It isn't so much burglars we're afraid of. It's young political activists. That big
blue-and-white sign on the front of the building, with the word "Investment," spells
hated capitalism to them. We don't want a mob to come storming in, or to bomb the
place.

But the bankers and investment managers who looked out on to the troubled Frankfurt streets knew what it was all about: the "investment that spells hated capitalism" is part of an age-old conflict between the pursuit of wealth and the pursuit of the good society. As one of the bankers said:

I can see their [the Jusos'] point. Real estate speculation has been threatening to get out of hand. All these skyscrapers going up while there isn't enough housing at rents people can afford. It's a mess.

A brief historical digression seems appropriate. The connection between wealth acquisition and power, and the criticism of both wealth and power, are part of the story of modern capital. What has always been particularly open to criticism, throughout history, has been the pursuit of exorbitant profits. Of course, one man's "exorbitant" is another man's reasonable return on investment.

Criticism of wealth acquisition for its own sake, indignation at the pursuit of private gain, predates the ancient Greeks' development of the first version of the "capitalist mode of production." Traders charging whatever the market would bear were probably the first capital accumulators who were not kings, warlords, or robbers.

Confucius delighted the ordinary inhabitants of Lu State. During his term as chancellor the marketplace traders "no longer charged exorbitant prices for lambs and pigs."

As barter gave way to trading for gain, it was within the human ken of such things that opinion would be divided. One can pretend that around 1000 B.C. a young Phoenician, endowed by nature with all the attributes extolled by Dale Carnegie's course, saw his chance. He charmed a fisherman into loaning him six fish. He took the fish down the road and traded four of them for two dozen figs from a man who had a fig tree in his garden.

Our young Phoenician returned to the fisherman and gave him 20 figs for the six fish—and the fisherman went off home delighted. And as our young Phoenician sat beneath a tree nibbling on fish and figs he probably wondered why he hadn't thought of it before.

Had the entire transaction been witnessed by six other Phoenicians, two of them would have said: "Hey fella, that's pretty smart." Two more would have asked for a share in the fish and figs, and the remaining two would have declared: "That's immoral. You didn't do anything to earn either the fish or the figs."

As barter gave way to trade for gain, Aristotle bemoaned the change. While toying with tortuous phrases (in the manner of a modern economist: "houses and shoes and beds are equated in the market where experience and experiment show at what prices they can be sold"), Aristotle still found time to lash out.

W. F. R. Hardie states in *Aristotle's Ethical Theory:*

. . . his sharp disapproval is directed against trade which has as the object to acquire gold and riches and to find out in what way the largest profit may be got . . .

Simple capitalism is also known by its older name, usury, or charging interest on money. It is nearly as old as man, and certainly as old as trade, with the successful trader having the money to place at loan, or at risk. The Phoenicians, preeminent traders before the rise of the Greek civilization, were just early forms of the modern multinational corporation. They established settlements close to the source of the resources (copper in Cyprus, fish in Spain) in which they traded.

That moment in time when men persuaded other men to accept money (Greek silver bars, Guinean cowrie shells) is, like the birth of trade, a missing link in economic history. The Greeks produced capital and capitalism—and critics of both.

What the Greeks invented the Romans perfected. Theodore Mommsen may have been contemporaneous to Marx but he was no socialist, though his scorn for the capitalists drips through. He deals first with Republican Rome in *The History of Rome:*

The crisis that sparked the Roman revolution arose . . . out of the economic and social relations which the Roman government allowed, like everything else, simply to take their course. From a very early period the Roman economy was based on two factors—the husbandry of the small farmer and the money of the capitalist. The latter, hand in glove with the great landowners, had for centuries waged a war against the small farmer.

Then, with the onset of Empire, as the Romans were ridding the Mediterranean of the last remains of the Phoenician trading heritage

by sacking Carthage, Roman capitalism is brought up to date by
Mommsen:

> The disproportionate accumulation of capital was preparing a second assault on the
> farming system. Formerly the small farmer was ruined by loans of money, which
> practically reduced him to a mere steward of his creditor; now he was crushed by
> competition of overseas, especially slave-grown, grain. The capitalists kept pace
> with the times.

The *History of Rome* provides the examples for all time. Marx,
too, has some marvelous moments with the Roman capitalists, using
phrases like "the wage slave, just like the real slave . . ."

Spain was to the Romans what the North American continent became for eighteenth-century and nineteenth-century Europeans and
Americans. C. H. V. Sutherland, taking a final look at *The Romans
in Spain,* could well have been describing either:

> We have, in brief, an economic system [which might have been called deliberately
> unscrupulous if it had not been simply unplanned and opportunist]. . . .

Rome declined, the Dark Ages smothered Europe for eight centuries, and the modern times awoke amid trade, thought, and the banish-
ment of the Crescent of Islam from southern Europe.

Rational thought, prompted by the Humanists of the fifteenth and
sixteenth centuries, was a throwback to the rational questionings of
the Romans and the Greeks. It was because the Renaissance scholars
could look back into history that a great questioning—one that led to
the Reformation—took place. And men in fifteenth- and sixteenth-
century Italy and northern Europe had time for such matters because
of the great increase in wealth from trade, discoveries, and invention.
These developments followed the ousting of the Islamic peoples from
Spain, breaking the lock on the Mediterranean, thus again throwing
the door wide open to commerce.

The rapid increase in wealth brought its critics. Europe was a
Roman Catholic civilization. The Church forbade usury, though it
was the greatest consistent borrower of those centuries and some of
its members became notorious lenders. Some of the popes joined the

other rich men who were hoping the camel could get through the eye of the needle.

Whatever the causes of the Reformation, its effect was not clear until Calvin crushed that stinging nettle, usury, in the palm of his hand. As historian R. H. Tawney makes clear, Calvin merely accepted that making a profit was part of the normal commercial practice of the day. Calvin never endorsed capitalism or profit-making, he just accepted its presence.

In the earliest stage of modern capitalism, Calvin severely limited the freedom of operation of the burgeoning capitalistic class, and loaded it down with responsibilities to match its wealth.

From this type of capitalism and usury to W. H. Lecky's nineteenth-century description of the acceptable face of capitalism is a very large step indeed. But Lecky, in his *History of European Morals,* made it in a single stride:

> When men came to understand that money is a productive thing, and that the sum lent enables the borrower to create sources of wealth that will continue when the loan has been returned, they perceived that there was no natural injustice in exacting payment for this advantage, and usury either ceased to be assailed, or was assailed only upon the ground of positive commands.

When affluence is on the ebb, even if that ebb is merely a normal tidal event, interest rates stand out like rocks uncovered by the retreating seas.

Marx was never more prescient than at the moment in *Capital* when he saw that under capitalism men and women were more likely to become consumer slaves than wage slaves. He used those terms. And modern consumers in the West, during a quarter-century of general prosperity, have taken interest rates as the price of possessing now that which one cannot yet afford. They have lived up to Lecky's nineteenth-century statement.

If affluence ebbs and inflation soars, and the wage earner sees "20% of his paycheck going on interest and repayment charges," capitalism's face is rendered grotesque. The twentieth-century battle over interest, the rebirth of the fight over usury that lasted through three bitter centuries, will come. It is the watershed of capitalism—the debate always comes back down finally to whether wealth is *entitled* to more wealth simply on the basis of already having wealth.

In the late twentieth century ordinary people are being made uneasy because they are being asked to make up their minds about things they have not thought about, or do not understand, or have chosen not to make decisions about.

The Western industrial democracies are already in the grip of a secular revolution not present in Western society since the Reformation. This time capitalism, not the Church of Rome, is the focal point for change.

Philippe Ségur, a young Frenchman caught up in the spirit of the American Revolution, sums up young men through history, in Harold Nicholson's *The Age of Reason:*

we espoused the cause of Liberty. Without having any certain objectives, or any assured principles . . .

Without having any certain objectives or assured principles, young men espouse many causes, but most of all those causes that find favor with their peers. Today the spirit of capitalism is up against the spirit of change.

Before hearing from some of capitalism's modern critics it is first necessary to look briefly at capitalism, at the connection between the pursuit of gain and power, and at the contributions that personal-wealth acquisition made in the development of democracy.

Can capitalism stage a counter-reformation? There is nothing in capitalism's makeup or manner to promote or produce self-reform except the sheer necessity of having to do so. Reform implies a commitment of will, a desire to change.

Educator John Cooney told the writer, in a note on free enterprise:

The capitalist's actions are always ahead of his ideology. He can be talking about the glories of free enterprise while operating easily in industries or markets primarily governed or controlled by contract or regulation.

Capitalism has a fixed principle: profit. To that extent, capitalism is not unlike a religion. Little wonder Max Weber thought he had found "The Spirit of Capitalism" in the Protestant Ethic.

Capitalism is a system that automatically springs up when wealth exists in excess of personal needs and expenditures; when the wealthy person wants to preserve or enhance that wealth; when entrepreneurs, or traders, or people with wealth-creating potential can persuade the wealthy to invest some of that wealth in them or their exploits in return for a share of any new wealth created, any extra value added, any extra worth extracted; when the political form of government permits or encourages such capitalism to take place.

The modern "capitalist mode of production" of which Marx wrote had its birth in the making of an economic system which could accommodate, codify, regulate, permit, encourage, standardize, transmit, and socially redeem "a mass of individual trades and individual dealings." Calvin socially redeemed capitalism by giving qualified approval to charging interest on loans—conducting business for profit. He removed the stigma from usury.

Capitalism has functioned in a democracy, as one *Financial Times* reader wrote in, "on the basis that a man may make a fortune by meeting the needs of his fellow men." Capitalism, the private ownership of the means of production, has existed by consensus agreement of the majority, who presumably saw it as being in everyone's best interest. But capitalism has been producing what is profitable for the private owners of the means of production without regard to the exhaustion of scarce resources, rational allocation, or national needs.

Capitalism is concerned with utilizing scarce resources for its own ends. Government is concerned with allocating them for its own ends—which in a democracy should be the ends promulgated by the wishes of the majority. There is no reason to think that capitalism's ends and the government's ends will, or might, always coincide— unless, of course, capitalists control or influence that government.

The capitalist mode of production is, among other things, the means by which the maximum amount of redeemable value can be fashioned into, added on to, or extracted from that which can be sold—fashioned into, added on to, or extracted from, that is, by production rationalized in such a way as to carry out these procedures at the lowest possible cost.

Capitalism is a system geared to seeking out and extracting the wealth obtainable in any situation, for the benefit of personal private gain. Capitalism could be described as the technology of wealth enhancement, "the systematic treatment" of wealth. The capitalist mode of production is concerned with wealth, not production. Capitalism is about money, not products. Profits are capitalism's only constant, as one Dow Company official told *Forbes* magazine:

> At Dow we like chemicals. They are the only thing we understand well. But chemicals to us are incidental to making money for our stockholders.

The pursuit of gain through trade, through venture capitalism, through personal risk, has been one method of acquiring social mobility. In a meritocracy the possession of wealth is one of the merits.

Disraeli penned the point lightly but permanently in his early novel *Vivian Grey,* and if the picture comes through clearly it is because Disraeli personally had lived the problem:

> In England, personal distinction is the only passport to the society of the great. Whether this personal distinction arise from fortune, family or talent is immaterial; but certain it is, to enter into high society a man must have blood, a million or a genius.

Ambition wakes up each morning with many people, with opera singers and cabinetmakers, not just businessmen and would-be capitalists or the would-be rich.

There is no attempt here to plumb those psychological depths that make men and women acquisitive, competitive, anxious to lead, or anxious to succeed. Each reader may reasonably muse about what makes one being satisfied with little and another dissatisfied with much.

If one accepts the comments of M. J. Herskovits in his *Economic Anthropology,*

> the elements of scarcity and choice, which are the outstanding factors in human experience that give economic science its reason for being, rest psychologically on firm ground

then one can assume that man's survival drives, along with his need for challenge, his acquisitive and competitive urges, similarly rest "psychologically on firm ground."

How much understanding of today's capitalism one can gain from looking at ancient history, or at the "economic life of nonliterate people," is a moot point. A rough continuity can be forged from both historical readings and the study of small-scale societies (what used to be called "primitive societies): from barter to trade for gain, and then, in some cases, to capital acquisition and investment. It is a crude chain, inelegantly holding together oddly constructed links, but it takes sufficient strain for the purposes of this book.

Scarcity, rather than abundance, demanded decisions, decisions affecting the provision of essential needs. Survival first. What came next involved satisfying the passions and desires.

What grew up with man's rudimentary organization of society was, among other things, the conferral of power, and, willingly or unwillingly, submission to it. In small-scale societies the matriarch or patriarch emerged: by might, skill, wit, wisdom, luck, or fraud. The role brought power; it could also bring wealth, however measured.

Wealth could be snatched from neighboring tribes. It could come to the leader in tribute, such as that which followed the harvest or the kill. Bridewealth could bring a measure of earthly riches to the man with many daughters.

And somewhere along the line men and women beguiled by the benefits of power, or lured by the trappings of authority or social prestige, sought to gain access to these apparently attractive situations beyond their normal expectation of birth, station, or role in society.

Disraeli spoke of the three legal ways one might enter the society of the great.

Power and possessions are not inseparable; often the transfer of a possession can involve the transfer of power. Take a simple possession, the finger ring. From earliest times (and still today in some wedding ceremonies) rings were used "as symbols of great respect and authority."

William Jones explains in *Finger-Ring Lore:*

> The impression from the signet ring of a monarch gave the force of royal decree to any instrument to which it was attached. Hence the delivery or transfer of it gave power of using the royal name, and created the highest office in the State.

One tries not to overstress these links between power, social standing, and possessions or wealth, and aspiration to them. But, along with the need to feel secure in worldly terms, this aspiration to power,

wealth, and social standing has always been present in many people.
And has always been criticized, as Goldsmith did:

> His best companions innocence and health,
> And his best riches, ignorance of wealth.

A prime reason for acquiring wealth, or one of the results of having wealth, is satisfying desires, including possible participation at
some level of the power structure or raising one's social standing.
Money, be it cowrie shells or silver ingots, is, as Malcolm
Muggeridge once suggested, "a pasteurized form of power."

Those with the drive or need to achieve power or social standing,
but who fail to gain it, usually settle for an imitation of it. They attempt to buy it or its mime. Social climbers are as old as wealth. But
many would rather be known as "parvenu" and "nouveau riche"
than be left out of the race.

In Ancient Egypt the power elite wore gold and silver rings, but
"the lower classes wore ones of ivory, or blue porcelain." To be
able to afford ivory or blue porcelain meant that these Egyptian
"lower classes" were the affluent, not metal-collar workers slaving
away at pyramid construction.

For the ivory or porcelain ring wearer, the "passport to the society
of the great" was, purely and simply, a silver or gold ring—even if
possessing it did not mean actual access to that society, it bought
social standing in the same way a person buys on credit one of the
twentieth-century furbelows of the "good life" advertised on the
glossy magazine page.

From "competition" to "power?"

In his nineteenth-century *Synonymes,* that indefatigable compiler
George Crabb drew a connection.

> Competition, from the Latin *competo,* signifies to seek together, to seek for the
> same cause. Emulation, in Latin *emulatio,* signifies the spirit of contending . . . and
> emulation frequently furnishes the motive for competition.

The 1911 *Encyclopedia Britannica* showed how wealth had long
been a form of self-protection:

> kingship [was] the earliest form of Phoenician government. The royal houses
> claimed divine descent, and the king could not be chosen outside their members.

His power, however, was limited by the wealthy merchant families, who possessed great influence in public affairs . . .

Leopold Pospisil links wealth firmly to power in *The Kapauku Papuans of West New Guinea:*

> Breeding and trading pigs is an activity which, if properly executed, may bring a Kapauku esteem from his neighbors, wealth, and the highest status in his society, namely that of tonowi, a rich man and a political leader.

"Tonowi" is *one* of the things capitalism is all about. Glimpses of "tonowi" are evident in Greece, Phoenician times, ancient Rome, Reformation Europe, eighteenth-century North America, nineteenth-century Industrial England and the twentieth-century global present.

The possession of money, or wealth, has everything to do with capitalism, for those who hold wealth for its own sake want to at least preserve it, and hope to enhance it. The mode of production that grew out of the eighteenth-century Industrial Revolution attracted the wealth that wanted to preserve itself or enhance itself.

The successful pursuit enabled men and women to move through society, or to satisfy their other desires. Burgeoning trade and capitalism at least provided opportunity in rigid societies where other avenues were few. Marjorie Rowling's *Everyday Life of Medieval Travellers* shows how the entrepreneur was offered opportunity:

> The oarsmen were freemen who were allowed to do some trading on their own account. The galleys also carried a fair number of bowmen of whom a certain proportion had to be of noble rank. They were known as "bowmen of the quarterdeck" and were chosen according to the Senate's decree by competition at the butts in Venice. They were fed gratis at the captain's table with his officers and any wealthy merchants who were on board. They also had a right to take a little cargo without paying freight charges. Thus, to impoverished young men of good birth, opportunity was given to gain experience in trade and seafaring.

Those less well born, and the poor marksmen, could always take up an oar and "do some trading on their own account."

Many a first and second son has climbed the ladder of success because his father pushed him up it. Hans Luther, the mineworker who became a part-owner of the mine, wanted son Martin to be a lawyer. The money and encouragement necessary to make it possible were placed at Martin's disposal.

Many a son and daughter achieved success because they were escaping from poverty or domination, or were trying to relieve the straitened circumstances of a parent or a home.

Success can be found in that peculiar kind of freedom of cutting loose from the past. This memorable passage by Ernest Watkins, in *R. B. Bennett,* on the Canadian frontier in the late nineteenth century, speaks for all frontiers:

> In Calgary he lived in a society that can be described as classless. Each man coming there wrote his own name at the head of a clean sheet in his ledger, and his neighbors were not disposed either to turn the pages back or allow him to do so. It was a society of second sons, some wastrels, some with more capacities than their elder brothers, but all men who had lived somewhere else and had chosen this place for themselves.

Success has come to people because their idea was swept up in popular demand: names like Ford, Bell, and Eastman are later names of the type of men who two millennia earlier had worked gold, silk, common metals, and mechanical objects into products, perhaps in constant demand, because they helped create or sustain that demand.

There is a point to be drawn from this brief digression into career opportunities and wealth acquisition potential: one must not be left thinking that in the human ambitions and actions of the present there is something different about man today than there was in the past.

Nor must one think there is something new or different about the criticism of wealth, whether in its early form of the exorbitant trader, or the anathema that faced the usurer, or the political and social animosity that has squared up against capitalism.

As the Reformation gave way to modern industrial society, one that began to produce a new social order of manufacturing wealth as a political faction, those who first confronted "modern" capitalism did so with the sense of exasperation. Weber describes in *The Protestant Ethic and the Spirit of Capitalism:*

> It is just that which seems to the [noncapitalistic] man so incomprehensible and mysterious, so unworthy and contemptible. That anyone should be able to make it the sole purpose of his life-work, to sink into the grave weighed down with a great material load of money and goods, seems to him explicable only as the product of a perverse instinct . . .

But as the Industrial Revolution's oppressive side became more apparent in an era that was already seething with men and women seeking answers and change, capitalism's natural antithesis, socialism, automatically developed more strongly. John Plamenatz, in *Man and Society,* writes:

> The early socialists contemplated the same economy as Adam Smith or Ricardo. But, whereas the classical economists saw it as a system ensuring that, on the whole, available resources were put to the most productive use, the socialists condemned it as wasteful.

Plamenatz further extends the point:

> The early socialists . . . were moved [above all] by the belief that poverty, insecurity and ruthless competition are degrading. Men who become socialists, even though they have a taste for abstract argument, are not moved in the first place by the pure desire that certain abstract principles of justice should be put into practice; they are moved by sympathy with the poor and are perhaps also offended by the indifference and smugness of the fortunate.

As the ability and opportunity to question moved down society, one finds rational men and women producing the democratic form: self in political society. Hand in glove with the political opportunity was the economic opportunity. Men produced an economic form of self in society: capitalism.

If modern capitalism were a religion, and if that religion had a theology, then its God, Mammon, is self. Mammon gets only a couple of passing references in the New Testament and owes his fame to his publicist, poet Milton. Many people, like Milton, prefer to regard capitalism as godless in two senses of the word.

At his strongest, critic Tawney, bringing on Weber's final denunciation, writes in the *Protestant Ethic* foreword:

> If capitalism begins as the practical idealism of the aspiring bourgeoisie, it ends, Weber suggests in his conluding pages, as an orgy of materialism.

And what is materialism but self-indulgence? Dr. Johnson insisted that austerity is the correct antidote to indulgence—and a West that has been indulging itself is beginning to pay the price in austerity.

From Aristotle and the prophets of the Old Testament, to Christ, to the early and modern socialists, wealth and then capitalism have attracted severe critics.

The political element in anticapitalism is so strong because the capitalistic element in modern democracies has been so strong. Capitalists achieved access to the political power as the new wealth class sought political participation. Christopher Hill, in *Reformation and the Industrial Revolution,* suggests how:

the Netherlands and England were unique in having successful political revolutions which led to greater commercial influence over governments.

There are those who see in the modern tendency of the government and major corporations and industries to seek working arrangements not the strong hand of government taking over, but the strong hand of capitalism taking over government. What one sees depends on where one stands.

Criticism of modern American capitalism covers quite a range: at its mildest, in *Fortune,* May 1974:

the public keeps raising the threshold of what it considers acceptable business behavior.

A more censorious note sounds like this from Bruce Carrick, an editor who summed up this author's views by stating:

we can't afford the damned system because a) it was based on an abundance of raw material we no longer have and b) it has produced the kind of imbalanced society we no longer want.

And a mite more anticapitalistic; from Assar Lindbeck, in *The Political Economy of the New Left,* who writes

Why should wealth—and thereby also income and economic power—be as unevenly distributed as it is in present capitalist societies? Personally, I have always regarded this as the main argument in favor of some form of socialism. It has to be admitted, however, that some problems of private capitalism certainly are not solved by collective ownership and that some new problems would certainly arise.

People who would not accept James Ridgeway's call to nationalize the national energy companies and their natural resources, might still agree with his charge in *The Last Play* that:

The domination of oil, gas, coal and uranium by large energy trusts has helped to create its own energy crisis, raising prices, changing markets, carving out new resource colonies, leading to growing disparity between rich and poor.

Or, using Paul Samuelson's words in his introduction to Lindbeck, if young economists "at American universities . . . under the banner of 'Radical Economics' do want to change the direction of economic research," and are able to change it, then they are returning to a brand of political economy which cannot but emphasize more sharply the disparities within capitalistic economies.

Many people who seek a "single standard of treatment for rich and poor" are not socialists.

The migrant agricultural laborer, the modern imbiber of juice from those grapes of wrath, has caught the national attention.

Ridgeway, maintaining that Appalachia was poor because the wealth was under its feet, could be paraphrasing the plight of the rural worker, through whose fingers the wealth passes though only the dirt sticks.

Europe has its "new proletarians" in the migrant work forces that have flocked from Mediterranean countries and North Africa to the cities and factories of the continent. Their hovels, the conditions under which they live, the general attitude of the society around them to them, make them social misfits, outcasts. According to Jonathan Power in *The New Proletarians,* published by the British Council of Churches, twenty percent of France's "manual working class are now foreigners." There are 10 million foreign workers throughout Europe, "doing menial jobs, poorly paid, with little job security."

No one will conduct a reformation on their behalf, but their plight, their barely heard voice, is added to the reform mix. Far more strident is the voice of European industrial labor: it has its rhetoric, and its reason. First, the rhetoric, from a handbill given out by the International Caucus of Labor Committees:

Capitalists are already beginning to outline the kind of future world they see emerging from the crisis—a post industrial swamp, in which workers who are "lucky enough" to have jobs will be subjected to vicious speed-up and below subsistence level living standards, while the bulk of the population will be on the dole [unemployment pay]. Under these conditions only a programme which united the employed and the unemployed, the organized and the unorganized, in their common interest in the expansion of production, can pose a realistic political alternative to the capitalist no-growth world of the future.

Not that the rhetoric is without its grains of truth. The problem is that the yeast of argument swells the truth beyond its capacity to sustain itself. That comment about men "lucky enough" to have jobs need not be necessarily just imagination. The following appeared in 1966, in George Paloczi-Horvath's *The Facts Rebel:*

> Those fortunate enough to work might become the elite, not for economic reasons, but merely because of the prestige of having a job—any kind of job.
>   [John Billera, Executive Vice-President, U.S. Industries, Inc.]
>   You cannot collect trade union dues from these machines . . . But you cannot sell them motor-cars either . . .
> [Conversation in an automated plant between a director of Ford and an American labour leader.]

Capitalists have to face up to the fact that the two economic trends of the present, toward near-exclusive governmental control, or toward workers' control, are the only avenues for reform open to those who would stop short of revolution. Self-interest would suggest that capitalists themselves must provide a third avenue, or a compromise avenue, if they cannot face up to the consequences of these trends. A *Business Week* reader wrote:

> Economic growth has brought with it the advent of full employment, which has provided the worker with an unprecedented level of power, bringing him to a point where he can negotiate with his employer. The labor market is no different to any other market—in a monopoly, the consumer must accept the product and the price or go without, while in a perfectly competitive market, the consumer may select the product and negotiate the price. The labor market has just become competitive and workers are less worried about losing jobs.

The advance of the international power of organized labor, though many unionists adhere to it in principle, is a sometime thing. For the last few years there have been concerted efforts, most particularly in the metalworking and chemical industries, to bring international bargaining to bear on multinational corporations. Not by any stretch of the imagination could it be suggested that a new era of international labor has arrived in which multinational labor negotiates with multinational employer as an equal.

International trade unionism has been a labor aspiration for more than a century. Socialists have regarded it as near-inevitable, a coming together of like-minded workers, bound together by common cause, forward together in a single, certain direction.

Just as Lenin said that "capitalism would not be capitalism if the pure proletariat were not surrounded by a large number of motley types," so trade unionism would not be a national frame of mind but an international one except for the motley types demanding their own regional, national, and personal interests. "Pure" trade unionism could not help but be international any more than "pure" capitalism cannot help but be international.

What may well make a difference in international labor will be one or two successes by international federations of trade unions covering single areas like metalworking or chemicals. Charles Levinson, secretary general of the International Federation of Chemical and General Workers in Geneva, is one example of how articulate late twentieth-century international unionism is becoming. The challenge he throws out to the multinational corporations is quite new, quite attractive to labor at large: he successfully turns *the* single most pressing economic problem, inflation, into a labor weapon. It has the same appeal as the cry:

"No politics! Long live the purely economic struggle!"

Levinson is no aristocratic anarchist like the Mikhail Bakunin who used the above slogan, but out of books and writings like Levinson's, will come, in all likelihood, the separate slogans that can further mobilize international labor.

What is remarkable, however, is that just as the politics of domestic government have to be apolitical on so many new economic problems (meaning it doesn't much matter which party is in power, there may be few alternatives or choices on certain economic issues), so labor is developing into an apolitical force. Apolitical, that is, if the cry becomes "long live the purely economic struggle."

That truly is the arrival of "the nonmarxist wave of our neocapitalist future."

There is a new brand of rebuttal from the avant garde of organized international labor these days. Levinson promotes it in his *Capitalism, Inflation and the Multinationals:*

In the decade ahead, structural change, the multinational company, and capital investment will be the new determinants of inflation. They will not entirely supplant

the others . . . [but] . . . it is to this new dynamic partial sector that more attention
and policy must be directed . . .

Keeping international unionism concentrated on the economic
rather than the political gives the better informed workers—who,
while often dissatisfied, cannot marshal modern retaliatory arguments—a sense of justified grievance without the difficulties of finding themselves politically categorized various shades of pink. Because there is as much political shading within trade union
membership as there is among Saturday morning supermarket shoppers, the "leftist" label has remained a great deterrent to U.S. trade
unionism joining any developing global force. If the shift away from
the political and concentration on the economic can be maintained,
apolitical world labor may yet become such a force.

There is another difficulty. International bargaining and wage negotiations have to contend both with the wage spread globally and the
consequences of national labor blocs attempting to influence multinational corporate investment toward their particular country. Labor,
too, must produce its version of the statesman-diplomat as at home in
the smoky working class clubs and union meetings as in the world's
political corridors and executive suites.

More "international," but as yet limited generally to Europe, is
labor's drive toward a variety of worker participation and worker
control programs. These may be programs that take hold only in a
Scandinavian country or two. They may sweep through the industrialized nations. They may pass the United States by. They are,
however, part of the structural change of capitalism inherent in a second, if secular, reformation. It is not a question of whether worker
"participation" is acceptable to the European nations. Political
leaders in Europe acknowledge some form of participation by the
workers as inevitable.

The questions are: How much participation? How much control?

"Capital sharing," "worker participation," and "worker control"
schemes cover a variety of actual or possible situations. They range
from programs designed to improve the workers' surroundings
(cleaner factories, lower noise levels) to total ownership of those surroundings.

No trade union group has gone as far as the Danish Landsorganisa-tionem (LO), the Danish Federation of Trades Unions, in developing a formula for a possible legal takeover by the workers. "Capital shar-ing" schemes have these features in common, according to the 1971 statement on *Economic Democracy* issued by LO:

i. They are intended to provide workers with the opportunity of acquiring wealth assets;
ii. these assets are initially or primarily financed by the employer;
iii. the amount of accumulation per worker is determined either by reference to the profits of the undertaking, or in relation to the level of wages, or rate of change of wages of the workers concerned. Essentially the schemes provide arrange-ments whereby workers receive some *future* benefits in the form of a monetary lump-sum payment or ownership of wealth assets from their employer. The capi-tal contribution is also seen as a payment over and above the increase in real wages which would have otherwise been negotiated.

Without putting any rhetoric between cause and effect, workers' control schemes in their final form insist that a basic contribution of wealth or ownership in the corporation be continually granted—over and above negotiated wages—until ownership passes substantially into the hands of the employees. If the first question raised is: Why should the capital holders agree? The answer is: If the state legislates that such a process be implemented, the capital holders have to agree.

The scheme discussed here, the Danish one, is examined because it is one single method by which ownership, over a period of 10 years to 20 years, could pass from the old capital holders to the "new" capital holders, the workers.

Not the sort of talk that's likely to catch on here, you say? Listen to this from Jaroslav Vanek, director of the Program on Participation and Labor-Managed Systems at Cornell University's Center for Inter-national Studies:

"Self-management is synonymous with the liberation of working people," said Vanek, in an Associated Press reported story which also quoted him as saying:

The founders of this country gave us only half of our total rights 200 years ago when they provided us with political freedom. We must extend these rights to in-clude economic freedom if we want to survive as a free democracy.

Is there much difference between this and Denmark? The AP story explains:

> Under self-management, voting shares become nonvoting shares. Their owners get an annual return—a percentage income based on total investment in the company or based on the company's performance. Voting power is transferred to the company's workers, each of whom gets one vote. They establish working conditions, hours, company policy—even their own salaries.

And so on.

A further reason for looking closely at the Danish LO's program is that when European trade unionists met in Paris in 1971, under the auspices of the OECD's Manpower and Social Affairs Directorate, to discuss capital formation programs, its main conclusion was that:

> It may be that the Danish proposals will, in time, come to be regarded as the most desirable way of dealing with this subject.

The Danish LO, in calling its proposal "economic democracy," justifies and explains the expression with the statement that

> economic democracy is, in the first place, a question of ownership rights to the means of production . . . [and] . . . it is increasingly recognised in wide circles that the existing inequality in the distribution of ownership rights to the means of production and to capital is undemocratic, and that ownership rights are connected with power and influence.

Whether ownership rights to the means of production and capital are undemocratic must immediately fall into the category of "subjective political reasoning," but there cannot be much argument with the statement that "ownership rights are connected with power and influence." LO clearly states its case:

> Democracy means co-influence and co-determination for a maximum number of persons, both in the production process and in society. Consequently, economic democracy means the entire influence of society on the economic conditions, for instance on the banks and other central parts of the economic sphere of influence . . .

(Not that U.S. multinational enterprises abroad necessarily take kindly to codetermination. According to Norman Birnbaum in *Com-*

mentary, July 1975, "the president of the West German Trade Union Confederation recently castigated American business in Germany for 'colonialist' behavior in connection with its opposition to codetermination in German industry.")

There was no doubt, either, about the need for fresh thinking regarding a growing problem limited not only to Denmark. Those countries that face the problem of the "flight of capital" cannot help but look at their remaining capital sources and consider how better to utilize them. As the *Danish Labor News* stated it:

> Modern industry has an enormous demand for capital investment, and a considerable volume of saving is needed to satisfy this demand. Otherwise it will not be possible to maintain and further develop industry and other important sectors of the Danish economy.

The "old" way of achieving greater savings and increased cash flow (to increase profits) results in

> . . . constant appeals to the wage-earners for restraint in demands for higher wages, so that the companies will be able to get the higher profits they consider necessary for the continued growth of production and investment.
>
> These problems cannot be dismissed, but in a modern society there must be another solution than using the purely capitalistic method.

The LO program for "economic democracy" is "another solution."

The program calls for a payroll "tax," starting at 1 percent and gradually rising to 5 percent, to be borne by the employer and the existing stockholders. The "tax" would be paid in the form of newly issued shares into a central fund administered by LO. The government sector would give 5 percent of its payroll, too, into the fund, and this cash would be invested in more shares. Legislation would first have to require all Danish corporations, public and private, to reorganize in such a manner that there could be shares to issue, though the final size of the economic entity to which "economic democracy" would apply was never finally decided.

All Danish workers, in the public and private sectors, would then have a claim against the fund, regardless of their particular salary level, because the government also would pay a payroll tax on its employees.

These corporate shares, held by the central fund in the name of the workers, would give the workers the right to place representatives on the boards of the corporations where they work. In other words, imagine the trade union central fund "as a kind of Orwellian mutual fund" or unit trust with the workers holding the shares in the central fund, and the fund holding the shares in all Danish corporations.

Disagreement is not over the need for industry to have capital, but over the old ways of producing capital, and sharing capital profits. LO sees the continued trend toward price increases, already accelerating faster than ever with the massive increase in oil and energy costs, coupled with full employment, producing "capital gains which, as far as productive capital is concerned—and together with the enormous increases in prices of land and real estate—contribute to substantiating and in certain cases strongly promoting the inequality of the distribution of wealth."

Given that

the required flow of capital to industry—and also risk bearing capital—must be secured, the public authorities should make a greater effort in this respect, and the banks should endeavor to meet the demands in fields where there is a special need for new development. The conditions of ownership rights must, however, be altered at the same time.

When LO presented its plan before fellow European trade unionists in Paris at the OECD meeting, it was billed as a Wage Earners' Profit and Investment Fund. LO's claim for the plan was that:

it covers all wage-earners:
it is based on solidarity, everybody getting an equal share.
it is a combination of investment wages and a general profit-sharing scheme.
it secures for the wage-earners a share in the future surplus (profit on capital plus capital growth) of the companies.
it decentralizes influence and the right to decide over the fund resources.
it will contribute to a stabilization because, in principle, the money will remain in the companies.

And the Paris unionists were impressed.

The Danish employers and capital holders were not impressed:

"Economic democracy? It's economic demo-crazy!"

All Danish political parties have an element—out of political necessity—of "economic democracy" or "worker participation" in their political platforms. The Danish employers and suppliers, representing the owners in effect, also believe there is an issue. As one spokesman told this writer:

Democratic economy: how to democratise the ownership of capital in private industry. That's the real problem.

The employers and suppliers are in principle prepared to accept that the ownership of capital be redistributed, that there be "more equal distribution of the ownership of capital invested in private enterprise." The employers' view of the method is a well-known and, in some corporations and industries in the West, the well-tried one of giving "every employee the opportunity to save, and invest his savings in private enterprise."

However, the Danish employers caution the worker about the wisdom of such investment.

Wage earners are the big majority of the electorate. For this reason almost anything has been done to give the wage earners and salaried persons as big an increase as possible. That means the return on capital, the income from capital, has gone down . . . from 9.1% in 1960 to 5.8% in 1972.

In Denmark, at the time the above comment was made, the return on investment in savings and bonds was 11.1 percent, and had risen to that peak from 7 percent over the period capital return was declining.

Denmark has another serious problem, as the employers see it—that due to the economic and political policies of the government:

labor has become more scarce than capital, because the public sector has been expanded so much. The public sector from 1960 to 1969 absorbed more than 80% of the net increase of the labor force.

What the employers see happening behind the LO proposal is an attempt to "centralise the power of both capital and labor with the same man, namely the President of LO." As the employers' spokesman said:

My personal opinion is that it is impossible for one man to pursue the aims of both capital and labor at the same time. He has to maximise wages and return on capital, which is impossible. I think there will always be some conflict of interest between capital and labor, which are the only two factors in production, and they will always compete.

(And yet, some form of worker participation appears absolutely essential, otherwise Chrysler U.K. would not have offered its workers a chance to participate in order to help solve serious corporate problems.)

The practical problems and the political problems inherent in a dramatic shift of capital and control from one section of a community to another are not sufficient arguments against it. Obviously any group determined on such a course expects to bear that burden. The range of problems must begin, however, with what happens to the democracy.

Competition between capital and labor is, in many European countries, the basis of the two-party system as the lines are presently drawn. It is not inconceivable that a new two-party system could emerge in a democracy that has suffered through the traumatic experience of "economic democracy." Lines could be drawn, for example, between the workers' party and the bureaucratic party. All this providing that the democratic system had been able to withstand the stress exerted on it in the shift of economic power.

The least desirable face of "economic democracy"—and plans like these are not without appeal to anyone with a taste for socio-politico-economic experiment—must be the tremendous risk of concentrating capital and labor in a single center of power, one quite capable of matching up to any government. Where is the major opposition to come from that is vital to the democratic two-party system?

It becomes at this point one thing to say that if capitalism is one of the prices we pay for a democracy, then the price is too high, quite another to suggest the alternative is not equally high, maybe even higher. On its own merits that is no argument for retaining capitalism. This indicates a likelihood in some Western democracies that they will go the route of even deeper government penetration of society rather than allow the basic tug between labor and capital, however minimized by that sheer weight of government presence, to disappear.

Having looked at the Danish plan, and even though it is thus far a political nonstarter, can it not just be regarded as one more attempt at socio-economic-political experimentation and left at that?

Not so. "Economic democracy" or "workers' control" is the direction in which European trade unionists and several European political parties are heading. As U.S. corporations now draw sizable profits from Europe, they must accept the political realities and obey the legislation of each country they invest in.

What are U.S. corporations offering U.S. workers? Corporations like Anheuser-Busch, Inc., are putting ever more stress on the benefits—and advantages—of employees all down the line buying shares in the company.

This is an old concept. During a 1975 interview, August A. Busch III told this writer that the company believed all the workers had the ability to understand how the corporation operates. "They do understand what cash flow is," said Busch.

The Anheuser-Busch president and chief executive officer said that the workers were told who owned the company, what yield those stockholders could expect, and how that yield compared with other investments such as "C.D.s (certificates of deposit) and Treasury bills."

A-B workers at least know where they stand in a highly-paid industry second only to the typographical unions for the best wage rates in the country.

European labor has been looking for something to fill the vacuum created by the abandonment of the "old left" economic solutions; it is highly political trade unionism in most European countries; it has already come up with one or two startling new ways of doing things. The most striking, if one will overlook the pun, is the workers' takeover of the plant about to be closed: the work-in.

No move is more likely to gain public support than the sight of workers voluntarily turning up at their jobs to continue to build ships, as happened at the Upper Clyde, in Scotland, or farm machinery, as occurred in Wales, when management decides to close down a factory, plant, or industry. It is a magnificent ploy. Government has to act, and it is a toughened government indeed that can evict workers who are demanding only that their jobs be protected or returned.

The Upper Clyde story is an amazing mixture of unionism, capitalism, communism, and government intervention. Simply stated, a decision was made to close down these old-fashioned yards, neglected through years of low or no capital investment, part of a declining shipbuilding industry that had been missing its opportunities for a half-century. But the decision to close the yard, already the object of government subsidy, was rejected by the workers. They instead formally notified the authorities they were "taking over" the yards. They continued with the work in hand and dispatched union leaders—some of them from communist-led unions—on a global search for new owners, or new orders, and made the government listen.

The eventual outcome was that Marathon Industries, Inc., of Texas, lured in by workers' promises and large British government grants and loans, agreed to take over the yards to build drilling rigs for North Sea oil exploration. Whatever the future may hold, Marathon and the Clydeside workers already have one rig out to sea.

Blending the imaginative and the pragmatic, trade union leadership can appear on occasion as something other than strike-happy and bloody-minded. So, in countries with both a strong social democratic or socialist heritage in their trade unionism, a ready-made package like Denmark's "economic democracy" plan gives them a sense of what worker control can be, and how it could be accomplished—accomplished, of course, if political circumstances arose that would allow the legislation through.

Finally, in Denmark there had long been "cooperative management" or "industrial democracy" through workers' councils involved in the day-to-day running, productivity and efficiency schemes. Danish employers were not unhappy with this form of factory-by-factory worker-management cooperation. It is fairly well tried in places like Germany, and at least is one more forum for ironing out problems without resorting to strikes and allowing workers to press for change without doing it at an annual bargaining table confrontation.

Yet even in Scandinavian countries, where labor-management relations are at their smoothest, where they are operating within a framework of "the best interests of the national economy" unpressured by government, the problems are severe.

When wages throughout an economy are programmed to keep pace with wages in the growth sectors of the economy, inflation is encouraged, unless capital investment in the slower sectors is working at eradicating the spread between the rapid-growth and slow-growth sectors, or unless government can devise ways of allowing for the difference through, say, selective taxation on "growth."

One of the points emerging from all this discussion is the well-established one that organized labor has, or can find, the power that enables it to stand up to management, to have its case heard. In Europe, more than the United States, there is also a political under-current to the argument, because finally it comes down to the "quality of life" the workers can expect. Such discussion does not take place without political ramifications.

On another front is the vulnerability of the highly capitalized production system to inadequate labor relations.

Michael Cooley, head of a white collar British trade union group of engineering technicians, designers, and draftsmen, shows the nature of the changes taking place within industry and commerce. He acknowledges that "technological redundancy" is likely as the computer starts taking over in the design field, but he goes on to spell out the rest of the process, a process that has been repeated, with variations, for more than a century. M. J. E. Cooley, in *Computer-Aided Design, Its Nature and Implications,* states:

> In the past when a clerical worker went on strike it had precious little effect. Now, if the wages of a factory are carried out by a computer, a strike by clerical workers can disrupt the whole of the plant.

Cooley explains that the same can now happen in the design area, where very high rates of capital investment are changing the nature of the work. Computer-aided design, Cooley suggests, has these effects on the remaining workers:

> firstly, it proletarianizes them, but secondly it also increases their strike power. The employers . . . will seek to designate these as areas of management in order to prevent them becoming effectively organized.

To summarize the politically oriented criticism of capitalism before looking at capitalists' responses to their modern predicament, let's range the gamut from Marx of the Old Left to Levinson of the New Labor.

Marx, separating the various layers of society, dividing them into units that would facilitate the class struggle, seemed to reveal the difficulties of promoting class struggle:

the intimate connexion between the pangs of hunger of the most industrious layers of the working class and the extravagant consumption, coarse or refined, of the rich— for which capitalist accumulation is the basis—reveals itself only when the economic laws are known.

Knowledge of the economic laws, or even concern about the economic laws is not the hallmark of the modern individual. Economics is not an attractive subject, and "political economy" demands a degree of knowledge (or fervor where knowledge has been passed over) that finds few adherents among the cognoscenti, the dilettanti, or the radical chic, let alone those hard pressed to reach Friday when they set out for it on Monday.

Supporting or rebutting Marx is a debate that takes place over the heads of the electorate in the United States.

Taking the work force of the West as a whole, or even narrowing it down to the unemployed or potentially unemployed American, does the working class struggle really ignite the feelings of the many in the working class? Does it really reach even a discernible minority?

In the United States, where the assembly line worker sees his children get into the state university, is the appeal from the U.S.-published *New Solidarity* weekly speaking to a major element of the U.S. working class?

. . . the capitalist class must ultimately reduce real wages by about 40% if it is to shore up its debt-ridden income in the present period of deepening depression. But the government cannot simply decree or even force the working class to accept such lower wages immediately.

Organized labor can apply pressure of a political and economic type on modern corporations and entire industries. Is there a new tendency here, the monitoring of corporate behavior by those inside the corporation at the nonexecutive level? Levinson explains, in an ICF document:

It was the Chemical Section of the ICF [the International Federation of Chemical and General Workers' Unions] who first drew attention to the scandal of the high profits being made out of the two tranquilisers Librium and Valium, and as a consequence the British Monopoly Commission reported that on these two tranquilisers alone £24 million profit had been made in six years, and they ordered this Swiss-based company to reduce their prices by 75% and 60% respectively, and to hand back to the government some £11 million which it was claimed was the amount overcharged. West Germany, Sweden, Canada, America and the European Community are also taking steps to investigate the high prices of these two tranquilisers being supplied to the Health Services and to their consumers. It is sad, but symbolic of the state of our society, that such huge profits should be made out of sickness. It is time, and high time, that we took profit making out of the social service and health care system on which the health of the people of the Western world is so much dependent.

Where does all the discussion lead? Back to power and the power struggles in society for control over the entire range of the social, economic, and political spectrum. The struggle is between those who believe that capitalism, even in its neocapitalist form, still can provide the good society, and those who do not.

Capitalism in Europe has been an evolutionary process tied to the Industrial Revolution, a political economic theory promoted—or opposed—by the political leaders of the day. On occasion, European capitalism, even outside of wartime and depression, has had to be subservient to survival economics: socioeconomic needs, reallocating scarce resources, and restructuring income distribution in order that the particular nation exist. For at least 150 years capitalism in Europe has been attacked on its home ground, probed, opposed, and, in one instance at least, overthrown.

At no point in history—not even during the Depression—has the United States come up against these phenomena with any real threat attached to them. Trust-busting in turn-of-the-century outbursts against the monopolies was not attacking the capitalist system, just its abuses. Syndicalists, communes, and Wobblies notwithstanding, there has never been the sort of concerted and sustained mass feeling against capitalism—present both in times of anguish and plenty—that for many European nations is a way of life.

U.S. capitalism has been a means of dividing up the new wealth. While there was a chance of some of that wealth trickling down to the bottom, or the opportunity for those on the bottom to reach up to where the wealth was, the United States made capitalism not just respectable but part of the national fabric.

How goes the spirit of U.S. capitalism in the final quarter of the twentieth century? It ranges from the optimistic to the nostalgic.

David Rockefeller, writing on the Op Ed page of the *New York Times,* presents the optimists' case:

> . . . if American capitalism is to maintain and increase its vitality, it must do a better job of integrating its economic and social functions.

Irving Kristol, who sees an environmentalist under every bed, and who labels John Kenneth Galbraith as an economist who "resists enlightenment," presents the following setting, in *The Public Interest:*

> Whenever and wherever defenders of "free enterprise," "individual liberty," and "a free society" assemble, these days, one senses a peculiar kind of nostalgia in the air. It is a nostalgia for that time when they were busily engaged in confronting their old and familiar enemies, the avowed proponents of a full-blown "collectivist" economic and social order. In the debate with these traditional enemies, advocates of "a free society" have indeed, done extraordinarily well. It is therefore a source of considerable puzzlement to them that, though the other side seems to have lost the argument, their side seems somehow not to have won it.

The sentiment evokes images of the old nobility watching the new democracy depriving it of its freedom of action and its powers—and the parallel is worth retaining.

Because capitalism is the sum total of the individual trades and dealings of every profit-oriented entity, there is not and cannot be a leader, a person who "represents" capitalism. Capitalism is not a great monolith acting out some Machiavellian capitalist plot. Capitalism moves after profit, and that alone is enough to give the impression to those who watch it that it knows where it is going and what it is doing.

But singlemindedness has cost capitalism dearly.

Listen to one of the leading global management consultants, who told this writer:

> This is incredible in retrospect but we never really felt that employer-employee relations, or industrial relations, were really our concern. We were much more concerned to look at things like financial analyses, cost benefits, and things like that.

Today we have men on our staff who would not have been hired 10 years ago. They are no less good. They are different: Men who understand that the human resources of a company are as important, or more so, than any other asset, and have to be managed that way.

Faced with curtailment of their activities and open hostility toward their motives, big businessmen are belatedly talking in terms of social goals, social responsibility, and fresh concepts of serving the public good while serving the private interest.

Apart from eliminating, repairing, or preventing obvious environmental damage, improving product quality, and keeping their noses clean (all huge undertakings, incidentally), capitalists are uncertain what the "public good" is, whether they can afford it, and how to go about it.

Nor is it surprising that capitalists are hesitant about which way to go: there is no national consensus on the obvious environmental, employment, and consumer issues, and no lead from the political leadership. So capitalists are left with fine phrases and anxious faces trying to think of programs to promote—programs they can support with a degree of real rather than forced enthusiasm.

Even then, most businessmen do not really believe they should be in the "social goal" business. Nor would they have to be if government took on itself national social responsibility, allocating and regulating in such a way that corporate capitalism could not counter the public will, but that its main value to society was in its value to the economy as a profit-making dynamo. Making profits is *all* capitalism is good at. Nothing else. That is its sole purpose, sole motivating factor, sole goal.

Capitalism will take stock of every regulation, every law, every encumbrance placed upon it, and still find ways of pursuing profit. Government should decide what those "social goal" regulations, laws, and encumbrances should be, should enforce them fairly, and still find ways of letting capitalism produce the profits that provide the taxes and jobs that provide the economy with some vitality.

The Swedish economy, hailed by many as the most admirably state-interventionist in Europe, is merely a capitalist economy (95 percent of the GNP comes from capitalist corporations) with a totally

Social Democrat government. Government uses capitalism's profits to pay for the social programs. At least the Swedes are under no illusions. As one executive told this writer:

If Sweden had 10 times its present population it would be among the biggest capitalistic imperialist powers in the world.

Former Social Democrat prime minister Tage Erlander explained to this writer:

Take away our social intervention and you are left with a generally capitalist economy.

Swedish big businessmen do not like the degree of government intervention and do not enjoy the high level of taxation, but they cope. The same story was true in Britain. When the British Labor government took office in the sixties, Neil Wates, head of Britain's biggest private building company, gathered his staff together and said: "Right, lads, now let's find out where to make a buck under socialism." They did. But will they always find out where?

That is what capitalism can do. It can keep its end goal, profits, in sight, and keep trying new ways—despite new obstacles—of getting there.

In a democracy, capitalist corporations should not be called upon to originate social programs. They should know what the social goals are and make sure they do nothing to prevent those goals from being met while ensuring that everyone connected with their corporation has the opportunity to participate personally in helping the community and the nation achieve those goals.

Setting the social goals for society is the government's job. It is a political job. That's what politics is. And two-party politics in a democracy is supposed to be two parties competing against each other offering programs to promote the common wealth and the national goods. But within this competition for public support there should be a strong vein of agreement across party political lines as to what the best interests of the nation are.

The modern litany of urban and social discontent, our permanent Greek chorus, is too well known to repeat here. Surely it is sufficient only to say that in broad areas concerning education and health care, preserving the national heritage, stamping down hard on all that is corrupt and venal and criminal while promoting a sense of direction and purpose for all Americans, there is a wide enough swath for developing a national consensus not purely dependent on which party is in office.

Within the vacuum that is the American consensus of the present, all corporate capitalists can do is take general aim in a general direction.

David Rockefeller on "social responsibility":

First, corporations must develop more effective tools for measuring the social, as well as economic, costs and benefits of their actions. A broadly acceptable format for detailed social accounting is probably a distant goal, yet there is much that can be done now. Social objectives can be formally incorporated into regular business planning . . .

Second, businessmen must take the initiative to spell out more clearly and positively the longer-range economic and technical implications of current proposals for social problem-solving. Too often, in the view of businessmen, critics seem simply to proclaim goals as solutions without taking into account the necessary processes, resources and economic dislocations. Critics of business, on the other hand, frequently brand those who point to the costs of social progress as mossbacks. Neither group is exclusively correct.

Arjay Miller, former president of Ford, addressing a White House conference on "The Industrial World Ahead":

Businessmen have for too long been stereotyped as men who always react negatively to any kind of social progress that interferes with traditional ways of doing business. Business can increase the hiring and training of minority group persons, introduce new technology and increase the level of job skills, improve the quality and serviceability of essential products and eliminate as quickly as possible the harmful air and water pollutants resulting from its operations.

Companies can do a lot more about social problems, but they should not pretend to be something they are not. A business is a business, not a philanthropy. Its actions should be justified essentially on business grounds, on enlightened self-interest, not on moral or ethical grounds.

Both men had to speak as if the broad mass of society even knows or agrees what is socially responsible, socially desirable, or socially relevant.

Internal initiative, those things that can be done within the corporations, has to come from the capitalists themselves, in conjunction with their workers. But external initiative must originate elsewhere in society, with capitalists called in to share in the debate as one more social entity.

The corporations individually and collectively must produce the internal programs, the range of alternatives, the compromises, that can be presented to their employees and society as indications of honorable intent. In the United States, where employees cannot yet even be sure that their pensions will be honored in many major corporations, where the major oil companies stand accused of manufacturing the energy crisis, the credibility gap is wide indeed.

From one corporation to the next, however, there are only ever-so-slight beginnings, even though over the last century there have been single notable examples of sound approaches to changing how a factory, or a business, or a corporation performs its functions.

All 9,000 employees at Sandoz, A.G. in Switzerland are "staff," not hourly workers, all paid on a monthly basis. Employees, even senior executive staff, may dress informally, and can start work anytime between 7 A.M. and 9 A.M., finishing sometime between 4 P.M. and 7 P.M. All are responsible for keeping track of their own hours worked. This type of minor structural change can be the start of considerable improvements within a single corporation.

Like cooperatives, workers' participation schemes, the attempts at the four-day week, Volvo's attractive abolition of the assembly line, or the employee-owned John Lewis Partnership (Britain's fast-growing department store and supermarket firm), many different approaches have been tried and are being tried.

This book never set out to discover why men strive; it was prepared to accept that they do. A feel for power, then, is the most difficult element to gauge or modify in the sort of self-reformation being demanded of capitalism. Harlow Ungar put the point into the context of corporate capitalism in *Investors Review:*

Companies like Monsanto, Corning Glass, Eaton, Texas Instruments are giving their workers more freedom to use their own judgement on the job by removing supervisors and other "bossmen" from the immediate work areas.

Some plants at General Foods Corporation and Procter and Gamble may go so far as to let worker teams run entire departments, entirely free of executive interference.

But most companies would scoff at such schemes, saying that they would be un-

able to work under such conditions. For, the conservative firms point out, power "to
do things my way" is as much an incentive to executives as monetary compensation.

Capitalism has no reforming pope to lead it on its Counter Reformation, so self-reform has to come as the sum total of all the individual
corporate attempts and successes at reform throughout each phase and
unit of "the capitalist mode of production."

Corporations that do not yet even have personnel men on their
boards of directors may well be a long way removed from having
workers there, or executives whose responsibility to board and stockholder, worker and customer, concerns corporate activities in a wide
range of social goal-finding activities and social problem solving. The
"corporate Jesuit," who must be more advanced than the "hierarchy"
he represents, could be the new ideal for those destined into the corporate structure. He would be the social technocrat in the industrial-
social sphere that the economic technocrat is in the industrial-political
sphere. He would have his counterpart among the workers, too, in
this best of all possible corporate worlds.

Capitalism has yet to come the full circle back to its own Reforma-
tion-endowed respectability. The only thing that made capitalism respectable—or if not respectable, acceptable—was its "heroic" quality: work in the service of the community, work of which wealth was
a "natural" by-product.

The spirit of modern capitalism has become something else, something indefensible:

an immoderate thirst for gain.

Can capitalism reform itself? Only if it can come up with some internal mechanism for moderating the maximization of profits by permitting that maximum to include expenditure, significant expenditure
of time and energy, on reforming its own structure—new ways of
including the workers within the corporate life and decision-making
process, including profits, and ownership perhaps; of setting social
goals as a result first of management and labor learning and carrying
out their joint responsibilities to society at large, as members of the
same entity, and then by encouraging all individuals within the firm
to find avenues for serving society as individuals.

Do not play down the conviction with which this must be done. This is not corporate boy scouting for adult labor and management. There are few social decisions that are not also highly political. There are few "longer-range economic and technical implications of current proposals for social problem solving" that do not call for wisdom rather than discussion.

The question is whether either management or labor can be selfless enough on behalf of those they represent, and whether executives and individual workers jointly engaged in making decisions can produce, in fact, worthwhile contributions to the community at large.

Simple capitalism is wealth. Complex capitalism is power. Men are reluctant to relinquish power, and can rarely do it gracefully. Capitalism at its peak—where the talk centers on 300 corporate multinationals running the world, "and who's to say the world would not be better off for it," as one oil man believes—is a power game. These men of power have passed the point where financial rewards count. To those who have never seen it close at hand, power may be an unreal concept. But over the wide field of activities in which man engages, there are power plays by men who aspire to or achieve the power that comes with leadership.

Power is the cruelest of all tests by which an individual may challenge himself. Think of national leaders who leave office dispirited or broken men; of former men of incredible stature and sway, in finance, in the military, in the law, or in the fourth estate, who have lost that stature. With the flame removed they themselves become shadows.

Power is white hot. Men grip it to see how much pain they can stand.

Modern capitalism has grown out of many forces, not least the need to cope with complexity. But one persistent prod has been the increasing insistence of holders of wealth that their risks be minimized. Even the smallest wage earner with the tiniest nest egg wants security, from which stems most corporate legislation and stock market regulation.

There is another reason for wanting to get close to the center of the political, economic, and social power structures. F. G. Bailey, in *Stratagems and Spoils*, writes

It is in this sense that knowledge is power. The man who correctly understands how a particular structure works can prevent it from working or make it work differently with much less effort than a man who does not know these things.

The power structure can be calculated and used to corporate or individual advantage. Hans Luther knew, by simply looking at the social structure of which he was a small strut, that for Martin to reach the highest obtainable peaks for that time he needed to gain an education, Latin, and to become a lawyer. Any Western parent determined that a child have every possible opportunity takes a similar reading of society as best he or she can from that particular vantage point.
   Bailey:

The man who understands the working of any organization or institution can find out which roles are crucial to the maintenance of those structures, and among these roles which are the most vulnerable.

The capitalist seeking to be close to the political power, seeking to understand its structure, readily realizes, as Bailey says in *Tribe, Caste and Nation,* that

political relationships are concerned with the distribution of resources and power.

There is one other problem within capitalism itself, that is, the division of capitalism into Finance and Industry. These two factors are not always in harmony. Indeed there may well be a trend toward that old dictum:

To survive, Industry and Labor must combine against Finance.

The following comments are by Peter Parker, a British corporate chairman writing in *Investors Review.*

We are all familiar with the separation that the modern corporation has tended to establish between ownership and management. Sometimes I see a new variation on this theme, an emerging separation between management and its own sense of freedom to manage. . . . The manipulation of shareholdings, a deft and often devious disregard of codes, and then the raid for the control of a company and its assets—this is not attractive to the industrial community with a growing sense of its social standards and values which are under challenge. Who is whiz-kidding whom that this sort of thing generates more wealth in the long term?

Parker was attempting to pin down exactly what sort of social responsibilities business should have. Because modern corporations have yet to concertedly attack this question with the techniques they bring to bear on other problem solving, Parker frankly admits to more questions than answers. But these questions, raised often enough,

may well startle our industrial community out of its well dug-in clichés of socialism and capitalism.

Parker, who believes management cannot alone solve the riddle of allocating corporate resources "to all interested parties," at least provides a clear-cut description of the change, deep change, that has affected management already:

Probably in the last ten years everybody in business has found himself somersaulting, or at least having to adjust, his private set of prides and prejudices to move with the inevitable post-Keynesian interventionist role of modern government. Something has changed when hard-faced businessmen feel that they can describe a price restraint as an initiative.

The beleaguered capitalist belongs to a house that may be divided. He certainly belongs to a society which is divided, but a society of people uncertain about the nature of those divisions, and uncertain about making a commitment to one side of the social argument or another. Capitalism is trying to survive in a society that does not know what it will settle for, a society led for the most part by politicians incapable of displaying before the public the limited range of options from which society has to make its choice.

Capitalism is being pressured to reform. The reform of capitalism is gathering up a wide range of reformist elements that have little to do with capitalism as such, gathering up complaints and hostility that more justly should be directed at government and the political system.

Capitalism is capable only of attempting, under the eye of a vigilant society, to keep its own nest clean. It cannot take on the political responsibility of social reform.

And yet the capitalist may not have the time or freedom now to even take care of his own nest. For the reasons described in earlier chapters the growth of Western capitalism is slowing markedly.

Capitalism needs growth situations to survive; that's where new wealth and fresh profits come from. E. J. Mishan, in *Growth, the Price We Pay,* says

> One may concede the importance of economic growth in an indigent society, in a country with an outsize population wherein the mass of people struggle for bare subsistence . . . But to be tediously logical about it, there is an alternative to the postwar growth-rush as an overriding objective of economic policy: the simple alternative, that is, of not rushing for growth.

To be tediously logical about it, where there is no growth, there is no capitalism. When an individual or a corporation or a country begins to live off its accumulated past wealth—such as Western nations including the United States are now doing—that is the very opposite of capitalism.

Capitalism means living off income. Capitalist nations living off their past wealth are living off their capital.

5

Goodbye, Middle Classes! Goodbye, Capitalism!

Intelligent economic policy should be based on reasoning that begins with human needs and desires, moves on to the resources available to meet them, and ends with decisions on the best ways of organizing and using the resources.

The primary object should be to meet human needs and desires more effectively.

Trade or self-sufficiency, private business profits or the growth of state enterprise, are all to be judged by what they contribute to that end; they are not ends in themselves.

Eugene Staley
World Economy in Transition
Council on Foreign Relations
1939

The demise of the middle classes is one of the things the decline of capitalism is all about. What kills off the middle classes is a combination of inflation, taxation, and stagnation. What kills off capitalism is the reallocation of profits away from the owners of the means of production, or a lack of profits, or a change of ownership of the means of production away from capitalists to government or the workers.

In the grand scheme of things, "intelligent economic policy" will eventually kill off capitalism in a democracy.

The great American middle classes traveled a long way in a short time. It was rapid, self-feeding growth. Economic circumstances produced the middle classes and the middle classes furthered those economic circumstances that would swell their ranks.

When the United States entered World War II it was still very much a working class nation. Using constant dollars, two-thirds of all U.S. families earned less than $5,000 in 1941 compared to only one-third in 1965.

Foundations of the middle class fortunes the booming fifties and sixties would bring were a far-off hope in the American dream in a country that had, in 1941, just emerged from the American nightmare: Depression.

It had taken a war, World War I, to introduce the American public to the stock market. Hugh Bullock, in *The Story of Investment Companies,* writes

several million investors who had not heretofore known the difference between a stock and a bond had become familiar with securities through the extensive wartime Liberty bond drives.

Ordinary Americans were only just getting to understand what should happen in the marketplace when the 1929 crash revealed all too clearly what could happen. By 1938, the worst behind them, the economy growing a little stronger, Americans were again picking up their threads of middle class capitalism. Once again they had a little money for which they wanted a safe haven.

By 1941 this aspect of middle class life, like practically every other, was part of Hollywood dialogue, too. Mid-twentieth century capitalism at its Hollywood glossiest could well be "Moon over Miami," an enervating post–Depression saga of updated gold diggers.

Cummings was boom, Ameche was bust—but about to start all over again. Charlotte Greenwood wanted to invest her $10,000 "in postal savings at 3 percent with the good old USA behind it," or was even prepared to speculate in "that South Texas Gas and Power Corporation, a mighty safe investment."

But the money was spent Twentieth Century Fox style, and Charlotte's two girlfriends blew it successfully chasing millionaires.

Most of that 1941 movie audience made it through the war and a major portion—half at least—made the move from the working class to the middle class in terms of income by 1965. By 1965, in fact, half of all U.S. households were earning between $7,000 and $13,000, having experienced a rapid upward mobility captured in its early maturity by John Kenneth Galbraith's *The Affluent Society*.

The consumer society by that time was rapidly turning to Weber's "final orgy of materialism."

The American middle class had seen its ranks swell rapidly before, but one had to go back to the Civil War to see a parallel situation in which "capital found itself in a flourishing position" and chose to combine that flowering with affluent indulgence and ostentation. When the Civil War broke out in the United States there were scarcely a handful of millionaires in the nation. When it ended, there were hundreds, as Turrentine Jackson points out:

> The unprecedented war prosperity plunged most of those who benefitted into a riot of extravagance and pursuit of pleasure. More charitable observers might attribute this to an attempt to forget the horrors of war and to keep up a brave front, but the true explanation was the accumulation of sudden wealth in the hands of those who were unaccustomed to it.

A century later the great consumer extravaganza of the 1960s washed away the remaining vestiges of an American sense of values. As Americans compared their improved lot in life with cameos snatched from Hollywood heartwarmers of the thirties and forties, the worthiness of thrift and hard work and—in the main—a nonflamboyant lifestyle evaporated.

Since 1965 it is the affluence that has started to evaporate. The American middle class, like the rest of the Western bourgeoisie, is being treated to a severe dose of cinéma vérité.

The West after World War II had been, in President Richard Nixon's words,

> a poker game in which the United States had all the chips, and we had to spread them around so others could play.

The Marshall Plan pumped life back into Europe. The first wave of GI Joes made it through college. Depression fears—for it was long expected that the Depression would return post-war—ended, and then were forgotten. The American middle class swelled like a successful soufflé between 1950 and 1965.

The "Moon over Miami" audience, the Hope and Crosby generation, was off on "The Road to Affluence." That audience became consumers then big consumers, small investors then big investors, small businessmen then big businessmen. All had disposable income in amounts their parents considered untold wealth.

Parents who had raised their children during the Depression were dying of old age as the electric carving knife, the electric toothbrush, and the plastic-coated disposable world were coming on the market. Their grandchildren were growing up in an age in which everything was available—and the money to buy it could be borrowed. The American Buddenbrooks yet to be written, with grandchildren maturing in the late sixties, will be a chronicle of most remarkable juxtaposition.

The old U.S. verities of thrift and moderation faded. The way of life in towns from Newtown, Pennsylvania to Orchard, Iowa, from Newtown, Connecticut to Orange, Florida, from New Town Village, South Carolina to Orchard, California, was being caught up in the new religion: instant prosperity for everyone. People began to live the dream, because financially it was coming true. From the second car to the second house, from Florida winter vacations to European summer vacations.

Affluence was bringing about an economic class mobility that in turn created a distorted view of the American dream, changed a general ethos of puritan work ethic into a blind faith, and promoted capitalism into a religion that incorporated people of all beliefs. When the American dream came true for so many Americans, they regarded the rewards as the natural outcome of their endeavors, when in fact it was as much the outcome of chance historical circumstance. There would have been, in any case, an historic rise in U.S. wealth eventually, just on the basis of its natural resources, self-sufficiency, technological ability, and purchasing power. Compressed into a quarter-century, however, Americans had come to confuse affluence with wealth, riches with reward.

The affluent society roared its way through the Final Boom until the 1969–70 "one-two" to the economic solar plexus took the whoopee out of its wallet.

The children of the sixties, those who wore their hearts and souls on their sleeves, or got lost on the road from Indiana to India in search of self, or who grew up looking for values in a society which had none, are already starting to get a little thin on top and fat around the middle. As the reaction to the waves of protest that rolled over the country in the sixties produced the children of the seventies, the nation has vaguely started to take stock of itself. The children may be doing likewise.

The middle class most certainly is.

Inflation, taxation, and stagnation. Inflation erodes middle class savings. Interest rates fall behind the rapid rise in the cost of living; the stock market fails to offer an alternative hedge. Profits were the froth for middle class capitalists and they are under pressure. What can the middle class do? It tries silver ingots, antiques, real estate, beef herds, property shares—and they all fall flat, taking savings with them. Back it goes to Wall Street to try again.

For the couple living off incomes somewhere in the $25,000 to $80,000 range, or with $100,000 tucked away from the sale of parental homes plus life savings, the race is to keep the money value from eroding. But if the money is being debased, and prices are rising, the only consolation the middle class has is that relatively everyone in that class is in the same boat.

There will be fortunes yet made in the stock markets. There will be rallies, and bear markets. But the setting is different now. These will all take place in an economy fighting a rearguard action with inflation and relatively declining prosperity. An entire class is feeling, and will continue to feel, the effects of the rundown.

The rich will ride out the rate of rundown, but even they will not be immune. The truly wealthy, the modern counterparts of those who never canceled a polo match throughout the Depression, have long since spread their risks globally—into real estate and ventures in other lands where the growth is still ahead of them.

The escape mentality is not limited to merely wealthy individuals. Banks think about it, corporations do it. One European bank, watching the threat of a socialist takeover in the country's approaching elections, was worried about socialist promises to nationalize the banks. All that bank's holdings were quietly transferred to another legal entity. Had the socialists nationalized the bank they would have acquired only a rented building.

As it happened, the socialists did not get in. But the illustration indicates how astutely and easily capital can sometimes move. That is the advantage of having so single-minded a purpose.

Because capital can exist as cash wealth, not necessarily as real estate, products, or services, but as money and credit, capital can at times move very quickly out of trouble—ahead of armies, laws, or ideologies.

Only acts of God move faster than scared capital, which is why acts of God are not covered by insurance.

Corporations scared of higher taxation and government interference can develop a complete "offshore" mentality. The Canadian company Hunter Douglas did exactly that. This multinational manufacturer simply decided that Canadian corporation taxes posed a threat, so it would register itself elsewhere. It did, in the Netherlands Antilles. The headquarters offices it transferred to Holland.

The really wealthy can participate in joint ventures in growth areas through financing and development projects. But going "offshore" is not a course for the middle class investor worrying about staying abreast of inflation to follow. An unwary investor following the wealthy overseas will fall right into the maws of this decade's version of the "offshore funds" of the sixties.

There is little access to overseas growth for the little guy in the stock markets of the world. People who lost money on the other side of the Hudson can take a complete shearing on the other side of the world.

Money under pressure does strange things and takes inordinate risks. Middle class investors in the second half of the seventies will be taking those risks, and a "new crop" not of "greedy suckers" but of "anxious savers" are falling victim to the unscrupulous.

What is happening to middle class savings reflects what is happening to the dollar as a store of value. It is the resettling to a lower plane, a reduced level. Inflation has to come out of something, and what it comes out of is the national wealth, the cash in hand. The wealthy can get out of cash only because they have so much of it they can take a beating in some cash while taking the profits that come from very long term appreciation, as in land or art. Middle class savers have difficulties of being unable to invest wisely, plus problems of liquidity. They need both, which makes land a poor investment because it is illiquid.

Organized labor can pressure for wages to be tied to the cost-of-living index. Hooked on to the conveyor belt of rising prices, labor may never get ahead, but may never fall behind. Relatively better off middle class workers will not get ahead but can fall behind.

Taking care of the poorest members of the society, funding the full array of social programs the United States so sorely needs, also must come out of the middle class. And does, in taxes, or by the back door in continued inflation through deficit spending. Either way it is the middle class living standard that is eroded—though eroded from a position of affluence that provided it with inordinately high expectations anyway.

Stagnation, "no growth," means that government must allocate what capital there is to those areas where the clamor is greatest. In a democracy of the middle class, governments pay heed to middle class interests, but the erosion of the middle class produces a larger "working class" as the formerly affluent gear their lifestyles to fit their new circumstances. Newcomers to the labor market are not finding the doors to affluence flung open wide as in the mid-sixties, so progression from college to the "middle class" is no longer assured.

Where once a family could make it with one parent working, the new middle class family is the two-income partnership—a very different economic unit with different priorities, probably more conservative ones. Home ownership may be the lower middle class' sole claim to being middle class—it may be all that the new middle class economic unit can afford.

Home ownership brings back the potential Western contretemps of interest rates once more. For if certain Western peoples are prevented from their natural aspirations for home ownership, they are prevented from attaining the single most important item for which they will settle.

If, in a low-growth economy, people have to answer not the question "What do you want?" but rather "What will you settle for?" the American tradition will include home ownership among its basic needs.

Home ownership is in the United States one of the "needs" *and* one of the "desires." To price home ownership out of the reach of the majority will bring down more governments than ideological debates ever could. Home ownership is, in fact, the little guy's sole hedge against inflation.

Remove all other vestiges of private property and materialism from the nation, bar three, and Americans will cling to their house, their television, and their car for themselves, and still hope for an education for their children.

This whole area of "human needs and desires" is what politics boils down to during a time of should-be austerity.

Economic slowdown produces two effects regarding the cost of money that make the whole question of interest rates germane to family living:

1. the consumer is more dependent on credit for essentials, like clothing.
2. stagnating income levels show up in the actual percentage of the weekly income going out in interest payments, in mortgage payments and the rest.

A society of informed consumers, capable of wide-ranging and often very justifiable criticism and complaint, demands reform in those areas which most affect its needs and desires. Interest rates will increasingly be featured, and the entire question of usury reopened. What has been most condemned in capitalism in the Old Testament and onwards is charging interest on money used for essentials. And the reason it was condemned 3,000 years ago was not because prophets and patriarchs were theorizing, but because the effect on their society was detrimental and divisive.

Department store interest rates of 1½ percent per month—18 percent per annum—would have been regarded as usurious in the sixteenth century even in a Geneva not opposed to interest per se. Tawney notes that Beza in Geneva, not long after Calvin's death, was roundly condemning the fact

that the city is full of usurers and that the ordinary rate is 10% or more.

This is not to suggest that credit—bank, mortgage society, or department store—is anathema to the majority, but that the difference between what interest rate is acceptable and what is not is subject to great change. Murmurings become outrage when people feel trapped or deprived, cheated or gulled.

Bank card and credit card and department store revolving credit systems look only to the increased business. During the recession those offering credit have been shaken by the number of defaults, but an improvement in the economy always helps erase the bad spots. What the credit providers do not look at is the end results of charging 12 percent and 18 percent interest on unpaid balances.

Customers do not just default, they agitate and advocate change and control. And credit controls more severe than anything banks and credit companies have ever been accustomed to is only a prolonged recession away.

But we are pulling out of the recession, right? Wrong. The recession is permanent. Only the degree will change. As a headline in *The New Republic* of July 1975 so nicely captured it: "Recovery Now, Relapse Ahead." The article was Charles Schultze's piece on "Another Oil Recession." Schultze? No left-leaning economist he, rather a former director of the Bureau of the Budget now at the Brookings Institution.

When a nation of middle class consumers and homeowners starts clamoring for government control over interest rates, and government starts to listen and act, society has begun to shake the capitalists out of the office blocks and down into the canyons in a peculiarly grass roots manner. Those who would control the interest rates are those who, under other economic circumstances, would have been expected to swell the middle class ranks as "popular capitalists."

Economic slowdowns also begin to further stratify the society. Social mobility is slowed and each group pressures for those particular forms of governmental interference most important to his group. When the nation had its mid-sixties mix of subsistence level poor (a percentage of U.S. society still unworthy of a modern democracy), capped by a large working class population, dominated in turn by the huge middle class majority, topped off by big wealth, the political activity of the nation reflected these divisions and the shifting displays of strength "twixt one and another."

As that middle class stratifies into subdivisions based on new economic circumstances the political mix of the United States changes because allegiances change. These are early days to do more than look at the potential for a new political mix. In sheer weight of numbers, one cannot help but believe politics is increasingly weighted toward more government intervention which in turn accelerates all the trends already described.

The middle class was the result of the wealth being shared out through the channels of capitalism. As those channels dry up or are blocked, the government does the sharing out and the lower end of the economic scale must in a democracy always increase its claim to a bigger share.

From high interest rates, as from other causes, capitalism will see a nominally capitalist society wielding the social and economic scalpels capable of ensuring a dismemberment of its own system.

High interest rates do nothing to help investment at that "Temple of Shares," the "Citadel of Capital," the stock market, as F. E. Armstrong referred to it in *The Book of the Stock Exchange*.

U.S. administrations do like to give the appearance of keeping their hands off the free flow of investment and the direction investment takes. But government does interfere drastically in the stock market, of course. Control over the money supply does exactly that.

Any government measure, taken for whatever reason, that props up a corporation publicly listed on a stock exchange is direct government interference in the marketplace. Public financing on a vast scale has repercussions on the stock market no less than government control over the interest rate and deficit spending money-flow.

World stock markets are going through their own internal difficulties: industries raising capital at the banks, rather than in the marketplace; the loss of the private investor or the decline in his numbers; and liquidity problems—liquidity being an essential function of the stock exchange.

Government has become a source of capital—at the expense of the stock market—in other ways. Development grants, perhaps to aerospace or electronics or other high-technology corporations, is a "governmental assumption of the leadership of the development process"—and a leadership hitherto assumed by the capitalist process.

Problems with the liquidity, viability, or acceptability of the stock market system raise, too, an old ideological rodomontade.

First there is, as Giorgio Pivato writes in *The Stock Exchange,* the intensification of oligopolistic phenomena within the industrial apparatus . . . while tax discrimination against shares is particularly strong. . . .

The fact that socialism has not yet produced any alternative to the market concept, means, Lindbeck says, that

among some individual authorities on the New Left it is sometimes admitted that a market system "unfortunately" may be necessary for some time even under socialism

even though capitalism alone has proved incapable of meeting all the economic needs of modern democracy, showing up

the inability of the market system, unaided by economic policy, to achieve economic stability [full employment and stable prices]; its inability automatically to guarantee social security and an acceptable distribution of income, wealth and economic power; its inability to provide collective goods and handle externalities such as various kinds of pollution without deliberate government policies . . .

The stock markets of the West grew also because there was a need for the little guy to have somewhere safe for his meager savings. He had banks and tontines, credit unions and cooperatives, insurance and post office accounts, and access to security through various other forms of institutional investment.

In the nineteenth century it was the Christian Socialists who had pressured the British government for new company law to protect the investor. Turrentine Jackson notes

tradesmen and working people had argued that they had the *right* to some means of investment for their savings that would be safeguarded, and the Christian Socialists had taken up their cause.

But the number of people investing in U.S. stock markets has declined for the first time in 20 years because no one safeguarded their savings. The small investor was rooked. At the tail end of the sixties the small investor had witnessed a Wall Street revival of men of 1900, men like Jay Gould ("when Gould went to pray, they spelled it with an 'e' "). On Wall Street in the sixties capitalism slashed one of its own arteries.

A slowed rate of growth blocks capitalism's other arteries. Deprive corporations of profits and the corporation also is deprived, not exclusively but generally, of capital. One writer in *The Times* stated:

No corporation manager wants to borrow 100% to finance investment. He knows that interest rates never sleep. He can cut down on dividends to the shareholders if investment goes wrong—but he must pay the interest.

Mishan, the antigrowth man, looks at Western prosperity up to the present and says of growth that the expansion of domestic markets

in conditions of material abundance must depend on man's dissatisfaction with their lot being perpetually renewed.

To sustain the growth, Mishan says, man must continually be demanding more. During the sixties in the United States he was certainly doing just that. Slowed growth, due to many factors, does not necessarily mean zero growth. But it may well mean "profitless prosperity." "Profitless prosperity" is when the nation is achieving sufficient growth to produce enough rewards to keep the huge industrial engines, capitalism's dynamos, turning over. The engines produce enough power (profits) to keep the workers employed and capital investment programs up to date, but do not generate enough power to produce high profits for the owners of those means of production.

What sort of growth rates could produce "profitless prosperity?" Kirschen looks at gross domestic product per head of population growth rates and comments:

We must be careful not to dramatise the general situation. A growth rate of 2.4% per annum in the standard of living entails doubling every thirty years and would have been thought very satisfactory in Europe, as well as in the United States or Japan, throughout the nineteenth century and the first half of the twentieth.

Kirschen was making his point regarding the growth rates in less-developed zones. But his observation as to what was once considered satisfactory tells Westerners this: their grandparents and great grandparents experienced improving standards of living, too. The rate was less. What this book says is that a doubling of the standard of living every 30 years may be the best the West can hope for. And it may be sufficient for living out a life of reasonable expectations.

Recommendations for lower growth rates are not just outpourings from ivory towers. Don't forget that in 1966 it was George W. Mitchell, chairman of the Board of Governors of the Federal Reserve System, who was urging a reduction in real growth "to about 2½%," albeit for a specific season.

Reduced rates of growth mean reduced standards of living, but in a United States showing no signs of opting for "intelligent economic policy" (policies forced on nations by outside circumstances as much as by internal preferences and predilections) the government still has to find ways of explaining these reduced standards to its electorate. Government, like capitalism, is better at promising goodies, designing panaceas and swallowable placebos, than telling the harsh facts and promoting essential if severe measures.

Taking this situation straight back to the stock market, the great Wall Street shakeout of 1974 was a preliminary in an economy that has to adjust to a lower rate of growth. It was part of the great flushing out of euphoria that sustained itself all the way from the Final Boom to the present. Wall Streeters are, finally, the last ones to believe that everything has in fact changed.

Growth depends, too, on people wanting to work more to get more. What if they are willing only to work less? Harlow Ungar wrote in *Investors Review* in 1971:

> Even among the older generation a changing attitude towards work is said to be becoming discernible. So concerned is the United States Administration that President Nixon was recently moved to make a public call for a return to the "work ethic," and top Administration officials are said to be worried by reports from businessmen of increasing drink problems among workers, more frequent absenteeism, more late arriving, a growing preference for leisure rather than work and the steady move towards shorter hours and working week.

In the United States there is the demand for the security of not being bankrupted by huge medical bills, and the security of being able to walk the streets without being robbed, raped or murdered; this boils down to little more than peace of mind, a comfortable state from which to grumble about the state.

Ideology plays little part in it. Peter Wilsher wrote in *The Times*,

> Most people today, having achieved a reasonable degree of freedom from want and freedom from fear, would agree that a desirable society should combine the max-

imum amount of personal liberty with a continued extension of general prosperity, and a reduction, if not an actual elimination, of the inequalities which generate so much envy and unproductive rancour.

Unhappily, no satisfactory way has yet been found to achieve these three desirable objectives at the same time. Any two, it seems, can only be pursued at the expense of the third. And as everyone has their own idea of their relative priority, the result is a general dissatisfaction with the way things are run.

Dissatisfaction with the "way things are run," with urban complexity and apparently ungovernable change, produced in the late sixties an age-old cry. It was the heartfelt call for more simple ways.

Aristotle had pined for them, for the more human era of barter. Luther's friend Karlstadt urged his students to return to the land, and returned with them. The early Industrial Revolution gave rise to the call for "two acres and a cow," and in the United States the rural commune movement of the sixties spoke strong testimony of man's ties to the soil when life gets tough.

One senses, however, that the moment of looking back has passed. There may well be, in the introspection of the young of the seventies, the willingness to work with what is. That may provide the determination and dedication to change things from within: but change them, not maintain the status quo.

There has been in the United States an incredibly deep-seated reaction against those who have despoiled the land and betrayed their trust. Americans unwittingly allowed their politicians and their corporate officers—to use Nicholas Colchester of the *Financial Times* quoting a U.S. businessman—to be

cradled like an artichoke heart, leaf by leaf into a state of complete amorality.

The charge made against the corporate state in *The Greening of America,*

an immensely powerful machine, ordered, legalistic, rational, yet utterly out of human control

finds a parallel in the political state, too. What has happened to the political state in the United States since World War II may well be that the bureaucracy, at the federal, state, and local level, so huge and sprawling and so often derided, has, for the last two decades especially, been taking the strain that should have been borne by the elected politician—leading the nation through change.

The bureaucracies, ill-equipped for originating ad hoc programs to cope with constant pressures, have nonetheless had to produce, and are still producing, those ad hoc programs. That is because at the national political level the nation's future in all its breadth, length, and depth has been practically ignored. The bureaucracies, generally devoid of long-term goals, are faced with producing a constant stream of short-term ones. This is a nation where there is much room for cohesive, nationally important programs that satisfy general needs and desires regardless of political party preferences.

Much that happened in the sixties had to do with the bureaucracies not being able to cope with the severe strains placed upon them. That part of the story behind urban decay and the breakdown of the national infrastructure is a much-neglected part. National political leaders have abdicated leadership to the bureaucracies, a task for which bureaucracies are not designed.

The pendulum of American history has just completed one sweep of incredible momentum, a forceful mass has moved right through trial, tribulation, and change of awesome complexity. And now, for just a brief period, the pendulum is stilled. It has reached the end of that arc. It is at rest. This, in dynamics, is the "moment of inertia." The United States is in its "moment of inertia." Soon its very weight, like that of the pendulum bob, will pull it down, crashing, rushing, surging through another vital, vibrant, evolutionary period into its new future.

Consider this, an editorial from *The Economist:*

The United States may be experiencing something that no other country has yet had to go through. It may be experiencing the first full flowering of the Protestant revolution.

What happened in the sixteenth century was the rebirth of an idea that had long lain dormant: the idea that the responsibility of the individual is the ultimate criterion of both politics and religion . . .

But its full impact was never felt by the majority of people. It remained largely a concept of the educated.

It is possible that the United States . . . the first to bring material plenty to most of its people, is now the first country to face the consequences of the fact that widespread prosperity universalises the revolution of individualism.

If that is the explanation of what is happening to America, the place could be almost ungovernable for a very long time: it could be living through the first onset of the war of all against all. The rest of us had better wave the Americans goodbye while we wait for the cataclysm to hit us in our turn.

Or could it be that the "war of all against all" is over in the United States? Is that what this moment of inertia is all about? The moment must be taken, or it will be lost.

Right now, as other Western nations experience degrees of economic disarray more severe than anything the United States is experiencing, America, by default but not shamefacedly, is back in her position as leader of the West. Two weights of responsibility, therefore, now press upon the American majority, the American power and wealth holders, the American electorate. The United States must enter a period of doing what is right for the United States, and not merely for the sum total of special factions or pressure groups within it; and the United States must do this with the future and balance of the West, with its role as Western and free world leader, in mind.

The onus on Americans is to first understand and cope with, not merely investigate, the problems facing their society, while understanding and participating in the problems facing the world.

Statesmanship is required from Americans not just as members of government, or corporations, or labor unions, but as Westerners too.

None of this augurs well for capitalism. Concern for the general good cannot, just as intelligent economic policy cannot, take specific account of private interests most of the time.

The capitalist perforce looks offshore and finds capitalism in disrepute there, too, even if capital itself is still welcomed.

President Kaunda of Zambia:

The capitalist system has as its dominant feature the exploitation of one man by another . . .

Iran's prime minister, Amir Abbas Hoveyda:

Neocolonialism is like a masquerade. It wears many disguises. It comes from the East, as well as the West.

Expropriation now is more subtle. Explained Charles Hargrove in *The Times* of London,

Outright nationalization would have been too costly for the Algerian government [which seized French-held oilfields] . .   it would also have made a bad impression in international banking circles, especially in the United States, where Algeria looks to finance its ambitious plans for developing natural gas resources.

Countries that seize property, with promises to pay, have acted out one of the risks of the game, and everyone nods knowingly as those invested there nod sadly.

There are in developing nations many of the old patterns of intuitive capitalism. One colleague reports that in Saudi Arabia the government offered easy credits and subsidies for irrigation so the nomads could become farmers. The nomads, as he described it, said "Praise be to Allah, we'll take the dough and hire Palestinians to do the work and we'll live off the profits."

Bob Okunedo, writing in *West Africa* magazine, described his return to Warri, his native city, *after* Nigeria became an oil producer:

The local businessman with capital has a variety of investment alternatives, each promising quick return and big profits. One such is Chief J. O. Edewor, who in the late 50s and early 60s was a small-time businessman. Today he is a tycoon handling a number of building and civil engineering contracts and owning a chain of estates which house many of the expatriate staff.

Warri, says Okunedo, "is witnessing the rise of a new plutocracy." And the West is witnessing the demise of an old plutocracy.

Change in the old social order is a difficult and risk-filled matter whether it be the emancipation of the tribal chief into a tycoon or the metamorphosis of the capitalist state into a neocapitalist one.

In the United States, as in the rest of the West, there has been a not-so-gradual revolution, remarkable for the ease by which it has so far been undertaken. The difficulties become more pressing as the struggle for power intensifies between the old elitist mix (based on money) and the new elitist mix.

Ironically, it was members of the middle class, seeking change and improvement in their society, who provided much of the social impetus that affects the survival of capitalism.

The New Democrats of the West, of the United States, have no more organization than did the peasants of the "Bundschuh" prior to 1500. Yet the new bases of power in society, the proliferation of strong minority groups (blacks, women, environmentalists, consumers) gradually transform a passive mass, a silent majority, into one not unwilling to be convinced by a dynamic minority.

Using "New Democracy" as the big umbrella under which all these protestors and promotors, the aggrieved and the aggressive, find fleeting—though effective—common ground on certain issues, thus do major pressures capable of causing significant historical changes build up in society.

The peasants' revolt was not the Protestant Reformation. But look at that peasants' war for what it was. In *The Radical Reformation,* G. H. Williams writes:

> The serious war was set off on 23rd June, 1524, when the Countess of Lupfen-Stuhlingen tried to send some of her peasants off to gather snails while they were intent on taking in their hay.

The decision by a group of disaffected automobile workers to cease work because management wants to speed up the assembly line, at a time when a climate demanding job satisfaction instead suggests the assembly line should either be slowed or abolished, may be no great remove from snail gathering.

Today's weapons are economic, and a battle may be fought with the bows and arrows of noncooperation. It does not matter in the conflict whether a decision to run an assembly line at a given rate can be justified. What governs the event is whether the persons attached by economic necessity to the assembly line are prepared to accept that rate.

In this Second Reformation, organized labor, organized consumers, organized environmentalists, organized radical economists, organized blacks, organized women, organized old-age pensioners, organized students all come together as unorganized New Democrats over certain issues at certain times. All draw what they can from this climate of reform, and their sum total of actions adds momentum to the pace at which the Second Reformation proceeds.

The incidents along the way, sparked by people who refuse to gather snails, serve as punctuation marks to the discussion and debate, as well as to reform's progress.

These modern peasants' revolts, of the housewife, of the blue collar worker, of the white collar man seeking job satisfaction, or the city dweller trying to save the countryside, show no signs of abating. These are the people of the Second Reformation. The debate over the future may not be going on over their heads. They may well understand many of the voices that speak of change and reform.

What has happened in the modern world, in the West particularly and the United States specifically, is that corporate capitalism has helped create technological and scientific man who in turn is creating "a new environment with which man and his institutions have to cope." Capitalism is only one of those institutions having to cope with this new environment, and is only one of the institutions—but probably the main one—caught up in the questioning and dissent regarding what has been.

Man *is* concerned with what is and what will be. The Organization for Economic Cooperation and Development, a multi-governmentally funded economic and social research unit, has published a "quality of life" set of social indicators. They serve as the New Democrats' Bible just as Luther's German-language Bible served the Reformation in Germany.

OECD's social indicators cover the Westerners' desire for good health services, a good educational system, satisfactory employment opportunities and employment, choice in the marketplace, social services, decent housing, personal safety, the honorable administration of justice, and social equality.

New Democrats would regard these all as rights, not privileges, would rather not overthrow the state to obtain them, would not be averse to the state's further intervention in economic life to provide them. New Democrats would need to add only a Genesis (more equitable wealth redistribution) and a Revelation (a responsive and uncorrupted political system) to have a complete Bible.

Certainly modern Western man wants to eat his cake and have it too, but that is not a sufficient contradiction to prevent him from trying for both.

The current reformation within Western democracies represents an attempt to renew democratic life "outside the rigid structures" imposed not only by traditional social, legislative, economic, and functional structures, but imposed, too, by the scientific and technological structures of modern times.

To set aside the old, to build afresh, is the kernel of reform—though the program of reform usually ends up trying to modify what exists in line with what one would build afresh. There is a great challenge to change. There is a vigor and dynamism created in "the minds of men abandoning old disciplines," men who welcome "the excitement offered by ever-widening opportunities."

Opportunities to do what? As Ségur said, "it can be change without having any certain objective, or any assured principles."

That "excitement" produced the Western industrialized civilization of the democratic brand generally acknowledged to stretch perhaps from the eighteenth century to the late twentieth. That same excitement is producing, and will produce, a new and distinct period.

Western industrial democracies in their various shades of government have been elitocracies under bombardment. Rule from below may mean a "below" farther down the social scale than has previously been envisioned. Democracy has been consent from below for the programs of the elite. The ruling intellectual and technocratic and political hand is increasingly finding its elbow nudged by the electorate's loudly voiced preferences as it tries to write the nation's future.

New Democrats gather in many ways. The movement's strength may come from individual ascetic conservatives, or puritan one-issue dogmatists, people with their teeth fastened into a single justifiable cause. Ralph Nader's brand of consumer advocacy is ascetic conservatism. Luther was a member of the Old Right. A second reformation led by New Democrats of the West must be austere to be successful.

Who will provide the guidelines for this reformation? Alas, the economists might be expected to.

And of economics Denis Goulet writes in *The Cruel Choice,*

> Economics has become the most abstractly mathematical and most practically applicable of all social sciences. It has achieved great virtuosity in handling means, but is no longer competent to evaluate ends or ideals.

Already the crux of another crisis is described. Those who would save us from economic disaster are capable of producing equally disastrous social and political morasses. The best way out is for government to say what it wants, have the electorate approve, and have the economists instructed to find out the ways in which these wants might be funded, or how the priorities might be staggered on the economic ladder.

But the government has to know roughly what the national consensus is. The government does not know. The electorate does not know.

As in capitalism, where the entrepreneurs, with the advent of large-scale corporations, handed over control to the managers, so in government the statesmen and the social reformers have handed over control to the bureaucrats and the political hacks. Peter M. Blau and Marshall W. Meyer, in *Bureaucracy in Modern Society,* believe:

> The bureaucratic form of organization, while it threatens democratic institutions in some respect, at the same time makes essential contributions to many democratic objectives in complex contemporary societies. Even if we could turn back the clock of history and banish bureaucracies, we would be reluctant to do so because of having to surrender the benefits we derive from them. Some authors have concluded that modern societies' need for bureaucratic methods spells the inevitable doom of democracy. But why interpret an historical dilemma as a sign of an inescapable fate? Why not consider it a challenge to find ways to convert the impending threat?

The American people have been betrayed by the shallowness of their political system, by the corruptibility of a significant portion of their political leaders throughout all levels of government, and by their own refusal to be involved.

There have been no checks and balances beyond the checks written out for political favors, and the bank balances of the recipients. The soured, corrupted, and corrupting political creatures who have seen and used our political systems for their own ends leer at us throughout Western history.

Is it to these that Western man has to turn when his democracy produces, in Goulet's words, the "big three"—government, industry, and the military establishment—a privilege system no less anti-democratic than that which characterizes "underdeveloped societies"?

Without the jackals of the public purse being thrown out of office, there can be no government by any political party capable of planning for the future in the best interests of, and mindful of the consensus majority opinion of, the nation. Without long-term policy, without "intelligent economic policy," the democracy is and will be subject to stresses not adequately buttressed, strains foreseeable but unforeseen.

Government of the people in their own interests means representation by the decent people of the cities and the towns. If that does not happen there can be no economic future worth considering, no democracy worth admiring, no quality of life worth living.

The whole question of the quality of life is a growing debate. The urban crisis was a debate. Black-white inequalities and the race riots of the sixties were buried in debate. But what happens to debate? Gunnar Myrdal, looking back 30 years after writing *An American Dilemma,* said that the major trend he had not seen was that the United States would allow the cities to deteriorate. City and town planning had been discussed at such a high level, the whole question of urbanization had been such a major debate in the thirties, that he was not able to reconcile the early U.S. knowledge and drive with the later cycle of decay.

America's economic predicament is being discussed at a very high level. In the recent past so have America's social and environmental predicaments—the litanies of despair. Inaction for the balance of this decade presents this generation, not the next one, with a "later cycle of decay" out of which it might not extricate itself at all.

In the affluent society, to paraphrase Denis Gabor, it did not matter whether the operation of industry was left generally to private enterprise or generally to the state (as in Germany or as in France), "so long as there [was] a free flow of credit."

In the post-affluence era it does matter and will matter, for the credit cannot flow as freely.

Having dealt with the somber side of Western democracy undergoing economic change, and the effects of these changes on capitalism, the following remains to be said: Small corporations will still prosper and grow larger, and their stock market value will reflect the change. Some industries may suddenly strengthen and gain in attractiveness and viability within the economy, and gains will be reflected there, too. The United States remains the West's largest homogeneous market, and as some corporations gain bigger shares even of stagnating markets—an affair well recognizable in the world tea commodity situation, for example—some will prosper and others will fade or fold.

But all this is capitalism played on a very different stage than

Americans are used to. Americans will have to look to Britain to see a parallel. Britain's economic peak was around 1870 and, in a much slower moving world, the island nation has been sliding down the economic scale ever since. In post–World War II Britain the rapidity of state intervention in a nation which had not recovered from the Depression completely changed the dominant capitalistic society of pre-Depression days to a new mixed economy of state ownership and capitalism.

U.S. capitalism, presently under duress, is increasingly to go the way of capitalism in all Western nations—to become first a minority economic factor, then a mere economic quirk, as the bulk of capitalist wealth is redistributed and savings are eroded.

When? No one can tell when. There are no wise men. Futurologists are not Old Testament prophets, they are panderers to man's age-old need to know the future. Journalists have no special access to tomorrow.

As Harry Hooper in his 1929 book, *The Evolution of the Flying Machine,* looked at all the available means of air transport, so this book has looked at all the available means of wealth-creation.

Hooper wondered whether the airship was still a first-class carrier capable of overshadowing the newly developed transatlantic flying boats. But he was not sure. No one had seen the risks yet of the airship, nor envisioned the advent of the jet engine. No Western nation has yet seen the risks of government domination in a democracy, nor yet envisioned new forms of wealth-creation satisfactory to an acceptable brave new world.

Perhaps the future will work. Substitute "government" for the "modern airway" and the "flying machine" in what follows from Hooper and take an optimistic view of the worst:

> By years of arduous experiment, by invoking every aid that science can offer, the modern airway has reached the position that it can operate in all kinds of weather, and on an all-year-round basis, with a reliability of over 90 percent. That is a proved established fact; and it is upon such a fact that the next phases of progress are based. The speed of the flying machine is not in itself enough. That speed must be accompanied by safety and dependability.

Modern democratic needs in a nutshell? Safety and dependability and 90 percent reliability, having invoked every aid science can offer to operate in all kinds of economic weather? Government-dominated democracy, like flying in the twenties, is still a young science.

Inflation demands sound economic planning. High rates of inflation must be defeated.

"Is inflation the final crisis of capitalism" rather than Marx's idea that massive depression would be?

Obviously any slowdown in the rate of inflation returns the confidence to what is, in the United States, a confidence economy, and the whole demand cycle picks up again.

But a slowing down in the rate of inflation has the electorate believing that government has triumphed again, when in fact government and nation alike may just be riding out one inflationary tide, the only skill required being that essential to avoid being capsized. If the United States, and the West in general, is suffering from the intermingling of separate inflationary trends—raw materials prices, deficit financing, and domestic wage and price spiraling—then the easing of inflation could well be just these items going "out of phase," a view this book holds.

The underlying causes remain. Western inflation has only one antidote: austerity. But doing without in the short term to benefit the long term is not one of the hallmarks of a consumer-oriented society of materialists. Instead, the West—or the United States, at least—has embarked on a new era of what could be called "profitless prosperity."

Modern political economy must cope with a balancing act between two major facts: government makes the demands, but industry makes the money. Industrial might survives, the nation survives, but the middle classes might not, or might not survive in the manner to which they have become accustomed.

Jobs are protected, so the bulk of the electorate-as-employee is safeguarded. That itself may be no mean achievement. Exports are guaranteed and government can play with the pulleys and levers as it strives for "90 percent reliability." Deserving industries and corporations are supported in the national interest—whatever that interest may be at the given moment.

Why do not the holders and owners of the means of production just sell out? To whom if the government will not buy? And having sold, do what with the money? Government bonds? Government-dominated, or -controlled, or markedly influenced industry may be little more than a government bond at two removes if government controls the profit level, and the taxes on those profits.

American capitalists knew which way capitalism was headed when the American Bankers Association moved lock, stock, and lobby from New York to Washington, D.C. Capitalism is going into the hands of government, perhaps to hold hands, perhaps to be tugged first in one direction then another.

Death comes to capitalism when old wealth can no longer create new wealth, when there is no more old wealth, or no more new wealth. When a nation is obliged to live within its means, that means allocation. If there is enough wealth or affluence so that people are satisfied to permit capitalism to distribute it, capitalism lives. When there is so little wealth that government has to distribute it, capitalism dies.

The Decline of Capital

A young man lived with his parents in a low-cost public housing development in Hamilton County. He attended public school, rode the free bus, enjoyed the free lunch program. After graduating from high school, he entered the Army and after discharge kept his National Service Life Insurance. He then enrolled in Ohio University, using his G.I. benefits.

Upon graduation, he married a Public Health nurse, bought a farm in Southern Ohio with an FHA loan. Later he went into the feed and hardware business in addition to farming, and got help from the Small Business Administration when his business faltered. His first baby was born in the county hospital, built partly with government funds.

He bought more acres and obtained emergency feed from the government; put part of his land under the Eisenhower Soil Bank program and used the payments for not growing crops to help pay his debts. His now elderly parents were living comfortably upon the smaller of his two farms, along with Social Security and old age assistance checks.

Rural Electrification Administration supplied lines, and a loan from the Farmer's Home Administration helped clear the land and secure the best from it. That agent suggested building a pond, and the government stocked it with fish. The U.S. government guaranteed him a sale for his farm products, and the county public library delivered books to his home.

He, of course, banked his money in an institution which a government agency insured up to $10,000 for every depositor. His son attended O.S. Univ. Engineering School, under the National Defense Education Act.

His daughter is in nurse's training under the Nurse's Training Act. He signed a petition seeking Federal assistance for an industrial project to help the economy of the area.

About that time he bought business and real estate property at the county seat, aided by an FHA loan; was elected
to an office in the local Chamber of Commerce. He wrote
his Congressmen protesting excessive government spending and high taxes; "I believe in individualism and oppose
all Socialist trends. People should stand on their own
feet."

Senator Stephen Young, column,
"Straight from Washington"

The elements of modern capitalism are linked together like children
playing "Ring Around the Rosie." It doesn't much matter which
hand holds which, all the players revolve together until one or more
falls down.

Sometimes one player falls down prematurely. The others may be
strong enough to pull that player back up. Money is currently the
most wobbly player in the game; devaluation and inflation are its
problems.

A stunned world saw the dollar devalued in 1971. Then it was
devalued a second time. The dollar supremacy myth was shattered.
Once that had happened, the dollar became subject to the same scrutiny as all other national currencies. It became vulnerable to changes
externally imposed.

Those who would buy dollars, or take payments in dollars, as they
engage in world trade—be it to buy U.S. grain or Arab oil—have
become sensitive about the continuing strength of the dollar. They
worry about its reliability as a medium of exchange at a given level
of worth.

They worry so much that the dollar's world value has been slipping
ever since 1971. Global and domestic inflation further add to the
dollar's woes. But why does the world regard the once-mighty dollar
as risk currency?

The impartial observer—impartial to the extent that he or she
wants to preserve the worth of his or her dollar currency assets—
looks at the value the dollar represents. It represents both the state of
the U.S. economy and that economy's "claims" upon that dollar. If

the government is going to have to delve further into deficit financing, automatically the dollar is cheapened.

What domestic pressures are there on the dollar? There is the pressure from the citizens who need social services. There is pressure from the increasingly rundown segments of the nation's physical plant, the crumbling cities. At some point the United States is going to have to pay that bill, or face severe social consequences.

What is there to support the dollar? Healthy corporations. But U.S. corporate profits are inextricably linked to (a) cheap energy; (b) previously cheaper raw materials; (c) traditionally lower interest rates than currently prevail; (d) a confident economy with a vibrant new issues market; (e) satisfactory unit production costs; (f) an expanding and homogeneous domestic market; (g) low inflation, allowing capital equipment and inventory replacement at something below the highly inflated replacement costs of today. Corporate profits for most major U.S. corporations are to some degree inextricably linked for the time being to overseas subsidiaries. Those 3,400 U.S. corporations with at least one factory abroad may be finding their foreign birds of paradise changing into albatrosses.

How else is the dollar being undermined? In the eyes of the foreign exchange buyer, there is always the current state of U.S. balance of trade and U.S. balance of payments to be considered. The would-be purchaser or holder of large amounts of U.S. dollars—and don't forget there are many billions of U.S. dollars floating around off- shore—cannot but be wary of the increasing U.S. dependence on overseas supplies for raw materials, especially, and always, for oil.

There is, further, for the foreigner, the realization or suspicion that the United States does not really understand its own predicament, and that there exists little machinery through which the administration and Congress can work on behalf of the people in informing the people what should be done, or what could be done, to halt the U.S. economy's continuing downward drift, then implementing such a program.

The U.S. dollar is no longer a measure of wealth or a store of value. It is a medium of exchange of continually declining value.

Are foreigners, generically referred to as "the gnomes of Zurich," unduly worried? Weyerhaeuser's profitable corporation, though capitalistic, has its president acknowledging the need for further government programs to aid the needy; Heldring is concerned that consumer demand is tailing off; Kerekes wonders about industrial growth; Kaufman talks of significant government intervention in the credit creation process.

The dollar's strength in the eyes of the world had come from the dollar reflecting the growing, burgeoning, profit-making U.S. economy supported by growing and profitable corporations. All those intangibles and tangibles that had worked to make U.S. capitalism supreme are now working against the U.S. economy.

U.S. corporations could expand easily overseas because the buying power of the dollar was so high. It was so high because it represented so much wealth. The keynote was confidence. When there is no confidence in the dollar, the dollar is suspected of representing very little wealth, very little further potential growth. As economic strength led to greater strength, so economic weakness leads to further weakness.

Where is the confidence? The nation cannot get a grip on its priorities. It can barely discuss them coherently. Yet Americans cannot retreat, as once they might, into grand isolation—they have become too dependent on the world outside. They can retreat politically, and see their influence wane, to the further detriment of their economic credibility. They can retreat militarily, and see their strategic security shattered, to the further detriment of their economic—raw material and oil—viability.

The world is witnessing the first layer of fat, the outside pelt of national wealth, being stripped off the United States. It is not a pretty sight.

That wealth is going, has gone, to pay the higher prices demanded by primary products producers and the oil cartel. It is going, has gone, to finance the overseas investments of the U.S. multinational corporations as expansion spending previously done in the United States is instead done to build up the economic infrastructure of others.

The wealth is going, has gone, to meet the payments of globally inflationary times, inflation due to artificially depressed raw material prices finally catching up, and due to more and more people bidding for limited resources.

It is a mark of how wealthy the United States is, in fact, that these prices are being paid with the minimum of national and personal dislocation and disruption. This statement is made not to minimize the individual sufferings of people caught in a severe recession, but to point out that many countries faced with similar problems are fighting off bankruptcy. The United States is capable instead of paying the higher prices—for the time being. Even the United States cannot continually meet the type of price escalation underway in the five years to 1975.

The British economy, in a slower moving world, has been sliding toward its present precarious situation. That doesn't mean the United States can slide for a century. The British have had severe doses of prolonged austerity. It has been almost a national characteristic for the greater part of this century.

Britain has constantly reordered and rearranged its national priorities. Today it is back at the national survival state, reordering even more: still a democracy, still a benevolent bureaucracy.

Britain, of course, was able to retreat—was forced to retreat—from world power status. The United States does not have that luxury. But the United States does have the capacity, and the need, and the time, to capably tackle the reordering of its national priorities.

It might be argued that the majority of Americans—and this is a democracy—do not want their national priorities to be reordered. They have little choice.

National priorities have to be reordered to prevent inflation. Slowing inflation is *the* national priority presently, and the majority want that inflation slowed even without knowing what new worlds anti-inflation tactics usher in.

It can be argued, and usually is, that government spending can be contained, and that alternate sources of raw materials—or raw materials substitutes—can be exploited. Theoretically it is correct regarding government spending, but the discrepancy is over "can be contained," and "will be contained." As far as alternate raw materials and alternate commodities are concerned, there are not sufficient alternatives to make this a reasonable short-term measure if one is discussing, as this book does, the West's being accustomed to "cheap" raw materials.

Alternate sources are just that. They are not necessarily cheaper, and indeed are less likely to be so than is happily posited. The only force making it worthwhile to even look for alternatives is the fact that existing materials are so costly. New sources may "shave the price" of existing materials somewhat, but none is likely to roll back cost increases experienced between 1969 and 1975.

Inflation is here to stay. Not a military takeover of the oil fields for oil, nor of Canada for water, nor of Zambia for copper, nor of the Moluccas for nutmegs would or could alter that situation for the United States.

The base of economic power is shifting away from the West. The United States is wealthy still, but the medium-sized industrial nations of Europe have lost ground rapidly to the Middle Eastern oil nations. The only source of strength remaining to Europe is any collective muscle it can flex by building up the Common Market as a political and economic unit—and that is a slow job, and one not certain of eventual fruition.

The West basked in the colonial possessions—and the United States—being depositories of cheap raw materials and/or labor. The colonial empires have gone, there is little if any influence remaining in former "spheres of influence," and the United States is no longer depository of last resort to the rest of the West. There are no other sources of cheap munificence.

The U.S. citizen basked in the solid, stolid infrastructure of a self-contained island. The United States possessed everything it needed and spread the wealth around among its own—unevenly—allowing plenty to spill over the sides and make its golden waves felt in many, if not most, parts of the world.

Take one more look at the figures. Just a quarter-century ago the United States *was* the most self-contained, the most productive island of wealth in the world: 25 years ago the United States produced 47 percent of all the goods made in the world—nearly half the world's global output.

Remaining only with oil by way of an example, it was only in 1974 that the United States was finally succeeded by Saudi Arabia as the world's largest oil producer, whereas 25 years ago it could export oil. These are the real shifts behind the raw-materials-related drop in the purchasing power of the dollar.

Easy access to the government printing presses for deficit spending is the other major element in the depreciation of the currency.

Money, then, is collapsing. And it is the rate at which it is collapsing that most affects the next link in capitalism's chain: the stock market.

Even assuming a 7 to 8 percent annual inflation in the years ahead, the dollar invested in the stock market on New Year's Eve 1975 will have to go into a growth stock of greater-than-average potential. By the time income and capital gains taxes are taken out of the rewards of such judicious stock market investment, the stock selected would need to be a high-class, high-level constant performer to merely keep up with the dollar's continuing decline in value.

The stock market is no longer the cradle of creative capitalism. In fact, it cannot even offer a 50–50 chance of keeping up with inflation for the investor. For the speculator, as always, the stock market offers unlimited opportunities to climb or crash.

These statements are not reflections on the actual worth of some of the investments currently available. Many U.S. corporations were undervalued in stock market terms in early 1975. Many of them climbed from their lows to a price more in keeping with the leaner economy and the leaner corporate facts of life.

But the market's bounceback is merely part of the general settling down of the total economy to its new reality. Corporate stock prices were unduly depressed. They came back to a more realistic high, and, in the free market process that produced that new high, many of them soared past their worth. There was, in other words, the same old cycle of oversell, overprice, overkill.

However, this time all these performances are taking place in smaller, less bustling, circus rings. Fewer investors, less disposable income, a less buoyant economy than at almost any time since the late forties, means the modest investor, the small outsider, becomes more likely than ever to fall victim to the smart insider. It also means that an artificial return-to-normal and business-as-usual atmosphere will return to investment and financial circles—for a while.

What will curtail any bull market will be the next round of pressures on the dollar and the economy from both internal and external sources. Higher oil prices, trade deficits, and possible balance of payments deficits will force the government deeper into economic management. The governmental hand is always an upsetting sight to investors, except when it is stimulating the economy.

Nor, as has been discussed earlier, are these the only problems facing the stock market. Banks, rather than new issues, are the source of new or ongoing financing for many corporations. The growth of the bank holding company is simply one more mammoth trust destined to eventually create its own governmental countervailing force. But until that time the banks are the lenders of first resort to corporations, and even in a new climate of optimism on Wall Street the banks are not likely to lose their premier position as long- and short-term lenders of first resort. The stock market becomes, therefore, more an exchange than the focal point of creative capitalism.

The managers were, of course, the new capitalists. They, once through stock options or other devises, were in a position to pay themselves into positions of great wealth on the basis of their promise to do the same, on a less grand scale, for the other owners.

If the rat race is tough, the rewards are more than generous for the executives who make it—if their measure of success is money, that is.

Corporate executives get their rewards as return on invested time, and energy, and imagination, and more. But for the corporate shareowner, who has invested only money, the return on investment is scarcely such a wonderful reward. Indeed, once inflation has been taken into account, many investors must wonder whether they can ever stay abreast of the game. If the only way to stay abreast of inflation through stock market investments is by hoping for capital gains, then the whole notion of investing has changed.

If there is so little return on investment, to the corporation or the investor, that the investor must turn to capital gains as a reason for being in the market, then the investor has turned into a trader or a speculator.

Modern refinancing of industry looks to profits, as does the investor. But if there are sufficient profits for retained earnings, and if those retained earnings can constitute a major portion of future capital investment, the corporation looks good on the balance sheet. But it looks equally good to the taxman, the government, and the employee. If profits are sufficient to provide reinvestment, then, the reasoning follows, there is sufficient money for higher pay, higher taxes.

And if those higher profits are enabling top executives to turn themselves into millionaires through stock options, how can the workers not demand their share: why should not the workers demand their share through higher pay and benefits, and the public demand its share through higher corporate taxes?

When executives are increasing their net worth from nothing into the millionaire bracket on the basis of performance, who are the capitalist managers to urge restraint on labor or those cared for through social services?

Indeed the only reason executive remuneration has not been explored more vociferously is that the public's gaze has been averted. The public gaze has been more on corporate outside activities, pollution, social responsibility and social accounting, foreign investment, and "job export" activities than on internal corporate matters. That the public will demand an internal accounting is inevitable.

For the corporate executive, still free to pursue his options, and with a marketplace to exchange them for money, hell on earth is when the market is illiquid. To the hustling executive, as to the speculator and unwise investor, the stock market has many of the elements of a "lottery . . . with entry reserved to a minority" of the population. This was once graphically expressed by a black militant who said that "either the numbers game should be legalized, or the stock market should be banned. It's just a middle class numbers racket."

If money is losing its value, and the stock market is losing its common stock role, what of the corporation losing its vitality in the face of the words of the Heldrings, the Kerekeses, the Weyerhaeusers, and the Kaufmans?

This book is not about investment as such. It rather is concerned with those trends destined to radically alter, perhaps eradicate, the whole system of privately accumulated capital investment, that is, the system of market capitalism itself.

This book is about that system. But one must at least take a passing look at the most ordinary investor, the ordinary person trying to accumulate and enhance or preserve a little money for old age. That question is, what does the collapse of capital mean to the average citizen who assumed that by accumulating capital all would be well—especially in old age or retirement?

Inflation will not go away. There are no guaranteed safe harbors.

For those who seek a degree of independence divorced from government support and/or control, the vehicles for long-term old-age security are scarcely yet developed. Or at least inflation-proof buy now, retire later, service-oriented facilities are not yet developed.

The whole area of retirement years and old age care in the United States is ridden with abuse and ripoff; or by neglect or substandard conditions.

Retirement and old-age care must increasingly become the concern of the nonprofit, service-oriented social institution. Where the government is not directly involved by building and/or operating facilities, then church, social, trade union, professional association, community nonprofit corporations have to take the responsibility. This has always been done on a minor scale. It must become a major movement.

When the old farming couple alongside the monastery in the fifteenth century became too old to cope, then they gave their farm, or paid a sum, to the monastery in return for care for the remainder of their natural life. Thus was the insurance industry born. The approach of old age strikes a persistent chord of concern regarding this guarantee of care. If the nuclear family refuses responsibility, the community family, the family of unrelated participants joined by bonds of location or preferred interests, has to assume it. There are no guarantees regarding decent treatment in old age unless there are persons who will responsibly undertake to assure that decent treatment is meted out to those in a dependency situation.

The industrial society is still coping with that one.

Individuals with personal incomes or accumulated wealth have been able to buy a level of security in retirement and old age that simply may not be available in the future except to those of extreme wealth. Savings and investment have been the main hope of most people approaching retirement and old age; and yet those on fixed incomes and a fixed amount of capital have seen in just these last few years how quickly, and permanently, all that can be erased by inflation.

The United States has been through severe inflation before. But the difference between inflation in the first half of the twentieth century and inflation in the second half is that the economy itself has peaked. In 1920 the United States was self-sufficient and expanding. Now it is not self-sufficient, but it still expects to expand, with consumption growing all the time. That simply cannot happen. Inflation will ensure it does not happen, for inflation is the price a nation pays for living beyond its means.

Now, indirectly, back to investment.

A person not in debt during a recession—a person therefore who is not liable to high inflation-era interest rates—may be likened to a person who has a job during a depression. His relative standing may be accelerating up the social scale sharply because the income base of others is being eroded so rapidly. But personal liquidity during a recession bumps right into another argument: one is supposed to borrow now in order to pay back in inflated (lesser value) dollars later on.

It all depends "on what helps you sleep peacefully at night." There is a difference between frugality and miserliness, between debt and investment. Frugality is the careful husbanding of one's resources, miserliness means doing without essentials in order to accumulate resources. Being in debt to buy a house is investment, being in debt to buy a color television is not. One is an essential commodity, the other still a luxury, however desirable. It all depends on the extent to which one wishes to mortgage one's future—which is what going into debt is all about.

Assuming a debt-free situation because of frugality, miserliness, or a high level of disposable income, what does one do with the excess capital? There have never been simple answers in noninflationary periods. Obviously the objective during an inflationary period is at least capital preservation, and hopefully some marginal improvement in value beyond inflation's deprivations.

The straightforward answers are that there exist, even in inflationary times, corporations that conduct their business well enough to produce income and capital gains that stay abreast of inflation. There are not many of them, and picking them out is not part of this book. Under less straitened circumstances men have spent lifetimes trying to pick the correct corporations in which to speculate, and today investment in the stock market has taken on the nature of speculation. Too few of the old norms by which one measured worth have remained intact. Inflation accounting for corporations is in its infancy.

Management is no better equipped to appraise inflation's continuing effect on corporate futures than the individual is to assess inflation's effect on his personal future.

What is known is that profits paid out in the form of dividends are paid out in "cheaper" dollars than the ones invested. Capital gains, if any, can be taken only in a rising market, which favors the inside speculators while placing the ordinary investor at a decided disadvantage—capital gains at a level high enough to take the sting out of inflation and currency depreciation, that is.

There is the whole question of the actual value of the profits themselves once inflation is taken into consideration. There is the nagging question as to whether one is paying too high a premium to get into blue chip stocks; whether in fact there will be liquidity when one wants to get out.

It could be argued that the investor who invests cautiously in a prudent company has a short-term opportunity of reasonable risk investment. But if a stock market genius is a "man with a short memory in a bull market," then a shrewd investor is one prepared "to take modest profits now rather than long-term promises later." These comments are talking to capital gains: what about long-term investment?

Assuming continuing inflation of 8 percent, a modest assumption, the small investor may well remain better off staying away from common stocks. He or she can no longer take the risk. The market in common stocks will never again be a vehicle for the long-term investment by the small investor. It no longer is a predictably liquid investment vehicle even for the biggest banks and the wealthiest capitalists.

What is happening to the stock market only strengthens the role of the banks in the rapidly oligopolistic world of national and international corporate life, or strengthens the government hand in the private sector. For the ordinary investor faced with fighting inflation it is either banks or bonds, with the emphasis on U.S. government notes.

Interest rates will not be keeping pace with inflation, but the risk factor is so lessened with government bonds that secure depreciating assets are better than insecure assets with capital gains potential. If liquidity is not a major factor, the small investor is still not really much better off. The house owned here, the piece of land judiciously bought there, the purchase of items of value of which the purchaser has distinct personal knowledge (the painting, the gold sovereign, the item of nineteenth-century U.S. furniture), all done on a minor scale, is about the only hope of spreading the risk while anticipating gains at some point.

But this is not capitalism, not capital investment in the sense one has come to understand it. Storing wealth, hoarding wealth, is simply not capitalism. Capitalism means *employing* capital to create more capital by exploiting a given situation.

Are there no answers?

Beware the futurologist. Beware the modern Tetzels selling econometric models and economic potions with the assiduity of a sixteenth-century mendicant. "Telling fortunes is more lucrative than telling the truth," commented Georg Christoph Lichtenberg. Futurologists are mere fortune tellers. The truth is that no one knows.

Nor is this book trying to forecast the future. The entrails of this soothsaying are the giblets of the system examined in the light of social, political, and economic trends. This is latter-day political economy. This book is one view of what is happening, based on what one sees at this moment. Capital is collapsing at this moment. It will continue to collapse. I do not know when that collapse will be complete, nor what brave or brash new world will be in its stead.

One is not cheering here for the death of capitalism. The collapse of any established order is an awesome thing. One cheers if the effect of an inevitable collapse is to reorder the economy in the best interests of the commonweal, and in the interests of the people who occupy and share that common wealth. But one does not necessarily mean the other.

That capital is collapsing seems as obvious and apparent to me as watching someone I know growing old. To me it seems no more complicated than that, and this book has been my way of trying to look at why and how I see what I see. Others may not see it this way. But I must finally review once more what I have seen.

The pressures are external and internal.

Externally the United States and the Western nations are faced with the various forms of primary product monopolies and cartels. Oil is the most obvious, others are in the making. None can make its presence felt in exactly the magnitude the oil cartel has, but each commodity, in its own way, can seriously disrupt the accustomed habits of home, industry, and commodities market.

With increasing amounts of money going to pay for constant or even reduced amounts of raw materials externally, the Western nations are faced with mounting trade deficits. The United States is the least able to cope psychologically with this aspect of being a trading nation. However, the United States is probably still the best able to cope financially with the problem of higher prices.

Smart cartels are demanding inflation-proof payments for their raw materials. Nations with balance of trade and balance of payments in deficit do not have inflation-proof money.

This means devaluation—either through devaluing against fixed rates or constantly reevaluating or devaluing in a floating exchange rate situation. Devaluation is currency depreciation, and is a stiff price to pay in order to sell one's manufactured product cheaper while simultaneously coping with the basic raw materials prices shooting even higher than before relative to one's currency.

To protect the currency, protect the economy, and stimulate trade, governments are increasingly becoming involved in national exporting to safeguard particular natural or national advantages they may have in world trade. This means that free trade, with its competitive edge and freedom to risk all for profits, gradually is giving way to government-to-government dealings, however disguised; otherwise the multinationals will begin to control them by their sheer ability to shift economic power.

For the Western nations, without a massive increase in global consumers much that the West has to offer is looming into obvious overabundance: automobiles are the most pressing case in point, even without the oil crisis.

As Western nations become a saturated replacement market for items such as automobiles and televisions, even airliners and military aircraft, the whole pace of world trade slows down. Military sales are made to new oil wealth, to Iran as the shah seeks to reestablish the might of the Persian empire, to Libya as it turns itself into an armed encampment, but these are not realistic new growth areas in terms of world trade. The populations are too small, or the rulers are too cautious about giving people too much too soon.

World trade in high-margin goods was carried out between high-income industrialized nations selling to each other, bolstered for the most part by less-than-realistic raw materials prices.

Governments are playing two roles and heading toward a third. First, they are keepers of the national currency; next, they are promoters of the national industry. Then they will seek more restrictive controls over multinational corporations either located in their countries or operating from their countries. This mood, still in its infancy, will envelop the multinational financial conglomerates.

Governments have no choice but to control the multinationals, which already are selling technology—their last resource—in order to maintain profitability. This is in direct opposition to the national interests of exporting nations. Technology is the West's oil.

Daniel Vincendon, writing in *L'Express* (Feb. 5–11, 1973), stated the problem quite simply when discussing IBM. "Can a great nation agree to the new international corporation, based on technology, more or less escaping its control?" The answer for the nation, in this case the United States, is no. The reply by the multinational corporation, in this case an IBM, may well be: "Try to catch us."

The breaking up of a large multinational corporation into national corporations interlinked only by technology may do wonders for antitrust sentiments, and local national pride, but it successfully puts all technology out of the reach of any one government.

The multination man doth protest. "The only power we have is the power not to invest, not to start new ventures, or gradually to run down the old ones." Thus spoke Dr. Ernest Woodroofe, chairman of Unilever, several years ago. He added: "And this power every local industrialist also has."

That last statement is not correct, of course, because the local industrialist does not have the range of external alternatives open to the multinational industrialists.

Looking at the multinational corporation's power from Dr. Woodroofe's point of view, the power to not invest is, in these times, the mightiest power of all: it is employment. New investment is what keeps existing employment levels up, and increases the amount of jobs for the future. No government concerned with holding on to power through the democratic process can let that one escape.

Multinational corporations have escaped, however, and will continue to do so unless new national and supranational forms come into being. Not an immediate prospect. That leaves only moral suasion, a limp plea to multinational corporate responsibility.

Technology has been the West's "cartel" against the developing and underdeveloped nations for more than a century. With the rise of the particularly sophisticated forms of electronic and systems technology of today, the West is reaching the frontiers not of knowledge but of easily commercially convertible technology.

As governments domestically and internationally pressure multinational industrial, service, and financial corporations over profits, so will those corporations be tempted to place more and more of their operations outside the jurisdiction of governments. The offshore world comes into its own, as the offshore mentality gains acceptance with its practitioners, though not with those such maneuverings seek to avoid: the national tax collectors.

To straighten out its own economy, the United States is going to insist that U.S. multinational corporations invest in the United States. This insistence, in fact, may coincide briefly with changes in the global situation, making the United States a not unattractive investment location.

The United States needs the U.S. multinational money invested at home.

The United States, economic keystone of the West, also has special burdens as a superpower. Disarmament and nonproliferation are the offered answers. The reality is that proliferation and arms spending will continue apace. Those who would see arms monies go to the crying world causes: to combat starvation, ignorance, disease, oppression, have their scale of values in the correct order. But this is a disordered world.

How disordered? The U.S. administration is still urging Western industrialized countries to develop some form of retaliation should OPEC push oil prices "too high." Any attempt to do so would be a contest only to see whose pips squeaked first. OPEC could deny oil while the West denied exports. The West would capitulate first.

How disordered? Just a couple of years ago it was assumed that within a matter of years, perhaps months, the Arabs would have used their petrodollar surpluses to buy up all the publicly listed U.S. corporations. By the summer of 1975 Arab investment in U.S. corporations was still less than the amount of British investment in U.S. corporations ($2.9 billion to $3.6 billion).

How disordered? Japan, the trading nation with the world as its oyster less than 10 years ago, chalks up record bankruptcy rates, and its major bank forecasts zero growth.

How disordered? Public distrust of the major corporations is pandemic throughout the U.S. population, according to the opinion polls.

How disordered? Michigan wants to pay welfare recipients $5,000 to leave the area, a harking back to lessons unlearned in Speenhamland, England, in the closing years of the eighteenth century.

Suddenly the welfare recipients are to blame for a disordered society, rather than a disordered society to blame for the welfare recipients.

How disordered? Crumbling cities with declining tax bases cannot survive because the tax money has fled with the middle classes to the suburbs. But the suburbs cannot be drawn into the city regional tax net—the middle classes won't allow it. Period.

How disordered? The new form of beggar-your-neighbor is providing "export credits" to allow another country to buy from you now and pay for it later. The public purse has become a huge and wondrous thing.

How disordered? The employed and recently employed are in revolt. They will not give up more of their income for taxes. The *Milwaukee Journal* polled its readers. The majority put taxes higher than crime as their major worry. Especially worried were homeowners, and those with incomes between $10,000 and $25,000—in other words, those closest to the welfare lines themselves.

How disordered? The large corporations, deep in debt, are trying to extricate themselves, just as banks, laden with bad debts and seriously overloaned, are trying to edge toward firmer ground.

How disordered? In a rapidly deteriorating situation due to a lack of governmental long-term economic planning and due to a lack of resource allocation, the latest fad is the belief that the nation's corporate problems stem from overregulation.

How disordered? Labor unions, those who finally have to promote export industries, are developing a witch-hunt mentality in tracking down foreign imports that compete with their goods. The bumper sticker that says "Buy a foreign car and put five men out of work" reveals only that those who believe such things don't realize that the money paid to Germans for a Volkswagen is the same money the Germans use to buy Boeing 747s.

How disordered? Rio de Janeiro is promoting its stock exchange. Brazil as the next capitalist nation? But if investors can get sheared on Wall Street—even with the Securities and Exchange Commission working on their behalf—what chance Rio?

How disordered? The Federal Reserve Bank of New York is beginning to act as the Bank of England traditionally did. When the pound sterling was under attack, the Bank of England would step in and prop up the pound by buying pounds sterling with its holdings of foreign currencies. Now the New York Fed does the same thing to support the dollar.

How disordered? The United States is uncertain what to do about its food-producing ability. Should grain be sold to the Soviet Union? Should U.S. farm policy provide surpluses, or function in the free market? But if the free market means selling to Russia and China, which pushes up the prices, can America live with a free market in grain and other foodstuffs?

How disordered? The U.S. still has no coherent oil policy or energy policy despite a breathing space of more than 12 months' duration.

How disordered? Inflation rates of 6 to 7 percent "at the start of economic recovery" mean more and higher rates of inflation ahead.

How disordered? There is no consensus of what Americans would settle for. They would agree that a person still has a right to private property (though the Supreme Court "now tends to see public benefits as 'property,' " too, according to *America* magazine).

How disordered? It was a *Business Week* reader who suggested a limitation on the amount of assets an individual could own, with $100,000 or $200,000 suggested as a possible ceiling. If *Business Week* readers can think such thoughts, politicians will, too, one day.

How disordered? Succeeding administrations are still suspicious of government ownership and control of corporate entities. Consolidated Edison was able to use this reluctance to great advantage. Con Ed can hold over the head of the government: "aid us financially or we'll collapse and you will *have* to run us."

Not every administration will be unwilling to grasp the nettle of government ownership. Not every administration will hold off breaking up the major banking groups and their economic grip on the corporate state.

Oddly enough, there seems to be genuine popular sentiment against breaking up the American Telephone and Telegraph system into smaller units. If that appraisal of popular sentiment is correct, then it would seem that the users and populace believe they are getting a good low-cost service from a reliable monopolist. Changes will be made affecting AT&T's would-be competitors, giving them a chance to compete, yet no major movement appeared to want this huge feather quilt of a company, AT&T, broken down into a number of equally cozy, though less large, pillows.

Electricity prices are not low, electricity service has proved itself less than reliable; the local power monopolists may not be regarded in the same light as the local telephone company. Major changes may yet be forced on both government and power utilities in this country before the decade is out.

And this, in turn, returns the topic to the question of capital investment. Utilities by and large do not have sufficient capital to meet the high costs of developing alternative power sources, nor even the profits in some cases to meet the high prices of existing fuels for current operations. It takes no special talent to foresee major government intervention at some point. The only questions are: how? and when?

As in utilities, so in vital export industries. So, too, in vital regional industries where unemployment would become prohibitive: the government cannot stay its hand from ever-greater involvement.

Controlling investment capital is what the capitalist free market has been doing. When the government controls how much investment goes where, and for what, and if those reasons have nothing to do with profits as such, then the government is not becoming the capitalist of last resort.

The government has become the economic manager.

When men no longer have the right to make fortunes meeting the needs of their fellow people; when capital depreciates more rapidly than investment profits can match that depreciation; when the market system is no longer a vehicle for investment but for speculation; when government involves itself with business for reasons of vital national interest divorced from corporate profitability; when the major private sector segments of the day, like the bank holding companies, are broken back down into smaller units; when the government takes major responsibilities for raising and directing investment capital, then capitalism has collapsed.

Note that none of this has an ideological base. These roles are acted out of economic necessity, not prior commitment to some ideology. Not "Vive the social animal," not "Vive the political ideal," but "Vive the economic unit."

Does democracy survive? As long as there is a reason for two parties of differing opinions, and with a reasonable chance of those two parties alternating in and out of government, then democracy survives.

Do we get a higher quality of life when we are adjusted to our new reality? "Quality of life" from the point of view of a democratic commonwealth has to mean reasonably equal opportunity for all to share in the quality, to share in the life. That seems further away than anything I can focus on.

When does the U.S. depression arrive? It may never come in our lifetime. Depression is when people have to scramble and scrap for physical survival. Recession is when an individual or a nation constantly adjusts down to a lower standard of living in material terms.

This is a continuing recession. Recession—or inflation—is sufficient to bring about the collapse of capital.

> "Ring around the rosie,
> Pocket full of posies,
> A-choo, a-choo,
> We all fall down."

Austerity

Austerity is the proper antidote to indulgence.

Dr. Johnson

The West has been indulging itself for centuries; the United States for decades. This book has tried to explain how that ability to indulge ourselves in material affluence has been possible.

When this book was begun, in January 1971, the energy crisis, the first dollar devaluations, were still ahead of us. It was inevitable that they occur sooner or later. The dollar devaluation had been long delayed; the energy crunch came half-a-decade earlier than anticipated.

This book is a report back from the front lines of world capitalism; a look at the economic "cold war."

My journeys in the last five years are full of name-dropping names and place-dropping places. Many of the questions and trends this book addresses have been raised in discussion and interviews with people as different as Sweden's left wing prime minister Olof Palme and Iran's right wing premier Amir Abbas Hoveyda.

The shifting sands of world capitalism I have discussed directly and indirectly with the leaders of multinational corporations, globe-girdling banks, and the secretary general of OPEC. Capitalists, labor leaders, economists, academics, politicians, workers, and the man in the next seat on interminable long-distance flights, all have had to bear the brunt of my questioning.

The night shift foreman at Mercedes-Benz, the taxi driver in Beirut, the Alaskan legislator at Point Barrow are solemn figures in a world drama the scenario of which is still being written. No one has answers. Many have hopes. Some have good ideas. Once I thought the socialists might be capable of providing that which the capitalists are not—a functioning egalitarian society. But the answer is not to be found, ready-made, in the ideologies of the past. Each national society must cope with its present, and its future, with the best it has at hand. In a democracy that means begin by asking an informed society what it will settle for.

This book is the summary of a lone journalist; that is both its weakness and its strength. Others going the same route would have had to marshal many of the same points and arguments. Their summaries and conclusions might have been different.

Journalists are observers and commentators. But that is not sufficient for a book such as this. There have to be practical suggestions or the observations are barren. A reprise of the problems without some attempt at recommendations is to avoid the crux issues.

I have tried to limit my recommendations to two areas, briefly explained.

Not too long ago I stood at the side of "the pit," as the trading ring at the Kansas City Board of Trade is known. The Board of Trade is the largest cash wheat trading center in the world, and the major center for hard winter wheat sales.

Hard red winter wheat is what the Soviet Union buys when it goes into the grain market, and for the last few days all eyes in the pit had been watching the wall where the white-suited men on the catwalk chalk up the ever-changing prices.

The Soviet Union was back in the market. Its presence was not unduly rocking the Board of Trade, but lessons were being learned about the growing volatility of wheat prices.

In 1972, when President Nixon announced $750 million in credits were being made available to the Soviet Union, it was several weeks before the bushel price of wheat was affected by even as much as 25 cents.

This time, three years later, the bushel price of wheat had moved up by more than 25 cents just on the rumor that the Soviets were returning to the grain market. The wheat-buying world is no longer complacent about assured American supplies as it once was.

These days the Soviet Union and China can make single purchases that overshadow the entire annual consumption of smaller nations. When rumor has it that the giants are going into the marketplace, all the others have to sit up and take notice immediately.

Export sales of wheat are an emotional issue because the price of bread is an emotional issue. The move by the longshoremen's union to refuse to handle the Soviet Union sales shows how emotional. The countermove by the governor of Kansas inviting longshoremen to his state to see what the wheat sales mean is a response both pragmatic and emotional. Just like the Chicago housewives going to the Missouri hog farms, the several Americas are worlds apart.

For the country to alter its economic drift, Americans have to understand those several Americas.

Walter Vernon, executive director of the Board of Trade, admitted his major concern was that because grain sales had such political and emotional overtones the government might move in to take over, and wreck the market by doing so. As Assar Lindbeck noted in an earlier chapter, the delicate market system cannot easily be replaced even by those who would change everything.

This country's greatest current and future problem is inflation. The cure for inflation is a strong currency. Currencies gain strength when they represent worth.

The "strongest" dollars the United States can earn are export dollars. The strongest dollars the United States can print are dollars that represent a stable and planned economy.

The price of the strong currency that can defeat inflation in the United States is domestic austerity and a growing export market. As the dollar first holds its value, and then gains in value, it takes fewer dollars going overseas to buy those needs that have to be bought in the world market.

The strong dollar, one representing a country with perhaps only 2 percent or 3 percent inflation per year, means that savings are secure, fixed incomes are not deteriorating at an abnormal rate, and the national hysteria level eases downward.

To directly answer Walt Vernon's worries: If government intervention in agriculture means a growing and orderly export market in U.S. agricultural products, then government intervention is necessary. If government intervention interferes with and prevents the possibility of a growing and orderly export market, then the government might leave well alone while better regulating abuses.

The greatest single economic problem facing the United States is the continuing decline in the value of the dollar. A strong currency buys more of what it needs from the world than does a weak currency.

The United States must take those steps necessary to stop the dollar's rot. And Americans have to be told why those steps are being taken and what those steps are.

Those steps call for two definite measures: domestic austerity and rapidly increasing exports.

How much austerity? Enough: sufficient austerity to rebuild into the march of the generations some sense of what "disposable" and "consumable" items really cost. Sufficient austerity is required so that Americans will realize how wealthy they are and how much of that wealth is in fact mortgaging the security and the safety of future generations of Americans.

One has to be realistic about the costs of imposing austerity measures: cutbacks affect growth, affect employment, affect affluence, affect inflation. But not doing anything will allow all these ill-effects to occur anyway. The difference will be that if nothing is done the ill-effects will be prompted by forces over which the government has no control—the strong cyclical forces of free world trade in goods, money, and credit.

The examples that follow are deliberately limited. For oil, read also the many other imported raw materials; for reallocation and change in transport read also reallocation and change in land use, military expenditure, tax structures, and the like.

A rational approach to stabilizing the U.S. economy means many big strides and thousands of small steps. Nothing should escape the attention of those considering the implementation of a just austerity.

Oil is the obvious example of an area where domestic austerity is essential. Americans by and large still have little grasp of the incredible volume of oil this country produces.

Austerity, and this is the first of my recommendations, means that the price of oil, to use only one example, should be deliberately tripled in the next five years. Gasoline should be close to $1.50 a gallon by 1980 for the U.S. economy to have shown to the world at large that it is realistic about the true cost of energy and energy dependency.

The petroleum, automobile, and trucking lobbies can marshal all their own evidence to the contrary, but this country simply cannot afford the amount of oil it currently uses.

Thomas O. Enders, assistant secretary of state for economic and business affairs, on July 14, 1975, told the Senate Finance Committee:

> However necessary, it is costly and painful to restrain demand for oil . . . nearly all the other members of the IEA [International Energy Agency] have taken action to decrease oil demand, by passing through increased crude costs to the end user, by new taxation, by such specific conservation as fuel switching. . . .
>
> In contrast the United States has lagged. So far the only major conservation measure with immediate effect that this country has taken is the oil import fees. . . .
>
> Between the first quarter of 1973 and the first quarter of this year [1975] Germany's oil consumption fell by 14 per cent, Italy's by 8 per cent, Japan's by 8 per cent, Britain's by 18 per cent and ours by 6 per cent. And yet of all these countries the recession, which of course reduced demand for oil, was far more severe *here* than elsewhere. . . .

There is more than just lobbies to contend with when the government, with the best interest of the country at heart, adopts a rational program of austerity. There is the consumer, too. But let us continue with the petroleum-saving example.

The major reason people have not been flocking to mass transit programs is not price, it is that Americans are accustomed to the speed and convenience of the personal transport system, the family car. What will make the rapid transit system, the urban-suburban bus system acceptable is making automobile travel inconvenient and slow, as well as expensive.

Banning cars from business and shopping areas is not just a fuel-saving device, it is good for cities and good for the alternative forms of transport—bus, train, subway.

Most urban-suburban driving is done in posted speed limit zones of

35 miles an hour or less. There is no need to have cars that can do in excess of 40 miles an hour.

The town car already has more cylinders, more gears, and more weight than it needs. There is no reason why Detroit cannot outthink that modest modern variant on the traditional car, the AMC Pacer, and come up with a really farsighted town car: lightweight, roomy, 55-plus miles to the gallon.

A federally imposed tax on the cubic capacity of existing automobile engines, escalating rapidly above 1,000 cc, would quickly get Detroit designers reaching much farther out for the engine of the future than anything presently on the drawing boards. Two-cylinder, water-cooled engines can be matched up to a roomy, lightweight car suitable for the needs of the average family.

There is no need to ban the in-town taxi, providing it is electric. Already the state of the art of the electric car and bus are sufficient for downtown cruising. Taxi racks only need the same sort of metered electrical outlets that golf carts currently use.

The government, deliberately imposing ever-higher taxes on oil, would be encouraging inflation. But that inflation would come in any event. The difference is that the extra income to government can be put to work developing other energy sources, funding new urban transit systems, and easing the plight of those hardest hit by economic change.

U.S. government is stodgy where it should be farsighted; relying on previously attempted solutions where it should be looking at realistic new programs; following where it should be leading; capitulating to special interests when it should have the special interest of the nation as its foremost concern.

When austerity is self-imposed, it can bring benefits because it is part of a plan. When it is imposed by external pressure, it can cause chaos. That is how simple a choice this country has to make.

Austerity must be accompanied by planning. If the country has to use its oil sparingly, the people at large are forced to accept that there are certain desires they cannot afford.

Everyone is going to be relatively less well off materially. That is the price this country has to pay for orderly economic survival. But that does not mean the country has to become an austere society. The American's capacity for adapting to new conditions is broad enough that Americans can adapt if they have to.

Why should Americans accept voluntary austerity? They won't, unless they have to, and then they will do it grudgingly. Americans have to be educated to the great American economic facts of modern life—that this country has peaked as a self-sufficient nation endowed with a potential for constant growth.

Who could educate Americans? ABC, CBS, and NBC could. Walter Cronkite and Eric Sevareid should be looking to their responsibilities, not just their abilities as reporters, raconteurs, and rhetoricians.

The major networks should include as part of their major news and news feature shows a "Sesame Street" for adults explaining without ideological slant the story of the American economy. The national media have one role they have constantly neglected—the careful unraveling of life's complexities in such a way that the ordinary citizen *can* understand the economic and social and political facts of life. The Americans are the most informed and the least educated people in the West. They are constantly informed of what is going on, but not educated to what it really means.

An "Electric Company" aimed at adult economic education is but a first step to economic literacy. Without it, Americans will never know what their options are—or were.

Affluence is a temporary state of affairs. Now that it is on the wane the disorderly retreat from plenty demands instead careful but constant adjusting of priorities. It also means that some basic economic redistribution still has to take place.

New societies cannot be built with depreciating dollars. Existing societies cannot even be maintained in their present state of disarray with crumbling dollars.

Those who would marvel at the "natives" of Far Eastern countries for their resigned tolerance of life's vicissitudes should marvel at the tolerance and restraint of the black and brown and white Americans trapped and impoverished in the rotting core of urban U.S.A. and the equally impoverished rural slums and wastelands.

Those who would nod vigorously at Caspar Weinberger's parody on Malthus, of the welfare recipients eating the nation out of house and home, should keep their heads still long enough to read the writing on the wall. It says:

The top 10 percent of all Americans has as much income as the bottom 50 percent; the top 1 percent has more than the bottom 20 percent. That last little statistic, in people terms, says that some 2 million-plus Americans have more take-home pay than the combined income of the bottom 40 million.

The writing on the wall says the nation is asking for trouble. But this is not a book about social problem solving. The concern here is to see the United States back on an economically sound footing in order to return—or force—its concentration toward its mounting social problems.

A strong dollar means that the nation has to better balance its budget from its existing wealth and its existing income. Writing checks against the future to pay for social services debilitates the dollar. If social services have to come out of someone's hide, it must be out of the hides of those padded with their own pelts.

As this narrative followed the case for large increases in gasoline prices through further than just the single statement, let's look further at more taxes on the middle and upper classes.

Is it right to throw more taxes on the guy in the suburbs who is already holding down two jobs (with his wife working) to pay the mortgage and get the kids through college? Yes. By any Western comparison the two-job carrying, mortgage-ridden, tax-burdened man in the gray flannel leisure suit—and the ring of sweat around his collar—is already wealthy. He is wealthier than he has any reason to expect; he is wealthier than the nation can afford. His rapid rise in income and affluence during the last 15 years has come from the unique circumstances the United States and its dollar found itself in after World War II.

Those circumstances have changed. Suburban man's lot is changing, too. He needs a house, but it will have to be smaller so the mortgage will be lower. If his kids *have* to go to college, they'll have to find a way to help out. If he is deadly serious about their college future, he might find himself living in a small townhouse—maybe even a rented townhouse.

What is certain is that suburban man has to start rapidly compiling a list of his own priorities and needs just as the nation needs to compile its list.

But what does that do for the cities? Anyone now familiar with urban core city rot will quickly explain that the tax base is eroding and the cities are going bankrupt. They will add that the suburbs need to be drawn into that larger metro-tax base to aid the cities. Precisely. But apart perhaps from Toronto—due to the provincial (i.e., state) form of federation giving the province far more power than the U.S. state has—no North American metropolis has successfully thrown that real estate tax lasso around the suburbs on behalf of the cities, and on behalf of those now trapped in them.

It will take amendments to the federal and state constitutions to adequately reorganize U.S. metropolitan areas into just economic units. For tax "central" funding purposes, there is no reason why the smallest tax base unit should not be at least 500 square miles (half the size of Rhode Island). There is no reason why the bicentennial celebrations should not lead directly into a constitutional convention. It would be a good start for the next 200 years.

If government spending is to come down, and if social services are a major portion of that spending, then those social services must be met out of new tax rates. But the imposition of more taxes should take into account the very realistic worry that many people feel taxed to the hilt already. And those people have to be shown that perhaps their material aspirations and expectations are beyond reasonable expectation, just as the national material expectations—man on moon, plus social services, plus gigantic military purchases, plus global benefactor, plus constant highway builder, plus depletion allowances—are too high, too.

(One is arguing here for a just society, of course. But this is a democracy, and perhaps the majority of people don't really want a just society if it means giving up some of the material gains they've achieved.)

Further redistribution of wealth, a scaling down of material expectations, is part of the austerity that will strengthen the dollar. The money to support the needy while rebuilding the cities has to come from the nation's existing wealth—pried loose from the nation's existing wealth holders. If it comes out of further deficit financing, paid for with money straight off the government printing presses, inflation goes up and the dollar continues to go down.

Two essentials, then, are to cut down on expensive raw material imports and cut back on domestic government spending, including military spending and deficit financing. Wealth redistribution? Don't forget it was a *Business Week* reader who suggested perhaps $100,000 or $200,000 as a possible wealth ceiling.

The third essential is increasing the United States' ability as a trading nation. U.S. multinational corporations have to be brought back home or their overseas investment has to be carefully monitored and controlled, and that overseas income taxed. The large pool of U.S. dollars floating around in offshore banks has to be brought back home, too, perhaps in exchange for U.S. government bonds, but certainly brought back to these shores in order not to be used against U.S. economic interests by speculators, corporate treasurers, foreign exchange artists, and "the gnomes of Zurich."

The U.S. banks should be brought back down to size and the Bank Holding Company Act abolished. Banks, through Eurodollar financing, can circumvent domestic U.S. monetary policy; through their holding company's acquisitions they can operate outside Federal Reserve Board constraints; and as controllers, in large part, of the major national industries they can pursue profits to the detriment of the national interest.

"Shell" banking—offshore banking—should be eliminated. Banks should be required to divest themselves of all nonbanking activities in order that the Federal Reserve Board in fact may regain some control—most especially over bank indebtedness. Limits should be set on the amount of control and interest single banks can have in major industrial corporations.

The U.S. multinational corporation and the U.S. multinational bank has only its own best interest at heart. The United States cannot afford that corporate luxury. Eventually the upswelling of already apparent antibusiness sentiment will show corporations and banks that they can't afford the luxury, either.

With banks returned to Federal Reserve Board control, the United States can have more realistic monetary control, and can begin a program of working toward reduced interest rates. If the dollar is a strong currency other nations will want the dollar and will bid up its price. Other nations will want to keep their assets in this country, which will permit the United States to have lower interest rates because those outsiders want the security of the strong currency.

Just as weakness feeds upon weakness to drive the dollar down, strength would feed upon strength to drive the dollar back up. But it will take a very firm hand, and a major commitment by Americans to the future rather than to the present.

Rising trade capabilities, more exports, can add to the caliber of the dollar. Not just balance of trade is important, but the quality of what is being traded, and the quality of the currency being used in that trade. The United States still has much untapped export potential. It must tap that potential—and do it from domestic bases, not by setting up ever more factories globally to fill the need.

One of the United States' greatest export growth stories in recent years has been agricultural products. The total value of farm products exported in the fiscal year ending June 30, 1975 was $21.6 billion, the highest ever. It was $300 million higher than the previous year; $17 billion more than 15 years earlier.

Japan was the United States' biggest customer. (So we do have to take in their electronics products.) The Soviet Union and China were next. The United States has exported more agricultural products in the last 14 years than in the previous 40: wheat, corn, soybeans, barley, oats, rye, rice, cotton, tobacco, and much, much more.

Agriculture uses a great deal of "energy," so the higher fuel prices go, the higher farm costs go. But export dollars are the strongest dollars the United States can get. The farmer and the export industries should get preferential fuel treatment, or rebates, conducive to existing international trade agreements.

Preferential treatment? Certainly, that is what the allocation of scarce resources is all about. What matters is to build up the strength of the dollar, and build up U.S. world trade. If that means further government intervention—into agriculture or into the export business—then that is one more price to be paid.

There is a simple rule of thumb easily stated but not easily applied. Where government aid, intervention, and preferential treatment can stimulate exports it should be given. Where it would hinder exports the hand of government should be stayed.

Tax breaks for export-oriented corporations and industries? Most assuredly. Government aid for export cooperatives? But of course. A much more viable and participatory role for the commercial attachés in the U.S. embassies and consulates around the world? Without a doubt. Simplified export paperwork? A premium on foreign languages and international trading experience? It makes sound economic sense.

Austerity does not mean that no industries are growth industries. It means a harsh look at the realities of American economic life, and some major programming, planning, and legislation to take account of those realities. Allocation and dislocation, yes, but that is better than the alternative: economic upheaval outside the national government's control.

National wages cannot be pegged to the wages of the growth sector. That's why the buggy-makers went into the car factories. If export industries are growing, other industries may be declining. Some industries might even be sensibly wound down in size—with government aid—as the British government helped eliminate most of its domestic cotton spinning and weaving capacity.

If all this means that there might be a "flight of capital" by wealth holders seeking sanctuary outside the United States, then that capital flight should be curtailed before it starts. If all this allocation and dislocation means a cutback in the national standard of living, then that must be explained. If the standard of living is going to double only once every 40 or 50 years, then maybe that is the reality and we must gear to it. But we must gear down, not be panicked into it by forces beyond our control.

Most Americans do not know they are living on the economic brink, or that the country is. Someone has to tell them.

The President who serves his term without initiating a national debate of economic and social priorities has served only himself, not the people. A Congress that does not press and carry legislation that can restore economic stability in the best interests of the nation has served only the special private interests of lobbies and individuals.

If the debate is not initiated, if austerity measures are not forthcoming across the entire panoply of American and Western self-indulgence, the decline of capital will lead directly and quickly into the collapse of capital.

And the collapse of capital will lead to the collapse of what could be a moderately successful, moderately just and equal, popular democracy.

Epilogue

Let us at least hope it is not toward a world of swarming
ant-heaps populated by highly mechanized barbarians, a
new Dark Age, with technocrats in place of theologians.

F. L. Lucas

The Harvard Club was cool and a world removed from New York
City outside, a city skirting bankruptcy. It was July 9, 1975.
Dark suits, red and black ties, and decorum prevailed. They always
do.

One by one members of the Analysts Club began to arrive. After
drinks they began to collect in an upstairs meeting room for dinner
and discussion. It was a gathering primarily of wealthy old men.

There was Lucien O. Hooper, whose 79th birthday it was. Hooper,
a columnist for *Forbes* magazine, still puts in a full day's work as
vice-president of Thomson & McKinnon on Wall Street.

There was Glenn Munn, the only surviving founder-member of the
Analysts Club, a group founded in 1926. Bradford Story was there.
Story, 74, is the courtly and clever head of Brundage, Story and
Rose, an investment firm that conservatively handles a conservatively
estimated $800 million in private money.

There was Anthony Gaubis, a "gold bug" and chartist; and among
the other veterans of Wall Street was Joseph S. Nye.

There were younger men, too, people like David Dunbar of Beth-
lehem Steel Pension Fund, and John Durham of the Delaware Management Company of Philadelphia. Investment advisers, chartists,
but Wall Street–oriented capitalists each and every one.

It was a fine setting for a discussion of capitalism and liberalism, capitalism's apologetics: paneled walls, linen napery, good food, convivial company, attentive waiters—and much business to discuss.

The Analysts Club tradition is that, before dinner begins, each member writes out an opinion of what will happen one month, three months, and six months ahead, to interest rates, Wall Street, and the economy.

The members were bearish about the month ahead, but after that they were as bullish as could be. Most of them, that is.

When the poll results were being read out by chairman Dunbar, Joseph S. Nye turned to his companion and whispered quietly, "I don't agree. I think it's down, down, down."

So the country goes down until it steadies on a new plateau. The market, social, and government forces work as before. Upticks and downticks, then inflation cuts ever deeper into that base, and the country once more sinks down to a new plateau.

That is the story of the erosion of a capitalist economy; the story of the decline of capital.

Index

Abel, I. S., 54
ACEC, 43
Aeroflot, 58
aerospace industry, 40–42
Affluent Society, The (Galbraith), 140
Age of Reason, The (Nicholson), 104
Agnew, Spiro, 10
Alaska, resource development in, 30, 32–34
Alfa Laval, 61
Algemene Bank Nederland, 61
Alien Land Act, 74–75
Alkhimov, Vladimir, 47–48
Aluminum Werke, 67
Amax Sumitomo, 67
AMC Pacer, 188
"America for Americans" (campaign slogan), 74–75
America, Inc. (Mintz and Cohen), 60
American Airlines, 81
American Bankers Association, 162
American Challenge, The (Servan-Schreiber), 56
American Cyanamid Company, 62
American Dilemma, An (Myrdal), 159
American Express Company, 68
American Metal Climax, Inc., 67
American Telephone and Telegraph Company, 181
Amtrak, 6
Analysts Club, 195–196
Anheuser-Busch, Inc., 123
Anne, Princess, 74
antitrust laws, role of in neocapitalist economy, 94–96
Arab-Israeli Six Day War, 24, 26, 27

Arab oil powers, 25–28, 178
Aristotle, 101
Aristotle's Ethical Theory (Hardie), 101
Armstrong, F. E., 147
asset management, definition of, 7
Association of German Investment Companies, 99
Atlas Copco, 61
austerity, proposed program of, 183–194
Australia, international investment in, 67–68, 70

Bahamas, international investment in, 74
Bailey, F. G., 134–135
Bakunin, Mikhail, 115
BankAmerica Corporation, 61
Banca Nazionale del Lavoro, 61
Banco Real do Canada, São Paulo, 61
Bank Holding Company Act, 5, 60
banking, international, 59–64
Bank of America, 68, 72
Bank of England, 180
Banque de Bruxelles, 61
Banque Nationale de Paris, 61
Barclays Bank, 61
Beguin, Jean-Pierre, 75
Behrman, Jack N., 83
Bell, Geoffrey, 64
Between Capitalism and Socialism (Heilbroner), 83
Billera, John, 114
Birnbaum, Norman, 118–119
Black & Decker, 45
Blaine, James G., 74–75
Blau, Peter M., 158

BOAC, 41
Boeing 747 airliner, 34
Boeing Company, 41, 42
boom of 1964–66, 14–16, 19, 40, 86
Bouteflika, Adbelaziz, 75
Brazil, capitalist future of, 180
Brimmer, Andrew, 63, 71
Britain, economy of, 65–67, 93, 94
British Department of Trade and Industry, 66
British Government and Business Economic
    Advisory Group, 65
British Labor Party, 67
British Petroleum (BP), 24, 94
Broken Hill Proprietary, 68
Bullock, Hugh, 139
Bureaucracy in Modern Society (Blau and
    Meyer), 158
Burke-Hartke bill, 71
Busch, August A., 123
Business Week, 180

Calvin, John, 103, 105, 145
Canada, economy of, 22, 31–32, 67–70
Canadian Development Corporation, 31, 69
Canadian Forum, 68–69
Capital (Marx), 103
capital, definition of, 15
capital and capitalism, distinction between,
    12–16
capitalism:
    definition of, 15
    future of, 12–16, 133–137, 175, 183–196
    historical development of, 100–137
    interlinking elements in, 164–182
    religious implications of, 104, 110–111
    role of in corporate multinational expansion,
        37–76
Capitalism, Inflation and the Multinationals
    (Levinson), 115
"capitalist equerries," 59
capitalist ethic, 15–16
Carrick, Bruce, 112
cartels, 175–178
Cayman Islands, as tax haven, 60
Chase Manhattan Bank, 68
Chicago Citizens Action Program (CAP), 9–11
Chrysler Corporation, 43, 44, 122
Clausen, A. W., 72
Cleveland, Grover, 75

coal, as factor in economy, 22, 29
Coca-Cola Company, 51
Cockroft, John, 53
Coexistence and Commerce (Pisar), 47
Cohen, Jerry S., 60, 61
Colchester, Nicholas, 151
Comecon countries, 57–58
Commodity Credit Corporation, 57
Common Agricultural Policy (CAP), 53
Common Market, 40–54, 64, 71, 73
Confucius, 100
Consolidated Edison, 180
Consolidation Coal and Continental Oil, 29
consortium banking, 59–64
Cooley, Michael, J. E., 125
Cooney, John, 104
Coppee Rust, 43
corporate multinationalism, 37–76
corporations, public distrust of, 179
Crabb, George, 108
Cronkite, Walter, 189
Cruel Choice, The (Goulet), 157

Danish Labor News, 119
Danish Landsorganisationem (LO), 117–122
Durraugh Letter, 74
Dassault aircraft, 42
Davis, Robert, 5
"decline of capital," definition of, 15
Deere, 44
Denmark, economic picture in, 117–123
depression and recession, distinction between,
    182
Díaz del Castillo, Bernal, 18
Diocletian, 91
Disraeli, Benjamin, 106, 107
dollar, devaluations of, 63, 64, 86, 164,
    186–194
"dollar diplomats," 59
Douglas, Hunter, 143
Douglas, James, 18
Dow Chemical Company, 106
Dresdner Bank, 61
Dunbar, David, 195–196
du Pont (E. I.) de Nemours & Company, 62
Dunning, J. H., 65

Economic Anthropology (Herskovits), 106
economic democracy, 117–123

economic imperialism, 37–76
economic literacy, need for development of,
    48–55, 189
Economist, The, 65, 152
El Paso Natural Gas Company, 26
Enders, Thomas O., 187
Engels, Friedrich, 99
Enskilda Bank, 61
Enterprising Scot, The (Jackson), 18
Ericsson (L. M.) Corporation, 61
Erlander, Tage, 130
Esso, 33
European Economic Community (EEC), 40–
    54, 64, 71, 73
European Free Trade Area, 52
Evence Coppee et Cie., 43
Evolution of the Flying Machine (Hooper),
    160–161
"export credits," 179
Export-Import Bank, 97
exports:
    importance of to international investment,
        37–59
    program for increase of, 192
Exxon Corporation, 68
Ezra, Derek, 93

Facts Rebel, The (Paloczi-Horvath), 114
Faulkner, Harold Underwood, 17, 18, 39
Federal Reserve Bank of New York, 180
Federal Reserve System, 59, 60, 63, 150
Financial Times, 48
Finger-Ring Lore (W. Jones), 107
"flight of capital," 54–55, 194
Florida Gulf Coast, 30
Forbes magazine, 77, 106
Fortune magazine, 44, 61–62, 112
France, economic picture in, 92
Friedmann, Wolfgang, 75
From Great Power to Welfare State (Samuelsson), 30

Gabor, Denis, 159
Galbraith, John Kenneth, 128, 140
Gaubis, Anthony, 195
General Agreement on Tariffs and Trade
    (GATT), 67
General Dynamics Corporation, 42
General Motors Corporation, 46

Germany, economic picture in, 92, 99–100
Goldsmith, Oliver, 108
Goulet, Denis, 157, 158
government, business's relation with, 77–98.
    See also state as manager; state as trader
Gray Report (Canada), 68
Growth, The Price We Pay (Mishan), 137
Gulf Oil Corporation, 62

Halverson, James T., 95
Hammersley Investments, 51
Hardie, W. F. R., 101
Hargrove, Charles, 153
Harrier aircraft, 42
Heilbroner, Robert L., 83
Heinz (H. J.) Company, 67
Herskovits, M. J., 106
Hill, Christopher, 112
Hinds, Robert, 10–11
History of European Morals (Lecky), 103
History of Rome, The (T. Mommsen), 101–102
Holland Aluminium, 67
Hooper, Harry, 160–161
Hooper, Lucien O., 195
Hoveyda, Amir Abbas, 153, 183
Huff, David, 8
Hunt, H. L., 20–21

IBM Corporation, 46, 49, 177
inflation:
    domestic and global forms of, 86–87
    effect on competition of, 82
    rate of, 180
Instituto Nacional de Industria, 69–70
International Caucus of Labor Committees,
    113
International Federation of Chemical and General Workers' Unions, 126–127
International Harvester Company, 45–46
International Labor Office, 67
investment, as link in capitalist chain, 171–182
Iran, international investment in, 70
Islam, revival of, 26–28
Islam in Modern History (Smith), 26–27
Italy, economic picture in, 93

Jackson, W. Turrentine, 18, 74, 140, 148
Jackson amendment, 48
Jaguar aircraft, 42

Jamaica, international investment in, 74
Japan, economy of, 50–52, 59, 179
Jeaumont-Schneider electrical group, 43
Johnson, Lyndon B., 45
Johnson, Samuel, 111
Joint International Business Ventures in Developing Countries (Friedmann and Beguin), 75
Jones, William, 107
Jusos, 99–100

Kaiser Steel, 51
Kansas City Board of Trade, 184
Kapauku Papuans, 109
Karlstadt, Andreas von, 151
Kaufman, Henry, 8, 12, 166
Kaunda, Kenneth D., 153
Kendrick, Alexander, 95
Kennedy, John F., 16
Kerekes, Gabriel T., 12, 166
Keynes, John Maynard, 83, 90
Kheradjou, Abol Gessam M., 70
Khrushchev, Nikita, 58
Kirschen, Etienne-Sadi, 73, 149
Kozmetsky, George, 7–8, 12
Kristol, Irving, 128
Krupp (Friedrich) combine, 92

Landsorganisationem (LO), 117–122
Last Play, The (Ridgeway), 112–113
Lecky, W. H., 103
leisure, definition of, 22
Lenin, Nikolai, 115
Levinson, Charles, 115, 125–126
Levitt (J. K.) & Associates, Inc., 43
Lewis (John) Partnership, 132
Lichtenberg, Georg Christoph, 175
Lightbourne, Robert, 74
Lindbeck, Assar, 112, 113, 148, 185
Lindemans Vineyards, 68
Litton Industries, Inc., 43
Lockheed Aircraft Corporation, 42
London, as international finance center, 59–62
London *Times* (Sunday), 66
LTV Aerospace Corporation, 42
Ludwig, D. K., 20–21
Luther, Hans, 109, 135
Luther, Martin, 109, 135, 157

Macrae, Robert M., 2–3, 5–7, 12, 16
Malman, Seymour, 97
Man and Society (Plamenatz), 111
Manhattan tanker project, 33
Marathon Industries, Inc., 124
Marx, Karl, 102, 103, 105, 125–126
mass transit, program for development of, 187–188
Mass Transit Act of 1964, 51
McDonnell-Douglas Corporation, 41
McKenzie, Fred A., 65
McLean, John G., 19
Mead Corporation, 43
Mesabi iron ore deposits, 19–20
Meyer, Marshall W., 158
Michaels, James, 77, 85
Michigan, welfare program of, 179
middle classes, 138–162
    dependence of capitalism on, 138
    historical development of, 139–154
    social impetus of, 155–162
Miller, Ervin, 90
Milton, John, 111
Milwaukee Journal, 179
Mintz, Morton, 60, 61
Mishan, E. J., 137, 149
Mitchell, George W., 150
Mitsubishi Bank, 52
Mitsui trading company, 51
Mobil Oil Corporation, 62
Mobutu, Joseph D., 56
Mommsen, Ernest, 92
Mommsen, Theodore, 101–102
money, as link in capitalist chain, 164–169
Monsanto Chemical Company, 62
"Moon over Miami" (film), 139
Morgan Guaranty Trust Company, 60
Morrison, Ian, 62
Moscow Narodny Bank, 58
MRCA (aircraft), 42
Muggeridge, Malcolm, 108
multinational corporate expansion, 37–76
Munn, Glenn, 195
Muslims, 25–28
Myrdal, Gunnar, 159

Nader, Ralph, 157
Nassau, as tax haven, 60
National Cash Register Company, 50

National Coal Association, 22, 29
National Coal Board (Britain), 93
National Feeder Pig Show, 9–11
neocapitalism:
  emergence of, 77–83
  importance of antitrust measures in, 96
  technocrats of, 59
New Proletarians, The (Power), 113
New Solidarity, 126
New York, as international finance center, 59
Nicholson, Harold, 104
Nicholson, Ross, 24
Nixon, Richard M., 140
Nixon-Moscow round, 23
Northrop aircraft, 42
North Sea oil, development of, 29, 124
Nye, Joseph S., 1–7, 12, 16, 195–196

Occidental Petroleum Corporation, 97
O'Connell, Arturo, 73
offshore resources, development of, 30, 32, 33–34
oil crisis, 20–29, 180, 187
Okenudo, Bob, 154
Opel (Adam), A. G., 46
Organization for Economic Cooperation and Development (OECD), 156
Organization of Petroleum Exporting Countries (OPEC), 28, 30, 178
O'Shaughnessey, Hugh, 73

Palme, Olof, 183
Paloczi-Horvath, George, 114
Panasonic Corporation, 51
Parker, Peter, 135–136
Parsons and Whittemore, Inc., 47, 48
Patterson, Ellmore C., 60
Paul, Roland (Pig), 8–9
Pearson, John, 69, 71
Philip Morris, Inc., 67–68
Philips, Mark, 74
Piedmont airlines, 51
Pisar, Samuel, 47, 57
Pivato, Giorgio, 147
Plamenatz, John, 111
Political Economy of the New Left, The (Lindbeck), 112
Pompidou, Georges, 26
Pospisil, Leopold, 109

Power, Jonathan, 113
power, psychological lure of, 106–109
power utilities, control of, 181
President's Commission on International Trade and Investment Policy, 53–54
Prime Time, the Life of Edward R. Murrow (Kendrick), 95
Prince of Wales, 74
Prospectus Preparation for International Private Investment (Robinson), 73
Protestant Ethic and the Spirit of Capitalism, The (Weber), 110, 111
Public Interest, The (Galbraith), 128

Qaddafi, Muammar el-, 25–26

"radical economics," 113
Radical Reformation, The (Williams), 155
RCA Corporation, 43
recession and depression, distinction between, 182
Reddaway, Peter, 58
Reformation and the Industrial Revolution (Hill), 112
resource dependency, 17–36, 48
resource diplomacy, 23–26
Ridgeway, James, 112–113
Rio de Janeiro, as investment center, 180
Robinson, Harry J., 73
Rockefeller, David, 128, 131
Rolls Royce, 49
Romans in Spain, The (Sutherland), 102
Rootes Group, 43, 46
Rowling, Marjorie, 109
Rust Engineering Company, 43

Saab, 42, 61
Sabena Airlines, 42
Samuelson, Paul, 113
Samuelsson, Kurt, 30
Sandoz, A. G., 132
Scandinavian Airlines (SAS), 41
Schakowsky, Jean, 9–11
Schultze, Charles, 146
Scott, Harold, 48
Ségur, Philippe, 104, 157
Servan-Schreiber, Jean-Jacques, 56
Sevareid, Eric, 189
"shell" banks, 59–60, 192

Simca, 43
Smith, W. Cantwell, 26–27
socialism, historical development of, 111–116,
   125–127
Société Financière Européene, 61
Sony Corporation, 51
Spain, international investment in, 69–70
Speenhamland, England, 179
Stanleywine Vineyard, 67
state as manager, 96–98, 181–182
state as trader, 57–59
Stock Exchange, The (Pivato), 147
stock market, as link in capitalist chain,
   169–171
Story of Investment Companies, The (Bullock),
   139
Stratagems and Spoils (Bailey), 134–135
suburban man, tax burden of, 190
Suez crisis, 24
Sumitomo, 67
Sutherland, C. H. V., 102
Sweden, economy of, 13–14, 30, 61, 129–130
Synonymes (Crabb), 108

Tacke, Gerd, 95
Tajitsu, Mrs. W., 49–50
Taussig, Frank, 4
Tawney, R. H., 103, 111, 145
Taylor, Joel, 56
Teledyne, 7
Texas Gulf Industries, 31, 69
Third World, 56–57, 70–76
Thomas, Anthony, 53, 94
Toronto, tax program of, 191
Trades Union Congress (Britain), 67
Tribe, Caste and Nation (Bailey), 135
TWA, 81

unemployment, "administered," 90
Ungar, Harlow, 132, 150
United Airlines, 81
United Nations, 71
U.S. Department of Agriculture, 22
U.S. Department of Commerce, 52
U.S. Federal Reserve Board, 59 60, 63
U.S. Federal Trade Commission, 95
U.S. Geological Survey, 33

U.S. Merchant Marine, 98
U.S. Navy oil reserves, 24
U.S. Office of Coal Production, 29
U.S. Senate Finance Committee, 19–20, 71
U.S. Steel, 70
U.S.-U.S.S.R. Trade and Economic Council,
   48
U.S.S.R., as state trader, 57–58
usury, 101, 145

values, disordered scale of, 178–181
Vanek, Jaroslav, 117–118
Vernon, Walter, 185
Vietnam, 27, 72
Vincendon, Daniel, 177
Vivian Grey (Disraeli), 106
Vogl, Frank, 97
Volvo, 132
Vought aircraft, 42

Wallenberg family, 61
Walpole, Sir Robert, 18
War Economy of the United States, The (Mal-
   man), 97
"War on Poverty" program, 10
Wates, Neil, 130
Watkins, Ernest, 110
wealth, distribution of, 190–194
Weber, Max, 104, 110, 111
Weinberger, Caspar, 189
Wells Fargo, 68
Westinghouse, 43, 68
Weyerhaeuser, George, 11–12, 165–166
Why England Sleeps (Cockroft), 53
Williams, Albert, 53–54
Williams, G. H., 155
Williams Commission, 53–54
Wilsher, Peter, 150
Woodroofe, Ernest, 177
worker control programs, 116–125
World Mitsubishi, T.T., 49–50

Young Socialists (Germany), 99

Zentner, Peter, 48
"Zurich, gnomes of," 165, 192